BECOMING ZIMBABWEAN

RECONSIDERATIONS IN
SOUTHERN AFRICAN HISTORY
Richard Elphick and Benedict Carton, Editors

BECOMING ZIMBABWEAN

A HISTORY OF INDIANS IN RHODESIA

TRISHULA RACHNA PATEL

UNIVERSITY OF VIRGINIA PRESS
Charlottesville and London

The University of Virginia Press is situated on the traditional lands of the Monacan Nation, and the Commonwealth of Virginia was and is home to many other Indigenous people. We pay our respect to all of them, past and present. We also honor the enslaved African and African American people who built the University of Virginia, and we recognize their descendants. We commit to fostering voices from these communities through our publications and to deepening our collective understanding of their histories and contributions.

University of Virginia Press
© 2026 by the Rector and Visitors of the University of Virginia
All rights reserved
Printed in the United States of America on acid-free paper

First published 2026

1 3 5 7 9 8 6 4 2

Library of Congress Cataloging-in-Publication Data

Names: Patel, Trishula Rachna, author
Title: Becoming Zimbabwean : a history of Indians in Rhodesia / Trishula Rachna Patel.
Other titles: Reconsiderations in southern African history
Description: Charlottesville : University of Virginia Press, 2026. | Series: Reconsiderations in southern African history | Includes bibliographical references and index.
Identifiers: LCCN 2025021895 (print) | LCCN 2025021896 (ebook) | ISBN 9780813954486 hardback | ISBN 9780813954493 trade paperback | ISBN 9780813954509 ebook
Subjects: LCSH: East Indians—Zimbabwe—History | East Indians—Zimbabwe—Social conditions | Zimbabwe—Social conditions—1890-1965 | Zimbabwe—Social conditions—1965-1980 | Zimbabwe—Social conditions—1980-
Classification: LCC DT3058.E38 P37 2026 (print) | LCC DT3058.E38 (ebook) | DDC 305.891405891—dc23/eng/20250821
LC record available at https://lccn.loc.gov/2025021895
LC ebook record available at https://lccn.loc.gov/2025021896

Cover design by Lindsay Starr

For my father, Bharatkumar Patel, who first taught me history, guided me in developing strong morals, and encouraged me to choose my own path in life

and for my mother, Hansa Naik, who instilled in me a love of literature, taught me the power of words, and gave me all she did not have growing up

Africa was my home, had been the home of my family for centuries . . .
we could no longer say that we were Arabians or Indians
or Persians; when we compared ourselves with
these people, we felt like people of Africa.

—V. S. NAIPAUL, *A Bend in the River,* 1979

CONTENTS

Acknowledgments | *xi*

Introduction   1

1. Undesirables and Pioneers: Crossing the Indian Ocean, 1890–1923   21

2. Between White Picket Fences and Black Reserves: The Development of Indian Trading Streets, 1923–1945   44

3. Purity Schools and Hindu Daughters: Indian Education, 1930–1950   68

4. The *Dukkan* and the Courtroom: Indian Legal Challenges, 1950–1965   90

5. "Rhodesians First, Asians Second": Politics, Modernity, and War in Salisbury, 1965–1980   112

6. The *Kumalos* of Lobengula Street: Anticolonialism in Bulawayo, 1950–1980   137

Epilogue: Air Rhodesia Flight 825   163

Conclusion   171

Notes | *181*
Bibliography | *213*
Index | *223*

ACKNOWLEDGMENTS

This book has been in the making for a long time. As an actual plan of study, it began in Keren Weitzberg's classroom at the University of Pennsylvania in 2014, when she convinced me that the history of Indians in Zimbabwe was one worthy of exploring, researching, and writing. As an idea, it began with a childhood existential crisis in response to the question, Where am I from? Three decades of reading, learning, listening to stories, and reflecting on memories culminated in this book, and it would not have been possible without the support of family, friends, educators, and, most importantly, the Indian community in Zimbabwe themselves.

My first thanks are due to my parents, Bharat and Hansa Patel. I could talk before I could walk, and rather than suppressing my voice, they encouraged it. They filled my life with books and music and stories of the lives they had led before I existed; tales of life in a place called Rhodesia that was not built for them but was a country to which they always returned as home. They let me choose my own path, pursuing careers and education that they were denied. But they also always let me return home, too, for which I am eternally grateful.

I only knew one of my grandparents in life. Haribhai Naik, or Bapa to me, didn't talk much in the eight years that I had with him. But he gave me solid, stable love, and when he died, it felt like a part of my heart was missing.

Mum has since filled that gap, telling me about his life, teaching me the ethics he gave her, and inspiring my own need to learn about what it meant to resist the forces and systems that oppress and silence. My desire to tell his story to the world is the inspiration for this book. I did not get to meet my grandmother, Lilavatiben, but her sister took her place, raising my mother and helping raise me. Kusumben, or Ba to us, did not live the easiest life. Her strength in raising her daughters, working behind the shop counter, and helping build the family home on Lobengula Street only became clear to me much later in life than it should have. I hope I do justice to her life and legacy.

Haribhai and Dahiben Patel died before I was born. Dada, as I would have called him, did not have the opportunity to pursue a formal tertiary education, but he read everything, collecting books on history, politics, literature, photography, astronomy, and science. Every year, my father gives me a book from his library on Father's Day, a way to honor the legacy of learning that Dada left both of us. Dadima left her own inheritance behind, not only in the chin dimple we both share but in the stories about her fortitude, her stubbornness, and the sacrifices she made to become the protective matriarch of the family in Salisbury. As her only grandchild, I can only hope to emulate her strength.

Being an only child, I sought love and community from extended family. In Harare, I grew up not only at 25 Firsgrove but also at 69 Glamorgan, 49 Glamorgan, 50 Denbigh, 4 Viking Way, and as the fifth Patel sister at 44 Hurtsview. In addition to my cousins, Anj and Bhavika became my sisters. In Bulawayo, M. V. Naik and Sons provided a home every school holiday on Lobengula Street, and I cherish the memories of childhood escapades with my little brothers Ush and Viks. Masiba and Motimasi and the Masajis helped make the United States home, and Rakhi as my doctor-sister always served as a role model. Ushumasi helped me become independent, and her homes in DC were always a safe space during transitions in my life. BM and SM as my second set of parents were always there for the important moments in my childhood, from birthdays to Friday nights. Arya, Sansa, Daenerys, and Ellaria may not be able to read this book, but their feline companionship and unconditional love have brightened our transnational family's lives. It takes a village to raise a child, and this village helped me become a woman I hope they are all proud of.

Friends too numerous to name have provided moments of joy, solidarity, comradeship, and shared memories that got us through a global pandemic, spanning the globe from Harare, to Philadelphia and New York, and to DC.

A special few deserve mention for their love and consistent support. Suite Hella Awesome (what remains of it) and survivors of J-school and the history department at Georgetown have been companions through the trials and tribulations of college, graduate school(s), and my first job as a full-fledged professor. Charley, Chris, Marielle, Matt, Nichole, Jackson, the Jasons, Jordan, Katya, Ross, Roz, Rebeckah, and Sudeep have remained steady and true friends even as we have all scattered across the country. In Denver, Alexis, Heather, and Steve all helped make an East Coaster feel at home. Roopesh, Thariq, and Yagnesh have been protective older brothers for as long as I can remember, always making sure I'm okay wherever I am in the world. In Harare, Dilan, Kirti, Nilan, Romola, and the Sunday session crew ensure I always come back home, and friends and community at Sunrise Sports Club give me a place to go where everybody knows my name.

The history department at the University of Denver welcomed me with open arms, and their comradeship helps make researching and teaching a joy every day. Thank you to Elizabeth Campbell, Liz Escobedo, Yasmaine Ford, Carol Helstosky, Rafael Ioris, Kimberly Jones, Jodie Kreider, Daniel Melleno, Angela Parker, Bill Philpott, Susan Schulten, Jonathan Sciarcon, Hilary Smith, and Ingrid Tague for their support. Hilary in particular has been a generous and caring mentor since before my arrival in Denver. Outside Sturm Hall 366, Kelly Fayard, Darin Stewart, and Dheepa Sundaram have been supportive colleagues and friends, and I have learned as much about the world from my students as they have learned from me. Ang and Kelly have also been mentors, fellow revolutionaries, and coconspirators, and, more importantly, dear friends who keep me sane.

As much as friends and family have made fun of the many, many years I spent in school, my time spent as a student was invaluable. At the University of Pennsylvania, Lee Cassanelli, Paul Hendrickson, Ben Nathans, Peter Tarr, Margo Todd, and Keren Weitzberg helped me become a historian and a writer. At Columbia, Paula Span helped me become a good writer. Carol Benedict, Ananya Chakravarti, David Collins, Alison Games, John McNeill, and Jordan Sand were invaluable teachers and mentors at Georgetown, in and beyond the classroom. Benan Grams, Kevin McQueeney, Molly Thacker, and Jackson Perry were the best examples of genuinely supportive scholar-friends. Meredith McKittrick was a wise and steadfast advisor, and Kate de Luna pushed me to think beyond the nitty-gritty of what I was researching to consider why it mattered to studies of colonialism more broadly. Together, they both created community for those of us who were the first PhD students of African history on the hilltop. Sana Aiyar took me on as a student and has since served as a mentor who has helped me become a professor in my own right. In Harare, Dr. Hasu Patel has been a guide and a teacher who has shared with me the wisdom and insight of his years, and I have big shoes to fill as the next "Prof. Patel."

This book was the product of work that began in Harare in 2015, when Dilip Chouhan asked me to help create a community archive for the Hindu Society, and I spent many months in a dark room cataloguing and scanning thousands of pages of documents that became the foundation for the history of a community that has until now been invisible in scholarship on Zimbabwe. Prof. Hasu Patel shared with me his own personal archive of documents and recorded oral histories. The staff at the National Archives of Zimbabwe put up with my daily presence for many months, patiently answering my questions and digging out documents that had not been requested in decades. I thank them, as well as the staff at the National Archives branch in Bulawayo and the Library of the High Court of Zimbabwe, for their time and generosity. In the United Kingdom, I thank the National Archives, the British Library, the Parliamentary Archives, and the Derbyshire Records Office for access to their collections, and in the United States, the curators of the James Madison newspaper microfilm collection at the Library of Congress. In India, I would like to thank the archivists at the Abhilek Patal digitized records section of the National Archives for scanning documents for my use, a vital resource during the pandemic when travel was difficult. Various grants and fellowships funded this work, for which I am grateful, including from Georgetown University, a Fulbright-Hays Doctoral Dissertation Research Abroad grant from the Department of Education, the Cosmos Club, and the University of Denver. Maria Snyder in particular helped navigate the bureaucracies of grants at Georgetown University, and her support when I was abroad conducting research in the field was invaluable.

Numerous sources have offered me valuable feedback. Versions of the chapters as well as individual pieces of work received critique and commentary from conferences and workshops held by the African Studies Association–United Kingdom, the African Studies Association, the newly renamed Workshop on Southern Africa, the American Historical Association, the Georgetown Institute for Global History, and the Johns Hopkins Africa seminar. I would especially like to thank Jon Soske for attending the African history seminar at Georgetown and providing feedback on early drafts of writing. Casey Golomski, Jill Kelly, TJ Tallie, and Liz Timbs have provided feedback, solidarity, and friendship as fellow scholars of Southern Africa. I also thank the editors and anonymous reviewers of work published in the *Journal of Southern African Studies; Comparative Studies of South Asia, Africa and the Middle East;* the *Georgetown Journal of International Affairs; India in the World: 1500–Present; Xenophobia, Nativism, and Pan-Africanism in 21st Century Africa;* and *Sports in Africa: Past and Present* for feedback on published work that was foundational to my arguments and analysis for this book. Scholar-friends provided helpful feedback of revised book chapters, including Sana Aiyar, Rosalind Rothwell, attendees of the Northeastern Workshop on Southern Africa, Matthew Chiarello, and Liz Timbs.

I knew the University of Virginia Press was the ideal home for this book from the first email I received from Nadine Zimmerli. She, as well as Beth Colón Pizzini, have been patient, generous, and thoughtful editors. I would also like to thank Benedict Carton and Richard Elphick for recommending that this book be part of the Reconsiderations in Southern African History series, recognizing its contributions to the field. I also thank William Nichols for his helpful edits on chapter drafts, and the anonymous reviewers for their extensive and extremely helpful critique and commentary. My appreciation also extends to the editorial, design, and production team for their care and attention to detail during the editing process, and to Susan Murray for her thoughtful work on copy edits. For their help in tracking down original photographs and permissions for publication, I thank Kirit Patel, Dr. Hasu Patel, Dilip Chouhan, the Bulawayo Kshatriya Mandal, Raksha Bhagat at the Hindu Society of Harare, Thundeza Mafungwa at the University of Cape Town Libraries, Kudakwashe Mazuru at *The Herald*, Bharat and Hansa Patel, Anila Naik, Saroj Desai, Chetan Naik, and Pushpa Vashi. I would also like to thank Kate Blackmer for creating a beautifully detailed map of Gujarat for chapter 1. Thanks also go to Hansa Patel for help with translation from Gujarati to English during interviews, and for translating transcripts of oral histories.

The most basic form of history is storytelling. It is also the most compelling way to learn about the past. I have left for last those Zimbabweans who shared their time and stories with me, memories that are the foundation of this book supported by archival research and historical facts. They welcomed me into their homes and trusted me with their words. Some I have known all my life, while others I met for the first time—but they all treated me as if I were one of their own. Many are not named in this book, but their stories and insights were still critical for piecing together and contextualizing the history of Indians in Rhodesia. There were many others I did not get the chance to formally interview, but their friendship and community informed and inspired this project. I am not the sole author of the book—they are just as responsible for its existence as I am. This book is as much theirs as it is mine.

INTRODUCTION

In 1964, the Rhodesian government issued an arrest warrant for Joshua Mqabuko Nkomo. Nkomo was the leader of the Zimbabwe African People's Union (ZAPU), one of the nationalist parties fighting for the end of white minority rule. He was detained by security forces on 16 April and banished to Gonakudzingwa, a detention camp set up for political activists in the remote southeastern region of the country.[1] That much is established fact. Between the issuance of the warrant and his actual arrest, however, lies the murkiness of myths told about his attempts to evade capture. Along the railway lines that extended from the capital, Salisbury, through the border town of Umtali all the way to Mozambique lived the members of an extended family. They were descended from Gujarati Indian migrants who first crossed the Indian Ocean to settle in the territory decades before. The Rana family operated a lucrative laundry business, and members of the family network ran outlets of the laundry in the towns of Kadoma, Rusape, and Chipinge. The laundry shops were also a front for the liberation movement. They often harbored those evading the law and funneled money to ZAPU's underground operations. Nkomo, upon learning of his imminent arrest, allegedly sought refuge with the Rana family. The women dressed him in a sari, disguising him as one of them. The men then drove him through Chipinge, stopping at family homes along the way to Mozambique.[2] But Nkomo was eventually discovered by Rhodesian authorities, and detained.

The accuracy of this tale cannot be verified in any written documents. It is instead a story handed down from generation to generation of a family whose origins in what is now Zimbabwe date back to the 1890s. That Nkomo knew the Rana family is not contestable—the idea that he was successfully disguised in a sari is the somewhat outlandish element of the story. What is verifiable, however, is that Indian families across the country were settled in urban locales, mainly as traders. The shop, or the *dukkan* in Gujarati, was a key conduit in this story. It was a political space which allowed Indian members of ZAPU to support the party's underground operations. It was an economic center which allowed Indians to develop material wealth passed down across generations. It was a social space, too. Many Indian families lived in rooms above or behind their stores, and extended family networks were key to sustaining the domestic unit and ensuring economic livelihoods.

What is left out of this story is equally important. Missing from this narrative are the imperial networks which enabled Indians to settle in what was then Southern Rhodesia in the first place, following in the wake of the displacement of Nkomo's ancestors. Most Indian families were not directly involved in the struggle for independence. Young Indian men were recruited into the ranks of the Rhodesian army fighting against the nationalist movement in the 1970s, albeit against their will. Within the confines of their shops, Indians lived relatively insular lives, protected by the boundaries of domesticity and tradition. But the first Indian men who settled in Rhodesia did not return to the subcontinent. They chose to stay in Africa, and their wives joined them. Their children were born in Rhodesia, and their grandchildren in Zimbabwe. The businesses they founded stayed in the family across generations, outlasting the end of white rule. The shop allowed them to generate wealth and privilege, but through the few who used it to resist, it came to symbolize Indian participation in overturning white minority rule for the many.

Joshua Nkomo was ostensibly the main character in this story, but it was not really about him. Instead, it inserted Indians into the nationalist myth of how Rhodesia became Zimbabwe. In this framing, the authenticity of the tale does not really matter at all. What does matter is the deliberate and strategic association of one Indian family in their oral traditions with a hero of anticolonial nationalism. In the stories they told about their pasts, they highlighted how long they had been in the country and their role in creating both the colonial state as well as their contributions to its independence from white minority rule. But their assertion of political belonging through mythmaking is only one aspect of Indians being Zimbabwean. By passing this story down from generation to generation, Indians emphasized that they were Zimbabwean through historical and geographical claims to belonging.

This book goes beyond simply inserting Indians into Zimbabwean history. Instead, it argues that Indians transitioned from being a diasporic migrant population to becoming a Zimbabwean community. In this framing, Indians are reconstituted as an African population, not a foreign one. Their shops were distinctly African institutions, enabling their settlement in a new land by setting down roots across an ocean. But the *dukkan* was more than a physical institution. It was also a metaphor for an Indian presence in the country, and the role Indians played in its history through their shops. Just as the store was an African institution, so did Indians claim an identity grounded in Zimbabwe over generations. The centrality of the *dukkan* to the story about Nkomo in a sari reveals that it was through the shop that Indians in Rhodesia could find a way to become Zimbabwean.

THE IN-BETWEEN WORLD OF THE SHOP

Zimbabwe was a country of many names, names which declared to whom the country supposedly belonged. It was once the land of the kingdom of Zimbabwe, housed at Dzimba-hwe, "the houses made of stone." It was also the land of the Kingdom of Mutapa, the Rozvi state with a capital that no one can precisely locate. Later, it was the land of Lobengula, who came from the south and named his capital Bulawayo, "the place of killing." With the arrival of the Pioneer Column in 1890 and white rule under the British South Africa Company came the name Rhodesia, a tribute to the vision and ego of the enigmatic Cecil John Rhodes. Within the structures of the British Empire, the territory was declared Southern Rhodesia, a bureaucratically separate territory from the one to the north. The administration of what had become South Africa envisioned that Rhodesia would eventually join the Union. But Rhodesia's white settlers had plans of their own. In 1922, they voted against uniting with South Africa. The territory instead became self-governing the next year, albeit still under London's dominion, a colony-not-a-colony. In 1953, it became part of the Central African Federation of Rhodesia and

Nyasaland. In 1965, with its rogue self-declaration of independence from the imperial metropole, it became known simply as Rhodesia, a land which continued to deny Black majority rule. In 1979, the unrecognized state of Zimbabwe-Rhodesia briefly flickered into life. The Republic of Zimbabwe was the final name given to the nation-state in 1980, a remnant of an imagined glorious precolonial era that claimed to bring the entire country under an all-encompassing postcolonial identity.

Indian migrants and their descendants have been in Zimbabwe for as long as the white founders of the Pioneer Column, and therefore for as long as Rhodesia existed. The first Indian "pioneers" to the continent followed in the wake of indentured labor crossings to the railways of East Africa and the plantations of South Africa. By the twentieth century, Africa had become a "New World" for Gujarati peasants voluntarily migrating to seek new futures in an old land.[3] Rumors about the discovery of gold in Southern Rhodesia enticed prospective migrants. In the shadows of the Pioneer Column, Indian migrants came from the east via Mozambique and from the south via South Africa.[4] While the earliest travelers were a mix of free passengers from Gujarat and the descendants of indentured laborers already living in South Africa, it was the Gujarati migrants, both Hindu and Muslim, who stayed. Their descendants make up the majority of the local Indian population today, along with a small population of migrants who came from the Portuguese territory of Goa.

Indians never made up more than 2 percent of the country's population. Early colonial racial categories included Indians as part of the general "Asiatic" population. In 1911, they numbered 2,912 as compared to the white settler population of 23,606, out of a total population of 771,077.[5] By 1969, "Asians" still only numbered 8,965 as compared to 228,296 Europeans, out of a total population of 4,846,930.[6] Southern Rhodesia was a settler colony, like South Africa and Kenya, meant to attract large numbers of British emigrants to manage the mines and farm the land. But white migration took place in constantly refreshing cycles of arrivals and departures, "a settler colony with too few settlers."[7] Unlike many of the white pioneers of Rhodesia, Indians stayed and founded branches of family lines which extended across the Indian Ocean. Most of these families never returned to India, a distant homeland that over the years became more symbolic than real.

When they first arrived in the territory, Indians quickly learned that the mines and the wealth held within were not meant for them. The British South

Africa Company denied prospecting licenses to anyone who was not a white European. Indian men instead turned to the skills they already had as the sons of farmers, growing vegetables in small gardens located on white farms to sell to European residents and African workers. They operated as mobile hawkers, first on foot, then bicycle, then truck. As land legislation pushed them out of rural areas, they applied for general trading licenses and leased premises in the colony's towns and cities, selling goods ranging from kitchenware to clothing and everything in between. Eventually, their wives joined them from India.[8] Their families expanded, and Indians extended their stores by adding on living spaces that intimately connected their domestic lives to their economic livelihoods. The shop was a social center, one where the traditions of caste, endogamy, and religion brought across the Indian Ocean were reconstituted in an African context. In colonial urbanity, Indians used the shop to situate themselves as settlers, economic middlemen between white industrialists and African consumers. The shop counter was thus a site of interaction between Indians and their Black African customers. The literal practices of bargaining between shopkeeper and customer over the prices of goods were a metaphorical negotiation over ideas of belonging between populations who intimately shared urban spaces. The pavements outside Indian stores became vibrant trading hubs where Africans who worked in cities could aspire to middle-class status through consumerism and participation in colonial modernity. Because of its centrality to urban life, the *dukkan* eventually became an anticolonial space where select Indian men could participate in the construction of Zimbabwe as an independent African state.

The shop became a way for a minority migrant population to find belonging in a territory established by white settlers and then inherited by a Black majority. It was both a physical space as well as a metaphor for Indians' historic presence in Zimbabwe. In all the stories they told about their lives, as well as in written archives, Indians were always associated with the shop. Just as it became a uniquely African colonial economic institution, one that survived the demise of settler rule, so too did Indians stay in Zimbabwe. During the process of fast-track land reform in the 2000s, white farmers were constituted as an alien other, a remnant of colonial legacies that prevented full African control of the economy. Many left the country for the United Kingdom in response, returning to their "ancestral homeland." Unlike in other countries in Central and East Africa, however, Indians were not expelled after independence. Their shops and their assets were not seized as part of Africanization policies. Postcolonial legislation automatically constituted Indians as "indigenous" because of the discrimination they had faced during white minority rule, a status that had to be actively fought for in places like Kenya.[9] In turn, the shop was legally established as an indigenous economic institution. In a postcolonial nation-state where race and citizenship are conflated, the *dukkan* is a focal point for the creation of an African identity specific to a southern African context that complicates definitions of who belongs. As the *dukkan* is inherently both a Rhodesian and Zimbabwean space, those who lived and worked from these shops challenged a racially defined Zimbabwean identity.

Descendants of Indians migrants are Zimbabwean, even as they maintain the cultural traditions associated with their origins on the subcontinent, and the *dukkan* was more than a physical feature of Zimbabwean urbanity. Existing studies in African history have used the Indian shop to dehistoricize South Asian minorities by presenting them simply as middleman economic agents who were part of unchanging, insular, and one-dimensional diasporas. But the shop was not only a site for selling consumer goods. It was a private space that protected the structures of domesticity and kinship. It was a public social and political location where intimate encounters between different racial groups took place. It was a place where different forms of modernity were confronted, transformed, and reconceptualized as Rhodesia transitioned to becoming Zimbabwe. The Indian shop and the intersections of modernity at which it was located demonstrates that decolonization in Zimbabwe was not only about getting rural agricultural land back from a white minority. It was also about contestations over who belonged in urban as well as rural spaces.

BECOMING ZIMBABWEAN

Indians in Africa are identified primarily through the color of their skin—in other words, their racial identity. They are automatically designated "foreign," as "strangers," both within the continent and beyond it. Race was indeed the main form of demographic classification for the colonial state in southern Africa, but it was not always one that made sense. Gender and generation were also forms of negotiation through which ideas about civilization and class, religion and endogamy, and tradition and modernity, all played out through and beyond the shop as Indians sought belonging in different spaces. Social constructions of gender roles became a way in which colonial conceptions of race and South Asian religions were reconstituted in a specifically African context. Older generations of Indian men metaphorically extended the shop beyond its spatial confines to create structures meant to "protect" Indian women from African men and to prevent transgressive Indian men with African families from corrupting the community. Women and daughters were central elements around which Indians organized their communities and their social lives in Africa, even as shops were passed down from fathers to sons. Women were expected to marry within the boundaries of race and caste, their labor sustaining both the family and the business. By attempting to isolate their homes from the outside world, Indian men consolidated the segregationist foundations of the colonial state. But that did not mean women were confined to the interior rooms of the *dukkan*. They ran the shop counter, went to school, and transgressed the boundaries imposed on them daily. The idea that Joshua Nkomo had to dress as a woman to evade arrest demonstrates the patriarchal nature of narratives both about the migration

Figure 1. Kusumben Naik, Lalitaben Naik, and Urmilaben Naik behind the shop counter of M.V. Naik and Sons on Lobengula Street in Bulawayo in 1980. All of their husbands had once been involved with the nationalist movement. (Personal collection of Anila Naik)

process as well as the struggle for liberation, where women were often erased in the stories told by older men.[10] By becoming a woman, he was supposed to become invisible. But the very notion that he was allowed access to Indian women, who demonstrated their own agency by helping him to intimately take on their disguise, disrupts tropes about social insularity and the idea that Indians lived completely separate lives.

Gender was a way in which Indians sought to protect their worldviews inherited from their ancestors on the subcontinent, grounding—and protecting—themselves in an African space. But they inhabited other worlds determined by different ideologies. Their sense of identity and claims to belonging changed over time as further generations were born in Africa. The first generation of "pioneers," mostly men, saw themselves as imperial citizens, their identities intrinsically tied to their imagined civilizational origins in the British Raj. The colonial project allowed their migration, and they upheld its basic principles by choosing to stay. Their children, some of whom also came from India, some of whom were born in Rhodesia, used their static conceptions of "tradition" to protect their families from rapidly changing outside influences. In turn, they reenforced spatial and intimate forms of segregation. But they also began finding lives outside the shop. The grandchildren of the original pioneers located themselves as part of Rhodesian society and Western forms of consumer culture, while others found affinity with Black resistance and protest. They transgressed the boundaries that colonial racial hierarchies imposed on them in both subtle and overt ways. What they all had in common was that they used the shop as a site from which to negotiate their identities as Rhodesians, and then as Zimbabweans. When they tell their stories, they highlight what they did for Zimbabwe, even if their ancestors never imagined life outside of a colonial experience. They insert themselves into well-known historical narratives, emphasizing their presence in key moments, even in the shadows.

As a racial group, Indians were not a homogeneous unit. Families experienced colonialism and decolonization in vastly different ways. But every Indian family in Zimbabwe is linked to a particular "shop" or family business across generations. The *dukkan* was an inherently African institution, deeply shaped by local contexts. Through it, Indians themselves became African. They negotiated their identities on the ground in ways that went beyond their racial identity, which on its own defined them as eternal strangers. But they experienced Rhodesia's history as Africans, not that of transient expatriates.

The history of Indians in Zimbabwe is an African history—not one of a South Asian diaspora. By making this claim, this book reconstitutes southern African history by arguing that the region's minorities were as critical to understanding colonialism and anticolonialism as were contestations between Black and white over who belonged in the imperial territory, and to whom the postcolonial state belonged. But Indians never claimed the country as theirs. They instead sought belonging in the versions of Rhodesia that existed before it became Zimbabwe. They did not always articulate these claims overtly. But their historic existence in the country through the shop was their assertion of belonging.

This in turn calls for historians to redefine who and what we deem "African." This book makes three assertions to that end. The first is that the history it narrates is African history, and a truly Zimbabwean history, despite Indians being marginalized both historically and historiographically.[11] Until recently, historians of Zimbabwe were preoccupied with contestations between Black and white, between the ethnic categorizations of Shona and Ndebele, and between the political divisions of the ruling and opposition parties. This scholarship was a retroactive response in a highly racialized society in which opponents of dominant state narratives of a singular political struggle against white minority rule have been rendered "foreign," a mode of exclusion inherited directly from the settler colonial project. These divides have also been articulated as distinctions between rural and urban forms of belonging. State narratives emphasize a history grounded in the land, in the rural spaces where *mwana wevhu*, or the "child of the soil," can find their roots and the origins of their claim to indigeneity and belonging. Dissidents of this exclusive history instead turned to the urban centers and peripheries which complicated the nationalist myths on which Zimbabwe had been founded, sites where colonial power and ideas about belonging were dismantled and negotiated by transplanted populations, including Indians, in a multiplicity of ways.[12] The narratives of individuals, families, and communities highlighted in this book demonstrate how their histories were a critical aspect of local Zimbabwean contexts rather than being stories of insular and isolated diasporic subjects.

The history of Indians in Zimbabwe suggests that to be African does not necessarily equate to being indigenous or Black, drawing from Afropolitanism as an inclusive lens for the hybrid roots and influences of African cultures and peoples.[13] "Belonging" to a certain place is therefore not dependent on a racial identity. An Indian Ocean framework allows for a transnational and desegregated approach to reconceptualizing racialized as well as national identities, even for landlocked spaces that were still connected to the ocean through migration, colonialism, and decolonization. A second framing of identity this book makes is that Indians are African, calling for a deracialization of that term.[14] In a colonial context, race was a defining factor of identity, leading to definitions of "African" based on ideas about indigeneity and nativism. Colonial administrations categorized conquered populations according to fixed "tribes," and debates by scholars of Africa about the "invention of tradition" focused on the construction of ethnicity by both European rulers and African elites.[15] Imperial administrations strategically used race to relegate Indians and other migrant groups as "alien" populations and to displace Black Africans from their lands and their livelihoods based on civilizational discourse.[16] Just as the colonial experience "invented" ethnicity, so did it form ideologies of citizenship and belonging predicated on racial hierarchies that carried through into the postcolonial era. In that framing, Indians were defined as permanent "others," or "settled strangers."[17]

But theories of race and belonging were also constituted on the ground in ways that transcended the colonial experience.[18] In South Africa, Steve Biko defined being Black, and therefore being African, as "a reflection of a mental attitude," a commitment "to fight against all forces that seek to use your blackness as a stamp that marks you out as a subservient being."[19] Going beyond the "inter-group suspicions" created by the apartheid state, Biko saw not race, but commitment to the ideals of resistance as a form of solidarity based on historical experiences of disenfranchisement, which could include Indian and Coloured populations.[20] Many Indians in Rhodesia did not directly resist white minority rule and were politically ambivalent. But their history, lived through the shop, made their experiences uniquely African. They migrated to Africa as part of the colonizing project but lived as colonized populations. In turn, they resisted colonial ideologies that relegated them (and other racial groups) as inferior, both overtly and subconsciously. An expanded definition of the term "African" allows for Africans in the diaspora as well as diasporas within the continent to make claims to specific national citizenships as well as a more encompassing identity of what it means to be African in the world. It also allows for populations such as Coloured people in southern Africa, as well as mestizo, creole, and other communities with mixed origins living throughout the continent to claim a specifically African identity based on their lived historical experiences.

The third facet of identity this book considers relates specifically to nationality. If Indian history is African history, and if Indians are African, then Indians born in Zimbabwe are Zimbabwean. By delinking race from an African identity, and then from the national identities created by African postcolonial states bound by their inherited and artificial imperial borders, Indians are given space to be Zimbabwean. "Indian" as a term refers to a modern national identity and is not technically a racial classification. Indians born in Zimbabwe, descended from parents and even grandparents who were born in Rhodesia, are not "Indian" by nationality, and therefore the term makes no sense as an identifying label. They do not have to be Black to belong. They are sometimes referred to as the hyphenated identity of "Indian-Zimbabweans," or as "Zimbabweans of Indian origin." But they can simply be called Zimbabweans, along with every other person born in that land. This book argues that Indians are Zimbabwean based on their historical and geographic claims to citizenship. They made generational claims to belonging by staying. Subjects interviewed referred to themselves as Zimbabwean, and African, and Indian, and Asian, at different times and in different historical moments. What was clear from all of their stories, however, was that their lives were uniquely shaped by their lived experiences in Zimbabwe, not defined by their origins in a subcontinental homeland. This argument complicates the specifically Zimbabwean postcolonial nationalist agenda which projected the country's history as a contest between Black and white for land. Indian participation both in the construction of the colonial project as well as in anticolonial resistance through the shop complicates this narrative and postcolonial definitions of national belonging to answer the question, "Who is Zimbabwean?"

HISTORIES FROM BELOW

This is not a political or economic history of Zimbabwe. By centering the stories and lives of individuals, families, and communities, this book is a social and cultural history of Indians in Rhodesia. It is told from their perspective from their shops and their homes. As such, they are the main subjects—not white settlers, nor Black Africans—and it is their histories in the archives that are the foundation of this work. White settler society constructed the scaffolding of a modern colonial state. The populations they excluded from power were the ones who shaped it and who challenged its constrictions from below. It is their lived experiences that made Indians African. These experiences were not isolated. Just as with white administrators, Black Africans are present throughout this book, even in their absence. Indians relied on domestic insularity from the majority Black population in order to protect structures of economic and social endogamy based on caste and race within settler colonial structures, all the while depending on them for their livelihoods, the focus of the first three chapters. Afro-Indian political and intellectual engagement becomes more visible and viable in particular historical moments, seen in the second half of the book. Rather than rewriting histories of Zimbabwe that center Black African narratives, the goal of this book is to add to existing literature, contributing another valuable perspective to foundational and newer works in the field.

Beyond Zimbabwe, the idea that the histories of Indian migrants and their descendants are African histories has implications for studies of colonialism and empire. Recent histories of the British Empire focus on the "forgotten officials and governors," tending to see the empire as a whole as imposed from above.[21] In political studies of individual colonies, the dichotomy of collaborator versus resistor lingers as a specter, still based on the old idea that colonizers imposed and colonizers resisted. Social and cultural histories of colonized communities in Africa instead see them as critical to the shaping of the colonial experience, with a messy space of negotiation in between. The character and trajectory of empire is best understood through the colonized, and through the quotidian mundanity of their daily lives. Through their shops and in the daily actions and choices that constituted their identities, Indians both upheld the idea of Rhodesia and resisted it at different historical points. Empire was built from the ground up, and done so sporadically and haphazardly, by white settlers and Indian migrants as well as African agents. The lived experiences of the colonized show how it was constructed and destroyed simultaneously and in complex, interweaving ways. Indians made themselves African in their historical participation in these processes.

Because of their transnational origins, Indians in Africa have always been considered "strangers" in African history. Older histories of Indian communities in Africa tended to focus solely on insular community histories at the expense of considering the existing worlds and modernities into which they relocated.[22] South Asian concepts of religion were highlighted as central ways in which Indian families organized themselves and set up boundaries of domesticity. But these limits were also disrupted. Diasporas did not migrate into vacuums.[23] They were remade over generations outside the subcontinent, reconfiguring the social institutions and structures of power of the places to which they migrated. In recent decades, the use of the Indian Ocean as a methodological framework has opened space for a consideration of narratives of diaspora beyond the scaffolding of the nation-state and the ways in which national and transnational affiliations intersected and changed over time and space.[24] Within the subfield of the South Asian diaspora in Africa, studies centering on African contexts marked a transition from a tunnel-vision focus on an Indian homeland to that of the ways in which diasporic populations have been important threads woven through the fabric of African history.[25]

This book was fundamentally influenced by that scholarship, and in particular by Sana Aiyar, who argues that Indians' "diasporic consciousness" in Kenya emerged from two political homelands, leading to shifting meanings of Indian, African, and Kenyan at different historical moments. In her work, Kenya is centered as the formative local context for the transformation of transnational Indian political ideologies.[26] Indeed, Ned Bertz has called for an integration of an Indian Ocean framework with urban African history, and for scholars to break through the boundaries between "diasporist versus nationalist historiographies" that isolate Indians from historical African experiences.[27] Indians in Zimbabwe drew from conceptions of culture and tradition in India, but in response to local conditions of colonialism. Hindus and Muslims lived together in Africa, even as the Partition of India and Pakistan tore communities and families apart. The trajectories of communalism which had split Hindus and Muslims on the subcontinent came back together as a singular racial category in a colonial context, even as both groups continued to debate ideas of morality and patriarchy. Caste and wealth became disassociated from one another, even as both were used a way to enforce class and social identities within the racial hierarchies of the settler colonial world. Miscegenation between Indians, Africans, and Coloureds took place, causing contestations across generations over the identities of the children born to these relationships. Domestic insularity based on traditions formed on the subcontinent did not equate to completely separate historical experiences but instead became a localized forum through which Indians and other colonized populations could negotiate ideas about class and gender and how they would share urban spaces, drawing from James Brennan's consideration of the negotiations between Indians and Africans as historical actors over access to space and property.²⁸ Solidarities and tensions between both groups took place in response to local dynamics of change and power, as shown by Shobana Shankar's work on discourses of race and caste in West Africa that transcended colonialism.²⁹ Political engagements between Indians and Black Africans formed because of the nature of social transactions across the shop counter mediated by ideas about gender and domesticity, and as Jon Soske has shown for apartheid South Africa, the Indian "thread" was integral to understanding Black political ideologies.³⁰

But previous studies continue to conceive of Indians as essentially diasporic populations, while India and the Indian Ocean remain centered. In Zimbabwe, these transformations took place through the shop, which was very much an African space. Nearly all works on Indians in Africa have only considered the shop as an economic or racial enclave, one that kept Indians and Black Africans separate as a product of wealth and privilege predicated on racial hierarchies. As a social space where conceptions of caste, gender, and race were remade, however, the *dukkan* becomes far more than a diasporic middle space in between the worlds of white Europeans and Black Africans. The use of the term "diaspora" has only recently been applied to South Asian migrants, with the caveat that the word was historically used to describe migrant populations who were forced to leave a homeland due to political and economic factors.³¹ Rather than seeing the term as a fixed one, however, diasporas can be remade over generations, identifying with locales other than the idea of an original "homeland."³² It was in this ambiguous space of generational gaps and relocation that Indians in Rhodesia reworked their conceptions of Gujarati, Hindu and Muslim, and Indian identities to mean something in a settler colonial African context. Over time, they evolved from being a diaspora to becoming Zimbabwean, even as their conceptions of South Asian traditions continued to define their lives in and beyond the *dukkan*.

FROM RHODESIA TO ZIMBABWE

Chapter 1 traces how Indians arrived in Southern Rhodesia and how they fit into the settler colonial order. The patriarchs who passed down their stories of migration co-opted the language of white Rhodesian pioneers to justify their settlement in a land that was not their own. Their narratives highlighted how long Indians had been in the country, locating the original founders of families still living in Zimbabwe today. A central element of these stories, told by men about men, was the sacrifice and hardships that the "pioneers" suffered to become successful businessmen. They became a critical part of the settler colonial project as economic agents through early variations of their trading sites, even as they found themselves facing hostility to their presence from white settler society. But Indians stayed, using their trading activities to situate themselves. Their claims to belonging were predicated on their identity as part of an imperial collective rather than on their racial identity or the direct displacement of Africans. In their origin stories, they remember their status as colonized peoples seeking new opportunities rather than as colonizing settlers, claiming belonging in a way that white migrants could not.

Chapter 2 focuses on the transition of the mobile Indian trading site to becoming the *dukkan*, a fixed feature of urban spaces that was the first iteration of "home" on African soil. The shop sustained kinship networks as wives began joining their families, providing necessary labor. By bringing their wives back with them, male heads of families chose to transplant domestic institutions that made their presence permanent. Indians engaged with African customers across the shop counter, negotiating their presence in a way that white settlers did not engage in with Black laborers. Set between white neighborhoods and Black townships, Indian trading streets consolidated the frontiers of spatial segregation. But some Indian traders continued to operate in African locations, transgressing the boundaries of intimacy. The census as a tool of analysis showed how Indians reenforced gender roles and social insularity as their families expanded through the shop. But it also demonstrated how intimate encounters between Indians and Africans that breached the divide of the shop counter disrupted segregationist norms, leading to Indian patriarchal anxieties over their children's futures.

As a result, Indian interlocutors metaphorically extended the shop to the creation of religious and educational institutions known as "purity" schools to reenforce the bounds of domesticity in an African setting. Chapter 3 explores the history of these schools, which only admitted the children of two Indian parents. They were funded by the colonial state but run by upper-caste Hindu men who used language of "purity" derived from South Asian caste hierarchies as well as racialized settler colonial society to negotiate their agendas with the government. Rather than colonial officials transplanting ideas about caste and tradition, it was ordinary Indians who informed education policy. Their readings of religion were constructed by Brahminic and colonial ideologies on the subcontinent but were renegotiated by local interlocutors in an African context in order to prevent miscegenation with the communities with whom they shared urban spaces. They were less concerned about the "corruption" of their wives, many of whom had migrated from India as married women, than they were about their daughters. Children born in Africa became the "essence" of Indian communities through their potential for physical procreation as well as the reproduction of custom, and their education became a point of contention with the colonial state as well as Muslim and lower-caste Hindu families who deviated from upper-caste notions of morality.

The colonial state frequently intervened in these conflicts, and negotiations over the boundaries of domesticity and the restrictions of a segregationist society often ended up in courts for mediation. Chapter 4 takes up the narrative of legal cases brought by Indians to the intermediary space of the courtroom, which brought the state into intimate contact with its residents. These challenges took two forms. The first was through contestations over immigration restrictions and family law that codified the rules for marriage and inheritance. Judges often had to consider personal law in India, and the children who were born to parents married in India were the ones who had to negotiate the outcomes of these transnational relationships. In turn, they sought access to the worlds outside the shop as a way to ground localized forms of belonging. The second type of challenge saw court cases against spatial segregation that limited where Indians could expand their shops, as well as where they could find social lives outside of them. Rather than the shop existing as a space of insularity from the outside world, it instead became a tool used by its owners to directly confront the state.

Investment in the judicial process shaped a faith in the system. Rather than challenging individual restrictions, Indians now wanted to become part of the system in order to change it. A younger generation started to build their identities beyond the confines of the shop, as shown in chapter 5. They compartmentalized their lives by wearing Western clothing, listening to British and American music, and rebelling against gender roles outside of the shop. At the end of the day, they returned to the safety of Indian traditions in the home. But social participation in white society made Indians want to participate more publicly in the political system. Indian men in the capital city of Salisbury began running for local office, developing an identity as "Rhodesians first, Asians second." Wealthier families began separating their homes and their shops as a form of upward class mobility. While the shop was no longer a physical domestic space, it was still a center of family life, and understanding Indian desires to both protect it and expand beyond it is key to understanding their participation in the system. But their identity as "Rhodesians" was threatened when Indian men who were meant to take over family businesses were recruited to the army to fight a war they did not believe was theirs to fight.

Farther south, in the city of Bulawayo, a select group of Indian men used the shop to become part of underground resistance networks to overturn the system rather than reform it. The *dukkan* became a front for the recruitment of members and channeling of funds to ZAPU, expanding it as a space of engagement between Indians and Africans. These stories of quotidian collaboration exist beneath the surface of glorified narratives of transnational Afro-Asian solidarity, which masked tensions as well as localized alliances. But chapter 6 is less a story of fraternity versus friction than it is of the daily participation of Indian men and their families in the nationalist movement. It was once again men who determined the nature of this collaboration, while women sustained the practical concerns of the home and the shop. In between the accounts of conflict between guerrillas and Rhodesian forces, and between factions of the nationalist movement, were the lives of the families who lived on Lobengula Street, which became a frontier between their identities as the descendants of Indian ancestors, and their claim to belonging in an African future where they could become Zimbabwean.

RETHINKING THE ARCHIVE

I am from Zimbabwe, and my family is of Indian origin. I am a "born free," or a child born after independence in 1980. I grew up among the people I write about, and their stories and histories were familiar ones. My objectivity can thus justifiably be questioned, especially in accounts of the history of my own ancestors and my family. At the same time, my personal location in the writing of this history aims to counter the exoticization and otherization by Western scholars of communities in the Global South, a legacy that still haunts many works of ethnography. There has been an increasing call for scholars descended from the colonized, rather than the colonizers, to enter these conversations. If a true decolonization of the academy is to occur, there must be more discourse between academics who are removed from the people and places they study with historians who come from those communities themselves.

For me, this means acknowledging that the stories of my ancestors and how I came to be Zimbabwean are ones to be proud of, but also a problematic history to reckon with. Indians in Zimbabwe are notoriously race-conscious and racist, predicated on precolonial ideas about colorism and colonial forms of privilege. Indians in Rhodesia were settlers as well as colonized peoples; they participated in structures which enabled the displacement of the African majority from lands that were rightfully theirs. I have benefited from the transgenerational forms of wealth earned by my great-grandparents and grandparents from the shops they built when they crossed an ocean to better their lives. All Indian Zimbabweans of my generation have profited, to varying degrees, from this legacy. And yet, they continue to disparage Black Zimbabweans, to join in the calls of white émigrés who argue that life was better in Rhodesia, even as their family wealth continues to come from a country ruled by a Black majority without whom their family businesses would have no livelihoods. They refer to Black people as "karyas," based on the Gujarati word for "black," an inherently derogatory term for people they see as inferior. In writing this book, I was influenced by the legacy given me by my maternal grandfather and my father, two men born in Zimbabwe who have used their privilege to counter the colonial forms of oppression which allowed them to live relatively comfortable lives. The inheritance they have passed down to me is invaluable. My inspiration also comes from my mother, born to a household on Lobengula Street which was revolutionary in that it raised its daughters to stand for the rights that all born in Zimbabwe deserved.

These "messy, multisided histories" call for a reading of the colonial archive for "destabilizing forces" against the settler colonial vision of a racially ordered society which predicated access to wealth and power.[33] Navigating these "life geographies" involved a consideration of the various layers of hyperlocal, local, national, and transnational stories across space and time, all the while confronting the politics of both written and oral narratives.[34] At the heart of each chapter are stories centered on individual families, contextualized within larger frameworks of community, city, colonial state, and empire. Biographies have recently returned to vogue as historical sources, centering the voices of those previously marginalized from scholarly attention.[35] I argue here for the idea of people as archives of their own lives, particularly in countries in the Global South, where official and institutional documentation is sporadically collected and catalogued.[36] In Zimbabwe, access to the national archives is heavily controlled, and due to inadequate funding, facilities are ill-maintained and documents frequently go missing. The Rhodesian Front physically destroyed official records dealing with the period after 1965 before they left power, and the Zimbabwean Ministry of Home Affairs continues to restrict the availability of state documents produced after 1980.

Achille Mbembe has argued that while the state does not exist without its archives, the archive's very existence is a threat to the state.[37] To locate the voices that contradicted official narratives of the Zimbabwean past, I conducted oral histories. The people I talked to were Hindu and Muslim but also informants from other racial identities who were knowledgeable about the history of Indians in Rhodesia. My familiarity with most of the people I interviewed, some of whom I met for the first time, others who I had known for my entire life, meant that I walked a fine line between writing within and writing without. People felt comfortable talking to me, but I also had to approach them as an outsider to a certain extent, formalizing conversations that would otherwise happen organically, the subtle presence of a recording device within sight. I recount the oral histories that are the center of each chapter's framework as they were told to me, highlighting their authenticity and what Indians understood as most important about their lives in becoming Zimbabwean. This is not a book about how memory works, but it is about these life histories and what they tell us about Zimbabwe's history.

Equally important to situating the lives of Indians in Zimbabwe's history were archival records, despite their limitations. The construction of the contextual layers of this narrative began in 2015 with a community initiative led by the Hindu Society of Harare to collect the personal documents of individual families. I volunteered to create a physical archive of these collections, and also created a digital record. I was initially tasked with sorting through and cataloguing only the documents pertaining to Hindu families—not anything related to the Muslim population. I included everything anyway. In any case, it would have been difficult to distinguish between Hindu and Muslim narratives because of the intertwining threads of their stories. Beyond oral histories and community archives, these histories were also found in records from archives in Harare, Bulawayo, New Delhi, London, and Washington, DC. Archives in London and Delhi provided a transnational overview of imperial immigration and policy. In the Zimbabwean archives, where searches are conducted manually, there were a significant number of records located under the specific label "Indian"—but some of the most interesting documents came from collections relating more generally to urban council regulations, immigration, and education, reflecting the integration of Indian lives into broader historical narratives of social and public spaces. In Bulawayo, municipal council records combined with records from state archives in Harare demonstrated the various attempts at racial categorization that took place. Census records were instrumental for the narrative construction of settlement patterns, and newspaper and magazine collections from Zimbabwe and the Library of Congress in the United States provided contexts for checking facts, timelines, and public responses and attitudes. Legal libraries in Harare provided access to legislation and court cases, but the views of ordinary people also came through in their petitions and the challenges they brought to courts.

As a student of colonialism, I attempted to read "along the grain" of these colonial narratives for "small gestures of refusal and silence amongst the colonized."[38] The voices of the colonized that come through in challenges to state-imposed racial categorizations are highlighted through this archival methodology. This was seen in correspondence written to the state and newspapers, as well as in individual census schedules filled out by heads of families. Their self-classification of their race, nationality, religion, and profession tells me more about how they lived their lives than if I had simply read the categories and data into which they were slotted in official reports. Through these types of documents, I read the colonial project as one that was as much constructed—and deconstructed—by the people it governed as it was imposed through official institutions and systems. In between these different worlds and forms of modernity were real people. Behind the words of these pages are the stories of their lives.

ONE
UNDESIRABLES AND PIONEERS
—
Crossing the Indian Ocean, 1890–1923

> The majority of the inhabitants are determined to oppose by every means in their power the introduction of Banyan traders into Umtali, as they consider that the displacement of white traders by Asiatics will be very prejudicial to the prosperity of Umtali and Rhodesia generally and take the bread out of a large number of the mouths of Europeans.
>
> —ACTING CIVIL COMMISSIONER TO UNDER-SECRETARY, Southern Rhodesia, 9 January 1899

In December 1896, Bhimjee Rao Naik arrived in Beira from Bombay. He was of Gujarati origin and was seventeen years old. The exact reasons he got on a ship and crossed the Indian Ocean, or the *kala pani*, are unknown.[1] He first worked as a clerk for the Beira and Mashonaland Railway Company in the Portuguese territory of Mozambique. He then began to follow the construction of the railway eastward, setting up his first trading stand in a village in the Machaze Province. By 1899, the Beira railroad had expanded toward British South Africa Company (BSAC) territory.[2] According to legend, Naik became the first "pioneer" from the east to settle in what would become the colony of Southern Rhodesia, sometime at the turn of the twentieth century. He established another small shop in the border town of Umtali, a layover on the railway line toward the settlement of Fort Salisbury. In the no-man's-land between the invisible boundaries established by European settlers and companies, Naik imported goods from the Portuguese territory to trade to the Africans who lived in the surrounding areas of the Eastern Highlands.³ Dozens more would follow in his wake.

The Gujarati community in Zimbabwe today continues to evoke Bhimjee Naik's name as a central character in the stories of their "pioneers," passed down from generation to generation. Unlike white settlers, many of whom published written accounts of their settlement, Indians passed their stories down verbally.⁴ Their descendants almost always begin their stories in Zimbabwe in the distant past, blurring the distinction between oral histories of their own lives and the telling of oral traditions of genealogical descent passed down over the decades. The transmission of oral traditions of the arrival of ancestors is "communal and continuous" yet also filtered by the oral histories focusing on the experiences of the last storytellers in the chain.⁵ In this way, Indians explained the historical roots of their claims to belonging in Africa. Rather than "memory becoming more important than history," however, oral storytelling as a practice presents a method for exploring the validity of both fact and fiction in telling the tales of migration that were never written down.⁶ The stories of Naik's success through the shop became a collective origin story for the entire community. In turn, the first physical iterations of the *dukkan* enabled the expansion of families and kinship networks, allowing migrants to establish their businesses and then pass them down to their sons and grandsons.

In stories told by men about men, the pioneers were remembered as successful in business, sacrificing ties with their homeland to better their lives. But women were erased in these narratives. It was men who first made the crossing, and women who followed in their wake. Naik returned to India in 1903 to marry his wife, bringing her to Southern Rhodesia in 1909, but her name is not mentioned even in written accounts of his legendary settlement.⁷ The gendered nature of pioneer stories reveals how Indians participated in the patriarchal nature of settler society as they attempted to find affinity in Africa as members of an imperial collective.⁸ Their narratives in turn erased the Black Africans who had been displaced from their lands by the colonial project. An indigenous African presence rendered migrant Indian claims to belonging fragile, and so like white pioneer tales, these origin stories focused on the adventure of the relocation process, rather than what—or who—was there before both white and Indian settlers arrived.

This chapter traces how Indians migrated to Southern Rhodesia, and how they fit into the settler colonial order. By choosing to make their lives as urban traders, Indians participated in the construction of Rhodesia as a settler territory. They became economic agents through their shops, and imperial subjects who used the language evoked by white settlers to justify their mobility. But Indians found themselves facing hostility to their presence. The white settlers who formed the first governing and legislative body of the territory as shareholders of the BSAC vigorously debated whether further migration from Asia should be allowed, centered around fears of Indian infringement upon white labor, agriculture, and commerce. Indian migration threatened the very concept of a colony which the members of the original Pioneer Column from South Africa intended for mass white settlement. They labeled Indian migrants as "undesirables" and began to restrict their entry in the construction of boundaries of belonging to the settler space. They argued for the exclusion of Indians as perpetually colonized strangers moving between imperial spaces, otherizing and foreignizing these men as unwanted members of settler society. By regulating Asian migration rights, the white settler government established critical parameters of entry that were foundational to ideas of who belonged in the territory—and who did not.

But Indian families, unlike white Rhodesians, whose population fluctuated through constant cycles of immigration and emigration, set down roots in the territory, even as they moved back and forth across the Indian Ocean in the maintenance of endogamous marriage and kinship structures. As a result, most of these Indian families today can trace their lineage back directly to an original migrating ancestor, or "pioneer." The first Gujarati men were attracted to Africa by rumors of gold. The British South Africa Company denied them access to both mineral and agricultural wealth, but still they stayed. Colonial administrators in settler colonies often described Gujarati traders in the Indian Ocean world as "birds of passage," transient migrants with no roots in the places they settled.[9] This trope ignored the fact that Indians were colonized populations seeking freedom of mobility and rights of settlement in the British colonial world. Through their shops, they transitioned from being diasporas to being fixed communities. They predicated their claims to belonging in Rhodesia by seeking membership in an imperial collective rather than on the direct displacement of Africans. When white society rejected their presence, they remembered their status as colonized peoples rather than as colonizers, claiming belonging in a way white families could not by highlighting their continual presence across generations against all odds.

LEAVING

In Zimbabwe, origin stories from the past are key in the creation of communal identities in the present. For the Shona, the symbolic power of the spirit mediums Kaguvi and Nehanda are a poignant reminder of the struggle for liberation from the white man.[10] The Ndebele are defined by the legacy of the conquering Mzilikazi and his son, Lobengula. White Rhodesians invoke Cecil Rhodes as the founder of "their" nation, his dreams of expanding the British Empire from the Cape to Cairo invoking settler nostalgia for the days when they traversed "Dark Africa" to bring civilization and glory to the continent. The Gujaratis of Zimbabwe orient their origins in a lesser-known ancestor, one whose name invokes the perils of passage, the hostile space of the immigration office, and failed dreams of gold and riches. Bhimjee Naik is central to their pioneer narratives, a symbol of the struggle and sacrifice it took for Indians to settle in Rhodesia. In the stories each family tells about their original pioneer, Naik serves as the collective ancestor and patron of the kinship networks that allowed Indians to migrate—and then to stay.

White Rhodesian pioneer narratives similarly begin with the arrival of the Pioneer Column, a quasi-military troop made up of British civilians organized by Cecil Rhodes to secure the frontiers of southern Africa in the areas known as Matabeleland and Mashonaland. They came from the west from Bechuanaland, working their way northeast. They were conquerors extending imperial visions of white settlement that dated back to the arrival of the Dutch at the Cape of Good Hope in 1652. Their trek extended forward in time to the Rudd Concession of 1888, which took away Ndebele rights to their land, to uprisings in Mashonaland and Matabeleland in 1896 and 1897, which encapsulated the violence of the settlement project. Indians, however, arrived in the shadows, and as part of centuries-old networks of precolonial trade and migration in the Indian Ocean world. Because many of them were illiterate, the stories of their experiences they passed down to their children were more fragile than those written by white settlers.

However, their migration was linked to earlier patterns of transoceanic engagement. The earliest migrations of Gujarati merchants to the Swahili coast date back to the fifteenth century, an age of growing "long-distance trading connections" built through temporary, "circular" migration patterns.[11] These earlier networks of commerce and mobility established the physical shipping routes and ports that predated European imperialism. The earlier passages of ancestors who had once traveled back and forth between East Africa and Bombay provided the imaginative power that made crossing the ocean centuries later conceivable.[12] But it was the nineteenth-century colonial system of sending indentured labor to East and southern Africa and the Caribbean which delivered the practical frameworks of bureaucracy and passenger ships. After the formal abolition of slavery, the British created the system of indentured labor in the 1830s. Africans could not yet be induced to work for Europeans, and labor was needed in the sugarcane fields and for the construction of railways. The 1870s in India saw growing "agricultural uncertainty," causing indebted Indians to accept contracts for periods of labor on plantations in Jamaica, Trinidad, Guiana, Mauritius, Fiji, South Africa, Malaya, Burma, Ceylon, and Zanzibar and for railway construction in Kenya and Uganda.[13] Most of these indentured laborers came from Bengal or the south of India, entering what was essentially a form of debt bondage.

Indenture was suspended in 1917 and officially came to an end in the 1920s. But the incentives for leaving rural India survived. The first Indian migrants to Rhodesia came from farming communities, not the old merchant families of Bombay who had dispersed to all parts of the globe. In 1899, the monsoon failed, which led to a severe famine in 1900. The numbers of young men leaving Gujarat in the early years of the twentieth century increased as a result.[14] Their stories were cast in similar terms to those of the first white migrants from South Africa and England to Southern Rhodesia, rumors of new opportunities casting a "spell over poor, unskilled, uneducated whites with the promise of elevated status and wealth."[15] Unlike white settlers who were encouraged to migrate by the British government, however, Indians "migrated into this Colony on their own accord ... moved by the same spirit which has driven men and women to seek wealth and adventure outside the confines of their native land."[16] There was no question of women traveling on their own, however; even the idea of young men leaving was anathema for several families.

In the village of Vankarwad in Gujarat, a young man by the name of Natu Patel, who would later go on to work for Bhimjee Naik, was struggling to find a job at a bank in the nearby town of Surat. "In the meantime my patience was exhausted," he said of those years sitting around back home waiting to find a job. "I thought it better I go somewhere outside India."[17] Another, by the name of Hari Patel in the village of Dharmaj whose father owned a few small plots of land "wanted to be more than a small farmer."[18] D. M. Desai's father was his family's only son. His father farmed rice and mango trees in Parujan, and though the family had "enough food and everything," Desai's father had ambitions of his own, attending school in Baroda and eventually becoming a teacher at the English school in the village. He earned ten rupees per month as a state teacher, but as the family story went, was one day slapped by his uncle who said, "What are you going to learn in a school like this?" And so he left home for Bombay in 1918 in search of a job.[19]

Even after obtaining a position, he dreamed of finding opportunity in new lands. In 1891, the first gold mine was opened in Southern Rhodesia. Stories of gold, allegedly in even larger supply than on the Witwatersrand, piped the tune of opportunity.[20] Gujarati men first heard rumors of Mashonaland, the land of gold, through neighbors, or a friend of a friend, or a relative who had already made the crossing. "Gold was important to Indians, and enticed them to come out," said the son of a man who left in 1904.[21] The fabled wealth of Mashonaland had also attracted the attention of Rhodes and the BSAC, who eventually found the rocky hills to be mostly depleted of their mineral wealth. But Indians were systemically denied access to prospecting licenses to search for what was left.[22] As a result, it was existing networks of migrants already in Africa that featured more prominently in oral histories, not gold specifically. The first iterations of the shop appeared from the start. The earliest migrants were already taking part in some form of trading by the time others heard of the colony's existence. When Natu Patel failed his matriculation examinations in 1918, one of his schoolmates had just set out for Southern Rhodesia. "From him I come to know there is one country where educated people could easily pass English examination," he later recounted. "I investigated myself, the conditions there, how Indian people can make a living," deciding that the prospects there sounded better than they did in Fiji, another destination for one of his peers.[23] Hari Patel's neighbor was already in Southern Rhodesia, and his father wrote to the neighbor asking him to assist his son with the transition.[24] D. M. Desai's father, while clerking for the governor of Bombay, met Maganlal Rambhai Desai at the train station in 1920. Maganlal was living in Salisbury at the time and had come back to India

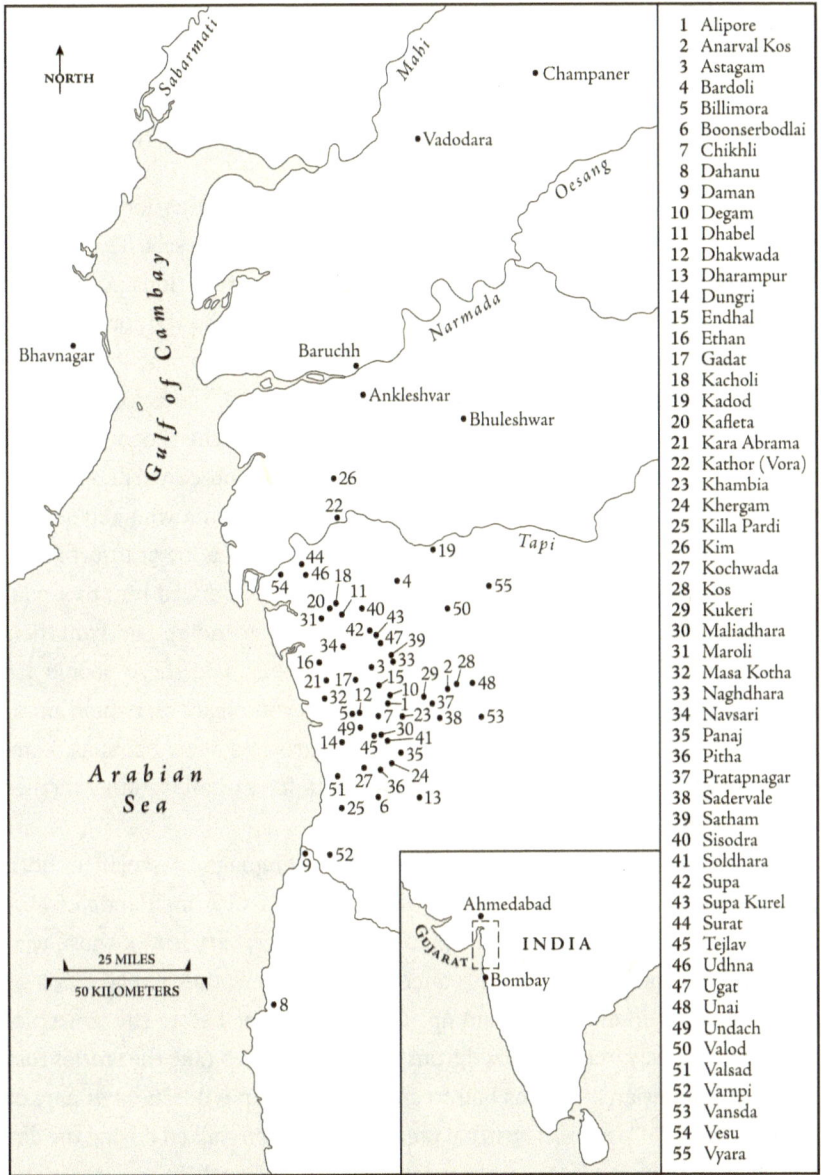

Map 1. Map of Gujarat indicating villages, towns, and cities from which many Indian families in Zimbabwe today originate. Gujarat as a state was created in 1960; before that it was a linguistic region of the Bombay Province created by the British Raj. (Map created by Kate Blackmer, based on information from "mind maps" drawn by Tulsidas Doolabh from memory and details supplied by Nagin Vithal; original maps from *Bulawayo Kshatriya Mandal 75th Anniversary Commemorative Magazine,* 1994, HSA CURE0011-133)

for a visit home. Their fathers had gone to school together, and Desai decided to go to Southern Rhodesia and join Maganlal, not telling anyone from the family that he wanted to leave for Africa. Borrowing six hundred rupees from a friend, and after applying for a British Indian passport in Bombay, he set off for Beira by steamer ship.[25]

The ships were part of the British India Steam Navigation Company, which at the time consisted of more than five hundred vessels. The journey from Bombay to Beira took seventeen days, stopping at various ports along the East African coast before turning south. The men bound for Southern Rhodesia docked at Beira, a port city established in 1890 by the Portuguese, where the steamer anchored for a week. Once on land, the colonial village networks of Gujarat were there to welcome newcomers. The shop was usually at the center of these systems of kinship, both real and constructed. Natu Patel met a man on the steamer by the name of Mr. Mehta who had settled earlier in Fort Victoria. "He was the man who gave us a lot of information on the road," Patel later recalled. In Beira, Mehta introduced him to a man by the name of Haribhai who was working for another Indian family in their store in Umtali: "Mr. Mehta, knowing this Haribhai, said these people are new and don't know anyone in Umtali, so will you please put them up at night?" The next morning, armed with some *puris* and a few bananas, Patel and a group of other travelers boarded the train for Umtali, heading farther into the depths of the unknown.[26]

Migration narratives were couched in the language of sacrifice, both physical and emotional. The journey across the eastern highlands of Mozambique was generally done in a piecemeal manner; very few of those who arrived in the early days had any concrete plan for how they would travel or where they would eventually end up. Those who came before the construction of the railway in 1898 walked from Beira to Umtali.[27] Like the stories told by white Rhodesians, Indians had to cross the African wilderness as part of their journeys.[28] To avoid nocturnal predators, the men walked during the day and slept in trees at night. In a somewhat fantastical retelling, one morning, Yusuf Adam's grandfather woke up to find a pride of lions sitting underneath the tree he had sought shelter in for the night; he was, according to this version of the story, forced to sit in the tree for three days, surviving on leaves, until the lions eventually moved on.[29] With the construction of the railway, that part of the journey became less perilous and more mundane, thanks in large part to village networks of friends and acquaintances whose trading sites were stationed along the way. Sacrifices here took the form of emotional rather than physical tolls. Some who arrived in Beira had only enough money to make it there and no farther. M. P. Patel's father mortgaged a set of golden buttons that his mother had given him to a man called Chotukaka who had already settled in Salisbury; with that money, he was able to board the train that would carry him onward. "It took him a long time to get that back from Chotukaka," his son recalled. "It was sad for him because that was a memory of his mother."[30]

These men told their sons the stories of their migration, which they passed down to their sons in turn. The tales they told were not just their own origin stories but also the stories of how the *dukkan* they would pass down to their children was established as well. The stories highlight a treacherous trek across wild landscapes, following in the footsteps of the Indian men who had passed the same way before them. From their shops, these men helped newcomers on their journey to setting up their own businesses. Women barely feature, except as figures who were left behind in India as wives and mothers. It is men's memories that we have to rely on to parse together the initial experience of migration, because they were the ones who were allowed to leave of their own volition. Their stories are also devoid of any engagement with the Africans whose lands they passed through. By erasing both women and Africans, Indians tethered their claims to belonging to white male pioneer narratives. They did not question their rights to mobility within the space of the British Empire, even as growing restrictions prevented their entry into South Africa and limited who could enter Southern Rhodesia.[31] British colonialism created incentives for them to leave India but also provided somewhere for them to go. Indians thus grounded themselves as imperial subjects with roots in another colonial space in their retelling of their origins.

The language used in Indian oral histories is reminiscent of white Rhodesia's commemoration and glorification of the "long-neglected heroes of the pioneer days"—not the imperial officers and colonial administrators, but the ordinary people who served as frontiersmen on the African landscape.[32] Indian men imagined themselves as frontiersmen from the east, consolidating the borders of British land. They subconsciously upheld the colonial violence which displaced Africans, an injustice that was "deeply gendered" as well as racialized.[33] Like white settlers, Indians participated in the creation of a patriarchal form of settler colonialism. They used the language of white pioneering for their migration narratives to highlight the founders of the community as male, suggesting that women were not important to the community's origins in Rhodesia. Men created a world into which women were meant to fit, one which both displaced and psychologically emasculated Africans.[34] But Indian men were settlers, not conquerors. They did not directly take part in the violent displacement of Africans, even if they did migrate to the country in its aftermath. The chronological instabilities and elements of fiction in their stories suggest a fragility to Indian claims of belonging because they were actively erasing Black African history from their origins in order to render themselves African. Unlike white settlers, however, they could not take their presence for granted. Even as they identified themselves as imperial citizens, the white state continually reminded them that they were, in fact, colonized subjects.

ARRIVING

The immigration office at Umtali was a hostile space. It was the first encounter a migrant would have with the official administrative network that would keep track of his movements. For an Indian migrant, it was his first encounter with the resentment of the establishment toward his presence. In 1903, the Legislative Council introduced an immigration ordinance, imposing a literacy test and income requirement on all those entering for the first time.[35] What had previously been a fluid border was now formally bounded, as those entering via footpaths or by train encountered the first checkpoint before they could move any farther. A sergeant was stationed at the train station to take note of everyone both disembarking and passing through. He could also decide whether to allow passengers to get off the train or whether to send them back to Beira, depending on whether both their papers and their reasons for entering the territory appeared legitimate.[36]

These restrictions extended across individual territories in the British settler colonial world. Indians who left the subcontinent did so because of their imagined membership in an imperial collective, but countries set their own rules and boundaries of belonging.[37] The Imperial Conference of 1918, part of the periodic gatherings of the leaders of self-governing colonies and dominions of the British Empire held between 1887 and 1937, explicitly addressed questions of migration within the Empire, including to Southern Rhodesia and South Africa. In setting a policy of reciprocity of treatment between India and the rest of the dominions, it was decided that each government belonging to the Commonwealth "should enjoy complete control of the composition of its own population by means of restriction on immigration from any of the other communities," and be allowed to determine the composition of its own population.[38]

On the ground, rather than there being a strict definition of a "desirable" migrant, the desirability of those seeking entry was determined through a process of elimination of unwanted characteristics. Most of these criteria were designed to eliminate Indians in particular. Immigration officials used the label "undesirable immigrant," a term characterized by a "state of destitution" or the "appearance" of not having the ability to pass the language test.[39] Knowledge of a "European" language was necessary—while authorities debated whether eastern European languages counted as valid, there was no question that Hindi and Gujarati were not sufficient for entry.[40] If migrants were allowed off the train, their second point of encounter with officialdom was with the immigration officer, the guardian of a border that was not fully consolidated and yet who could control who would be allowed—and who would be denied—entry. They were then subject to a medical examination as well as a language test. In some cases their fingerprints would be taken, depending on the resources available at each immigration office. In 1914, 176 people were turned away at Umtali and Bulawayo. Of those denied entry, 121 were "Asiatic"; the rest were Afrikaners, or "S.A. Dutch," entering from the southern border.[41]

In 1907, one of these "undesirables," Babulal Nathoobhai Patel, met Bhimjee Naik in Beira. He was only seventeen years old and had traveled from the town of Dharmaj. Naik was renowned in pioneer narratives for aiding travelers through the immigration process at the border to Southern Rhodesia, guiding them through the immigration test, which included helping those who did not speak English to fudge their way through the literacy exam. Stories involving Naik contained elements of both the factual and the fabulous; his entrance into origin narratives took on a mythical quality, blurring the lines between oral history and oral storytelling traditions. Naik's shops in turn were central to his identity as a leader. New arrivals were frequently told to seek out Bhimjee, often "without knowing each other, no relations at all."[42] Like a benevolent genie, he would appear.

Naik seemed to have connections at the immigration office, operating as a fixer of sorts. By aiding Indian migrants to "cheat" the system and enter on false grounds, he enabled a forced construction of belonging to the new colony. The price for Naik's aid was usually employment in one of his general trading businesses; a tangible connection to Bhimjee was recounted as a point of pride in oral histories. In the story told by Babulal's son, his father allegedly had no idea what was happening around him. Offering to help Babulal get to Southern Rhodesia, Bhimjee asked him what his qualifications were. He asked Babulal to show him his signature, which he did in "longhand, beautiful writing." That was the extent of his ability to write in English, however. Bhimjee, explaining that the written test required that the applicant write a paragraph about why he wanted to come to Southern Rhodesia, wrote out an answer for Babulal. Leaving him for a month, he instructed him to practice copying out the paragraph. Babulal, not understanding a word of what he was writing, kept at it, writing it out six or seven times a day. Upon his return, Bhimjee took Babulal to the immigration office, instructing him not to speak a word unless asked. But the officer barraged him with questions. Remaining silent, he allowed Bhimjee to speak for him, who explained to the officer that Babulal had "just come off the boat" and was suffering from a bad bout of "seasickness," miles and weeks away from his actual oceanic crossing. The officer agreed to skip ahead to the written test. As soon as he was given the paper, Babulal started writing. The immigration officer stood watching speechless. "This is the first time I've seen an Indian who's written so fluently," he allegedly told Bhimjee. "Take him with you." And so Babulal left with permission to stay, and accompanied Bhimjee to Salisbury to work for him. It would be the beginning of a lifelong partnership in both business and friendship.[43] These myths of encounter became a way for immigrants and their descendants to construct networks of belonging and kinship against restrictions through a common imagined "ancestor." Elements of the story Babulal Patel's son later recounted were wildly implausible. Whatever the exact circumstances of their meeting were, however, Babulal went on to become one of Bhimjee's longest-serving employees.

Unbelievable as this story was, its message was that Indians were determined to make their way into the colony, even when the white man attempted to keep them out. Like Babulal, others attempted to come in on false grounds when formal applications were denied. At Lourenço Marques, five Indian minors who had previously been denied permission to travel on to the Union of South Africa returned with new names and, more astoundingly, new "fathers," having spent months living in hotels waiting for new passengers to disembark from the ships who could be persuaded to bring the previously "prohibited" immigrants in as their "sons."[44] Mohammed Bhika, known today as the first Muslim to enter Southern Rhodesia in 1904, was turned away at Umtali because he could not speak English. He walked back to Mozambique on foot and waited for the "next lot of people trying to enter Rhodesia," who took him with them and told him not to "utter one single word," somehow bringing him in under the cover of the rest of the group.[45] Bribes became another way for those prohibited entry to attempt to enter the territory by more insidious means, the price ranging from four to twenty pounds.[46] In 1912, Keshaw Rama was alleged to have bribed an immigration officer through an Indian interpreter by the name of Jaffer Khamisa to "assist him in entering the Territory well knowing that he was a Prohibited Immigrant, he, Rama, being unable to read and write in any European language."[47] The case revealed an intricate network of bribery, run by intermediary Indian fixers like Khamisa and Bhimjee Naik.

Led by the legendary Bhimjee, ties of family and friendship continued to be consolidated through the immigration of friends, relatives, and workers centered around the *dukkan*. The shop became a space where kinship networks from villages in Gujarat could be re-created on African soil. A common way to start a business was to open a garden on plots of land owned by white farmers or the BSAC, and then sell vegetables, transporting them by foot or bike. Migrants did not necessarily come from trading castes and instead had to create that identity for themselves as a way to make a living in a new land. Indians also found space in African townships in developing urban settlements, opening up eating houses for African customers, or laundry businesses for white customers. They began to make formal requests to immigration authorities to bring in more of their "own people." In 1909, a group of "Indian Dhobies," or laundrymen, requested "permission to introduce Asiatic assistants" of their own caste in a petition penned by the one and only Bhimjee Naik. Naik also requested permission to bring in a cook for "High Caste Hindooes" in the colony, making the argument that he and his compatriots could not eat food prepared by someone from a different caste.[48] His request was eventually denied, but others wrote similar letters to the government. In 1912, Ranchod Naron, Valabh Fakir, Prag Kesav, and Nursi Premji requested permission to bring in twenty-one assistants for their laundry business, stating that they were prepared to send the men back after a contract period of three years.[49]

The kinship networks sustained by the shop depended on male labor. No requests were made for female workers—women who entered the territory in its early years came in smaller numbers, usually as wives. The *dukkan* was set up as a space run by men. Younger men would join older relatives, becoming store assistants as part of a rite of passage of experience as well as a means to save up funds to become a full partner or set up their own business. Women served only as mothers providing sons who would one day be expected to join their fathers. After setting up their businesses, many men traveled back and forth from India, having children in intervals and creating transnational families. They were setting down roots on African soil, even though the branches of their families still extended across an ocean. That would change with later generations. But in the early years of Southern Rhodesia's foundation as a colonial space, networks of male kinship were required to maintain the *dukkan* and allow it to expand.

This small but steady flow of "undesirables" did not go unnoticed. Their often-illegal presence, as well as their movement back and forth between India and Africa, was a reminder that the borders of the territory were still fluid, and needed to be fixed. The "most significant feature" of the creation of the Southern Rhodesian state was the presence of "a considerable portion of immigrant races which created problems calling for additional constitutional mechanisms."[50] "Undesirables" included not just Indians but other European ethnic groups who did not come from Britain. In 1907, of the entire white population of 1,689 residents, 7 percent were noted as having a birthplace in a European country other than Britain, while 11.5 percent came from the Afrikaner Transvaal and Orange River Colony.[51] The presence of these "immigrant races" in turn instigated the creation of legislation that aimed to keep the territory "white," and further, the right kind of white. Patriarchal colonial notions of gender and miscegenation informed this judgment. Select ethnic groups of Europeans were disparaged, with Afrikaners characterized as "an inferior breed" of white "whose culture was way beneath their own."[52] Greeks, Portuguese, and Italians in particular were castigated for being the "principal offenders" when it came to the "habit of cohabiting with native women," and families rather than single men were encouraged to migrate to prevent further interracial relations.[53]

But Indian migrants stood out, especially when they cheated the system. The languages they spoke, the food they ate, their willingness to live among their African customers, and the color of their skin marked them out as even more "undesirable." Unlike other less attractive white migrants, they could not eventually blend in. With the growing influence of white settlers rather than temporary company administrators in legislative bodies, the BSAC worked to ensure the "right" kind of immigration to the territory, based on settler standards of desirability—respectability, morality, acceptable behavior, education, a certain level of economic stability—but above all, English origins.[54] The representative body of elected white settler officials to the Legislative Council conflated economics and culture as a way of measuring the suitability of prospective migrants. "The main body of settlers in Rhodesia should be of English origin," concluded a BSAC-sponsored report on land settlement; by no means should a potential settler be the "bucolic oaf of the caricaturists, but a highly civilised individual with all the abilities and tastes and habits and ambitions of an Englishman."[55]

Race and class were conflated in strategic ways in order to maintain this desire. The trading businesses in which Indians grounded their proud origins became the reason for their designation as a lower class of migrant. Even if not explicit, "undesirability" was by this stage firmly associated with racial characteristics and vague ideas about how nonwhite populations lived according to colonial conceptions of Indian customs relating to religion, marriage, diet, clothing, language, illiteracy, and proximity to Africans. Indians were inferior not only because of the color of their skin but because of how they lived. Indians were also associated with the spread of disease, in contrast to Afrikaner and Greek communities, who made sure to distance themselves from their African customers and workers.[56] In 1918, during an influenza epidemic, Indians along with Coloureds and Africans were banned from traveling by train in order to prevent the spread of the disease. The government ordered the restriction on the basis "that it was necessary to take prompt steps to suspend all intercourse and trade among natives for the present" and that "British Indians are almost exclusively engaged in the country in trading with natives."[57] Because of their increasing presence as traders, as well as how they lived through their shops, Indians became targets for hostility. In response, they showed that they were not going anywhere, because they belonged as much as any British settler.

STAYING

Bhimjee Naik was the first recorded Indian to obtain a trading license from the BSAC in Umtali in 1898.[58] His businesses eventually expanded across the railway line from Beira to Salisbury, enabling his ability to help fellow migrants with the immigration process and employment opportunities. But while they had come into the territory in the shadows, their trading stands were visible structures that attracted hostility. White settlers saw Indians as "foreigners," ironically ignoring their own history in the region. In calling for restrictions to Indian mobility and settlement, white residents reenforced the boundaries of belonging being implemented at the border. In 1895, the Bulawayo Chamber of Commerce issued a resolution stating that "Banyans were of no good to the community." They argued that the Indian was not "an ornamental or beneficial member of the community" as he "undersold his white counterpart in business, hoarded money and sent it to India, spent nothing in the country in which he had made his wealth and made no contribution to the strength of the state." They claimed that "Indians were imperfectly rooted in the colony"; their real "home" was seen as being elsewhere.[59] In Umtali, similar sentiments were expressed. In December 1898, at a meeting of the Umtali Sanitary Board, white residents of the town raised the issue of the outbreak of bubonic plague that was taking place at Delagoa Bay. They passed a resolution asking the BSAC that "measures be taken to prevent the influx of Banyans into this District in the event of the outbreak of the plague of Beira," the main port of entry for those migrating from India to Southern Rhodesia.[60]

BSAC officials thought that was the end of the matter for the time being. But white residents decided the best way to protect their interests was to throw out Indians altogether. In the new year, Inspector Birch from the police force in Umtali received information that "a scheme had been organized" by a group of white townsmen "to raid the Banyan stores that evening, to load up their goods into wagons and to transport both Banyans and goods across the Portuguese border." The next day, on 4 January 1899, at nine o'clock in the evening, a mob of about 150 men "gathered in the vicinity of the Banyan store at the North end of the town with the object of carrying out their scheme," taking with them a wagon and oxen. That store belonged to Bhimjee Naik. They demanded admission to the shop, and when denied entry, "burst open the doors, made their way in, handled the Banyans very roughly, and threw their goods about." Several other Indian stores were attacked that night. Inspector Birch, along with twenty-four other men, arrived at the scene. The mob eventually left, threatening to return if the "Banyans" did not leave by the following morning.[61]

The ideals of white supremacy on which Southern Rhodesia was founded were being enforced from the ground up rather than being implemented as part of colonial policy from London. The next day, Inspector Birch and G. O. Robertson, the acting resident magistrate, returned to the Indian trading area. They found the "ring-leaders" of the mob, who were identified as police officers and justices of the peace.[62] The men eventually dispersed but initially resisted orders to turn in their arms. A few days later, the leaders of the mob resigned their posts, stating that they could not "support the Government's present policy on the Banyan question."[63] They argued that they were "at one with the sentiment of the majority of residents here viz, that [they] wish this to be an European community where trader, employee or artisan can earn a living and hope to find employment for his children in the future."[64] They were, ironically, men tasked with protecting all residents of the town, and they were eventually arrested. Naik was not the only one to face violence. After the Umtali incident, Nathoo Vadey and Allarakia Hassim wrote a letter to the secretary of state for India outlining white hostility to their shops after they were granted dealer's licenses in 1899.[65] More complaints followed.

In the official report of the Umtali incident, Bhimjee Naik was a footnote to the violence. In oral traditions, he was front and center as the champion of Indian rights. His success as a businessman set him up as the main character in this narrative, and his persistence became symbolic for Indian determination to stay despite the attacks. Almost seventy years later, Natu Patel, who ended up working for Bhimjee at his store in Salisbury, recollected the incident as told to him by Bhimjee. In his version, Bhimjee's visibly growing prosperity attracted the ire of the European settlers: "They saw a coolie had started business, said he has no right to be here, they thought." In this version of the tale, only fifteen to twenty men came with an ox wagon, telling him to "pack up and go back to Portuguese territory." Bhimjee, fearing their threats, wrote notes to the magistrate and Inspector Birch, who then arrived on the scene. In this telling, the respect they had for him was the reason they came rather than their having heard about an attack themselves. After dispersing the mob, according to Patel, two African constables were assigned to protect Bhimjee's two huts. Naik allegedly also wrote a letter to Queen Victoria asking that the BSAC grant his initial license. She then in turn replied personally to him as well as to the Dominions Office, "saying Indians must be protected and given equal rights."⁶⁶ In other versions of the story, he sent the queen a telegram after his store was attacked. Thereafter, the story goes, he was provided with mounted police as protection.⁶⁷

Incidents like this countered the romantic elements of stories of the migration process but did set up a new stage in Indian timelines of their history when it came to settling. Through the stories told from Naik's perspective, Indians were doing well despite hostility to their presence, setting up a viable livelihood through their shops. They continued to enter the country and to consolidate their social networks around their economic activities. According to their versions of history, the queen of England herself believed they had a right to be there and to make a living for themselves. Even those who crossed back and forth from time to time to maintain their families in Gujarat always returned. Their trading businesses became sites of settlement that allowed them to sustain transnational networks but also to ground themselves in a colonial locality. It was within this context that the first generation of Indian migrants to Southern Rhodesia began to construct their own distinctiveness as "British Indians," subjects of the British Empire who had the right to mobility between *and* settlement in imperial spaces.

In response, white legislators began to restrict not only who could enter Southern Rhodesia, but who would be allowed to prosper. The first real challenge to Indian residency came in the form of the Asiatics Ordinance of 1908, created in response to settler agitation. London would not allow Indians to be expelled en masse, but the local administration attempted to at least monitor and control them. Based on similar legislation in the Transvaal, the object of the ordinance was "to restrict the Immigration of Asiatics into this Territory, and to provide for the Registration of such Asiatics as are already resident therein." "Asiatic" here was defined as "any person belonging to any of the native races of Asia, including the so-called Coolies, Arabs, Malays, and Mohammedan subjects of the Turkish dominions, not being a Malay born and resident in any British Colony or Possession in South Africa." All "Asiatic" residents over the age of sixteen were required to carry a Registration Certificate, and anyone who left the country for a continuous period of more than three years would lose their residence.⁶⁸ This was significant for those men who traveled back to India for long stretches of time to get married and begin their families before returning. It was also the first law to directly target Indian migrants. The ordinance shocked Indian migrants. Rather than challenging "overtly non-racial" tests that checked their language skills and employment prospects, they now had to confront laws that were "explicitly anti-Indian in content." Criteria for entry were no longer applicable to all migrants but applied specifically to Indians on explicit racial grounds.[69]

Indians resisted. In their letters and petitions, they self-identified as *British* subjects, first and foremost. They saw their rights to belonging as inherent, coining the term "British Indian" to identify themselves in the census, which was not, in fact, a legal status. They highlighted their similarities to white settlers, and in their letters and petitions, they self-identified as British subjects and Rhodesian residents. They emphasized Indian participation in the very structures of empire, from fighting in British troops during the world wars, contributing to the colonial economy, and the role that Indians were playing in creating the British Raj.[70] But they also focused on the local conditions that were discriminating against them. They created a localized British colonial identity as a way of claiming belonging outside India, one based on a transnational collective but rooted in local contexts.

The British Indian Association was the first formal institution created by the Indian residents of Salisbury to claim these rights. Their goal was to protect their shops and their trade by pushing for the continued migration of labor networks that would ensure the survival of the *dukkan*. They made clear their desire to stay, as well as their continued rights of mobility. Natu Patel recalled the first meetings that were held, led once again by Bhimjee Naik. The exact year of formation is unclear, but their letters to both BSAC administration and London began as early as 1908, with the imminent implementation of the Asiatics Ordinance. As part of their campaign, representatives met with the colonial administrator. With the implementation of further immigration regulations in 1914, the association sent a delegation to meet with the resident commissioner for Southern Rhodesia the following year to request that Indians not be "subject to fingerprinting" when returning from trips back to India.[71] In 1916, the Umtali, Bulawayo, Gwelo, and Salisbury branches of the British Indian Association each sent a petition to the administrator, protesting the denial of marriage certificates based on Hindu and Muslim rites, difficulties in engaging laborers from India, bureaucratic problems of the Portuguese authorities, and the struggles of obtaining trading licenses for the shops that were critical to their livelihoods.[72]

They had basis for their petitions and claims to certain rights. Rhodesia was not initially meant to follow its own path. At this stage, Southern

Rhodesia, Natal, and the Cape Colony were following similar legislative trajectories. Southern Rhodesia's first Order in Council was drafted in 1898 and literally copied various pieces of legislation directly from that of the British territories farther south; Rhodesia was meant to be, in many ways, a shadow colony of the Cape. In the following years of settlement, many within the administrative framework of the BSAC assumed that Southern Rhodesia, when its "development" was "suitably advanced," would "take its rightful place as a member" of the British South African territories after the Anglo-Boer War.[73] However, Southern Rhodesia was never designated an official "white colony" by the British government itself, with the settler government taking its own initiative to attract mass white settlement, and until 1965, Britain "retained a considerable deal of control in order to protect the African population"—including imperial power of disallowance when it came to discriminatory pieces of legislation.[74]

Discrimination against Indians as well as Africans was often a concern. The India Office, which was responsible for the coordination of the activities of the British Raj from London, took a particularly critical stance when it came to the implementation of immigration regulations, which would threaten the concept of a colonial commonwealth by limiting Indian mobility. Administrators in India had already objected to the importation of recruited labor to Southern Rhodesia after the abolition of the indentured labor system. They encouraged Indian mobility, but not as part of a coordinated scheme, and plans to import Asian labor in 1903 failed after the interjection of the India Office.[75] The Indian National Congress party had similarly begun paying attention to the "plight" of its subjects abroad with a letter from Kunti, an indentured laborer in Fiji, that appeared in an Indian newspaper in 1913 and outlined the bleak conditions she faced.[76] With more Indians themselves taking on roles in the Indian Civil Service, consideration of the needs of the diaspora became a greater concern for the Raj. Along with Gandhi's newspaper from South Africa, publications produced by the Indian diaspora across the globe required the government of India to take notice, "the transnational dimension" of political agitation by Indians abroad underscoring "the extraterritorial imaginary of nationalists who took up the concerns of diasporic Indians in their emerging discourse about nationhood," a connection "reinforced by the experience of being colonized subjects" in both India and Africa.[77]

But while Indian nationalists on the subcontinent were extending the imaginative boundaries of an Indian nation, Indians abroad were more concerned about their rights on the ground. Naik and other elites connected themselves to transnational politics but did so on the basis of the local conditions they were facing rather than as part of a broader Indian nationalism. In 1908, Naik penned a petition on behalf of 182 other Indian residents to the secretary of state for the colonies in London regarding the introduction of the Asiatics Ordinance. Objecting to the new legislation, the petitioners "humbly venture[d]" to remind the secretary that "Southern Rhodesia being under Crown Administration, the Imperial Government are directly, as well as ultimately, responsible for the preservation of the liberties of British Indians subjects of the Crown resident therein."[78] Their voices were heard. Although the settler Parliament passed the act, the Colonial Office in London essentially canceled it through a policy known as the "imperial power of disallowance" after pressure from the Indian government as well as local Indian residents.[79] The cancelation of the ordinance was an early marker in what would be the start of constant tension between colonial policy to prevent overtly discriminatory legislation based on the pressures of political resistance and agitation across the Indian Ocean, and the desires of white representatives on the ground, who faced pressure from their constituents to solve the "Indian problem."

Southern Rhodesia's white electorate had plans of their own for the territory. In 1922, they rejected Jan Smuts's proposal for the region's annexation by South Africa, leaving it as a Crown colony with responsible government after the BSAC was expropriated by the British government.[80] By this stage, the Ndebele state had been destroyed, and any form of sustained African unity between the Shona and Ndebele had failed with their defeat in 1897. Africans were systemically removed from their own lands to make way for settler colonial agricultural initiatives. The displacement of Black Africans as well as the status of Indians became key issues around which Southern Rhodesia's white residents were beginning to envision themselves as an exclusive "nation" to which only they belonged and held full rights of citizenship. Elections held in 1924 for local legislative assembly members centered around the exclusion of Indians.[81] By the time Southern Rhodesia attained self-governing status, informal policy was to restrict the further entry of single, adult Indian males, moderated through the standards of literacy and financial standing required through existing immigration legislation. Although the Asiatics Ordinance had failed, its principles survived.

White Rhodesians founded their state based on the idea of the creation of a land for the white man, one sustained by their own pioneer myths. Indian migrants disrupted that vision. They took on tropes used by white settlers in their own origin stories, claiming civilizational parity with the English, but they were not "British." Even though they may have originated from the jewel in the English crown, they and their stores threatened both white livelihoods and a "way of life" that was foundational to a Rhodesian identity. But that founding was in many ways based on a myth; the nature of the white population was constantly shifting due to both immigration and emigration, with only fifteen of the seven hundred original pioneers still living in the country in 1924.[82] Indian "pioneers," on the other hand, stayed in the country, had families, and settled. Many families today in Zimbabwe are able to trace back a direct genealogy to a "founding member" of the family who arrived with the first generations of white settlers. The trading businesses they founded lived on through generations, allowing their stories to be passed down. As a result, they had more at stake in guaranteeing their rights within the colony than some of the transient European settlers did, with this stability and permanence reflected in the strength of their migration networks grounded in their developing trades and shops.

Yet without a large population of women, Indians had not fully settled in Africa. As their businesses developed, that changed. They transitioned from being diasporic, transnational migrants to becoming settlers whose lives would become deeply entrenched in local institutions and social experiences. With the attainment of self-governing status, Rhodesia prevented the entry of new Indian adult males and restricted how long they could be out of the country to maintain residency. To sustain their livelihoods, that meant the founding patriarchs of Indian society would now have to rely on bringing over their sons and younger male relatives—and their wives. The shops were key to the extension of transnational kinship networks and family lines that were setting down roots in Africa. The first generation of male migrants established the foundations of their communities through their identity as traders. As a result, the shops they set up would sustain patriarchal notions of tradition and identity once women began to arrive. That in turn became the foundation of their belonging to Rhodesia rather than to India, even as their colonial origins gave them the impetus to leave Gujarat in the first place.

Their claims ignored the Africans who had been displaced. Indians set themselves up against white civilization for comparison, erasing Africans from their rhetorical roots. The fragility of their claims to belonging are in turn reflected in the instability of their origin myths. But the pioneer stories on which their collective identity is founded ultimately recall them as colonized peoples, not colonizers themselves. They occupied a higher social status than indigenous Africans and were relatively less oppressed than they were. However, even though they were settlers, like Black Africans they too found themselves facing discrimination in a new imperial space. That collective oppression, albeit hierarchical and relative, meant that while white Rhodesian farms were taken away from them a century later, Indian shops were safe. Whereas elite patriarchs aligned themselves with white ideals of civilization, ordinary Indians lived their daily lives in shared intimate spaces with Black Africans on the ground in urban spaces. It was that experience that sustained the economic space of the *dukkan* but also allowed Indians and the other racial groups with whom they shared urban spaces to engage and establish the terms of their belonging as Indians continued to make their lives on African soil.

TWO

BETWEEN WHITE PICKET FENCES AND BLACK RESERVES

—

The Development of Indian Trading Streets, 1923–1945

> As the commercial front-line, North Lobengula Street went out of its way to attract African shoppers coming out of the Location. K. M. Naik's Tanda Bantu store at 57A Lobengula Street—"where everybody shops"—still stands and trades today as a survivor of this colorful past. Africans could buy basics in the Location. They came to Lobengula Street for "fashion" and for luxuries. The street's store windows were crammed with brightly coloured clothes and accessories, including the suits and shirts and gloves and shoes to which the Location dandies aspired. African market-stalls, attached to the stores, lined the streets. There was an atmosphere of carnival. "For many of us," says Mark Ncube, Bulawayo's oral historian, "Lobengula Street *was* Bulawayo."
>
> —TERENCE RANGER, *Bulawayo Burning*

The first men who crossed the Indian Ocean to Southern Rhodesia were farmers. While they came in search of gold and riches, those dreams were swiftly dashed. Some found employment in the mines, but most others made a living in rural spaces, based on the skills they had and the life they knew. White farmers granted Indians small plots of land to grow vegetables that they would then sell, including in the "market gardens" on the outskirts of Salisbury. A typical trajectory for a new Indian migrant would be to transition from small-scale trading in a rural setting to eventually owning his own urban shop. One of these traders was Mohammed Bhika, allegedly the first Muslim man to enter Southern Rhodesia in the early 1900s. Experienced as a farmer in India, Bhika opened a small market garden before obtaining a general dealer's license and opening his first shop, first selling grocery items, and then clothing.[1] The first generation of "pioneer" Indians operated in growing urban settlements and forts as well as rural spaces. Trading businesses that allowed them to change and meet the demands of their customers was a way for Indians to make a living and therefore earn the means to stay in the country.

In 1930, the settler government introduced land legislation that relegated Black Africans to reserves and left most agricultural land under white control. Rural-based Indians stubbornly refused to leave African zones, running shops and "truck" businesses in reserves. Other men set up homes with Black women, having children and creating mixed-race families. Some remained on the outskirts of urban settlements, building their own homes and running eating houses and trading businesses in African locations. Their presence outside established norms of morality created anxiety for male elites. In a patriarchal colonial society, immoral Indian men and Black African women were cast as transgressive elements that needed to be controlled. White administrations designated Indian shops in African spaces as "unhygienic," African chiefs saw Indian men as "immoral," and upper-caste Hindu elites castigated those who breached the boundaries of community. By the 1930s, nearly all Indians were forced out of African spaces.

They transitioned from being mobile hawkers to leasing permanent stands from urban municipal authorities. Most, including Mohammed Bhika, became "general traders" selling goods ranging from cooking oil to clothing, intermediaries between white-owned wholesale department stores and industries and Black African customers. Their businesses were allocated space in specific zones, becoming part of the racialized segregation of urban locations as they separated white neighborhoods from African townships. Indian trading streets became a central feature of colonial urbanity, a social and economic hub for the growing numbers of Africans in towns. As the shop grew, it became a critical facet of urban life, allowing Indians to engage with the other communities with whom they shared the streets of towns and cities. It became a settled space that could be passed down to their children, some of whom were now being born in Rhodesia rather than in India, sustaining their livelihood across generations.

The shop was the first physical space that Indians could call home on African soil. As it grew, however, the domestic boundaries of the *dukkan* remained intact. The earliest iterations of the *dukkan* enabled the expansion of kinship networks through employment. As restrictions on the entry of male adults increased, men began to bring over their wives and children, transplanting entire familial units across the ocean. A second generation of migrants entered the territory, consolidating the *dukkan* as both home and business. Informal female labor became critical to maintaining the shop. By bringing their wives back with them, men transplanted domestic institutions to make their presence in Southern Rhodesia permanent. The domestic separation between Indians and Black Africans is often taken for granted in African colonies. That separation, however, was deliberately constructed by elite patriarchs across racial lines. Indian shops and homes were a critical part of urban life, and the divide of the shop counter kept intimate, private spaces separate. As their numbers increased, Indian women contributed to the setting up of the shop as a space firmly entrenched on Indian trading streets, where their presence helped sustain the domestic boundaries of the *dukkan*.

Colonial attempts at racial division were reflected in the development of the census as a tool of consolidation and classification of the colony's diverse peoples. The census ordered schedules according to a hierarchy, with "Europeans" filling out C1 schedules, "Asiatics" C2, "Coloureds" C3, and "Natives" C4. The growth of Indian families and the enforcement of gendered labor and social roles by both Indian men and the colonial government were reflected in individual census schedules. Political hierarchies were meant to mirror physical forms of segregation. But even as Indians helped consolidate racial segregation in urban spaces, some continued to transgress domestic boundaries. In a colonial African context, they renegotiated their identities of race, caste, religion, and nationality to make sense in their class role as middlemen between Black and white through their shops. The neat categories of the census were not reflected in the chaos and messiness of actual lived experiences. These transgressions are revealed by a close reading of individual census forms, which lay hidden beneath the surface of collations and summaries of official reports.

Enforced policies of domestic separation did not mean that Indians were isolated from larger contexts or that they were "strangers" to African urban life. Indians continued to negotiate their belonging, using their economic identities to recontextualize the forms of identity they brought with them from the subcontinent. Over the shop counter, Indians and Africans haggled both over the prices of goods as well as how they would share the cities and towns they inhabited, a form of contact not mediated by the colonial state. Ideas about "belonging" were complicated and not always articulated in a formal identity. Instead, Indians developed their African identities as they negotiated the terms of their settlement with white authorities as well as the populations of Coloured and Black Africans with whom they shared intimate urban spaces. Many families today still own their properties on what were formerly Indian trading streets. Through their shops, Indians found permanent space for themselves in urban settings.

MARKET GARDENS, EATING HOUSES, AND TRUCKS

Mohammed Bhika transitioned from rural gardening to urban settlement at the same time that his family began to grow. After obtaining a general dealer's license, he rented a shop from a Hindu man, Hasu Patel's father, who had migrated from Dharmaj in 1911.[2] He did not have "a good education," but according to his son, he "must have had a very brilliant mind" to establish his business. His first wife died, and in 1925, he married a woman born in Bulawayo. Together, they had six children, four sons and two daughters. His sons, when they were old enough, worked for an Indian concern called Mehta and Company for a year before joining their father, helping him expand into other businesses on Moffat Street in Salisbury, as well as purchasing undeveloped land not far away on Charter Road. By 1950, the family had built their first commercial building. The entire time, the family lived in rooms behind their shops.[3]

Indians initially attempted to take on other forms of employment. While they had been drawn to the colony by the promise of gold, very few were allowed to work on the mines. In 1921, Gopal Naidoo's application for a prospecting license was denied because it would create a precedent for other

Indians.[4] In 1922, Maken Lalla was granted a license, but the police intercepted him and took it away before he could use it.[5] In 1923, B. M. Patel applied for a license near the town of Gatooma, but his application was denied.[6] The government believed that Indians should be completely excluded from the gold mining industry based on stereotypes about their "desire for gold" and their corrupt trading practices, which would lead to them illegally selling gold to African mine workers.[7] While not an official regulation of the British South Africa Company (BSAC), it was "the invariable practice not to issue licenses to coloured people or Asiatics.... Indians have been refused Licenses not specifically as Indians but as individuals."[8] The government was also responding to white protests against the encroachment of Indians into skilled employment on the mines, often as truck drivers.[9] On the Morven mine near Bulawayo, fourteen Indian engine drivers were listed as employees in 1901; by 1936 there were only eleven Asians employed on mines throughout the entire territory.[10]

Not allowed to prospect or work on the mines, Indian men instead turned to petty trading, an early version of the institution of the "shop." Market gardening was the most popular way to earn an income for those who had grown up on the farms of rural Gujarat. These men would approach a local farmer and ask for a piece of land on which to open shop, quite literally, with early European settlers depending on Asian gardeners for small-scale production of fruits and vegetables before the rise of plantation agriculture.[11] The gardeners would then go door-to-door selling their goods as mobile storekeepers; by 1912 they appeared to have "acquired a monopoly of the trade."[12] Some families set up laundry businesses for white settlers. Vivek Solanki's family history in Southern Rhodesia began when his great-grandfather, Nanjee Rana, first arrived sometime in the 1890s. He had come to work as a coal miner but instead ended up establishing a laundry in Bulawayo as the railway line to Wankie and Victoria Falls was being built. He set up the washing business by a riverfront—some of the trees they planted still stand today—and eventually expanded outlets of the original laundry alongside the train tracks.[13] According to their descendants, "they had some basic utensils and the number of males who lived in the same room cooked together. They had very little furniture, if any. They lived frugally and simply and worked hard for long hours in order to save as much as possible as it was everyone's wish to ultimately acquire their own shop."[14]

Indians also found markets among Black Africans, creating space for themselves in "native" locations. While their entry to the territory was regulated by the state, they made their living on the ground by providing a vital service for their customers who desired both basic foodstuffs as well as the goods associated with colonial modernity. Africans were confined to "Native Reserves" dating back to 1898, when the BSAC provided land for African occupation. More reserves were created in 1913, in areas with little rainfall and some distance away from railways.[15] Farming and mining operations relied on Africans as a cheap source of labor. Black Africans were denied land tenancy rights and forced to take on limited forms of paid work in order to pay off taxes as part of the *chibaro* system of migrant labor. Land was overcrowded and overutilized, making it difficult for residents to sustain a living without sending male workers to mines and farms. Because of the distance of these locations from major lines of transportation as well as market towns, Indian traders saw opportunities to expand their customer base. They were "virtually located in all parts of the country, even the remotest corner" of rural land.[16] The Indian shop initially functioned as a mobile form of capitalist activity, going to where the customers were located as opposed to consumers coming to a set place, more akin to the trading networks which dominated the region before colonialism.[17] Single men engaged in what was known as the "kaffir truck" trade, transporting goods via trucks to African reserves.[18] They set up trading stands in the reserves, using their ability to move around the country to become intermediaries between urban and rural markets.

The flexibility with which earlier traders were able to move around the country to seek out markets was coming to an end, however. Southern Rhodesia was by now an exporter of chrome and tobacco. It was known as a "quiet but stable backwater of the British Empire where life and property were secure," a haven for white settlement and small-scale commercial activity.[19] That haven needed to be secured. The Land Apportionment Act of 1930 divided rural spaces along racial lines as had similar legislation in South Africa, creating four types of land: white-owned land that could not be acquired by Africans; purchase areas for those Africans who could afford the lease; Tribal Trust Lands designated as the African reserves; and Crown lands owned by the state, reserved for future use and public parks. Approximately fifty thousand white inhabitants were given 51 percent of the land, with 29.8 percent left for over a million Africans.[20] The effects of the 1930 legislation were far-reaching and would deny Black Africans access to arable land in the territory well into the 1970s.

In-between populations, such as Indians and Coloureds, were not formally accounted for in land legislation, even as they were systematically denied access to both agricultural and mineral wealth. Rural segregation had in fact begun long before the implementation of the 1930 law. An Indian presence had not gone unnoticed, and Asian market gardeners were gradually forced off rural land toward urban settlements. As far back as 1905, the BSAC denied the renewal of a rural trading site license in Dondoza to a man known in the paperwork only as "Gunsam." No more renewals were granted to Indians from that year on.[21] Bhagoo Bhula's application to lease land in 1911 was refused.[22] In 1914, BSAC officials argued that "the Company's terms of land settlement" only applied to Europeans. Indians could apply for licenses to trade, as long as they had the permission of a village's local authority.[23] But by 1933, Ismail Mulla's application for a trading license in the rural district of Chibi was denied.[24] The percentage of Asian males formally employed in agricultural activities between 1911 and 1941 fell from 22 percent to 12 percent, while those who took on commercial licenses increased from 31 to 51 percent.[25]

Their removal was justified on the grounds of their "corrupting" influence on Black Africans, and Black women in particular, revealing the deeply gendered anxieties of a patriarchal settler society. Miscegenation was a particular concern. Early laws specifically targeted relationships between Black men and white women through the Immorality and Indecency Suppression Act of 1903.[26] By 1921, however, an investigation conducted by Native Commissioners found that "as a result of the establishment of a settled European population and the consequent force of public opinion, the evil is rapidly diminishing" and there was no need for legislation barring miscegenation altogether.[27] Indian men, however, became a new focus of concern, especially as there were only 223 Asiatic women compared to 1,027 Asiatic men present in 1921.[28] Both African patriarchal elites and white officials articulated concerns about the presence of unattached Indian males in the African reserves, denigrating them as "mostly immoral and promiscuous in their affairs."[29] "Natives" who left their wives and villages to go work in the towns left African women prone to prostitution, according to discussions by Native Commission officials.[30] Black women were not given any agency in these complaints, and their sexuality became a trope for concerns about immorality.[31]

The immorality of African women was closely linked to their liaisons with Indian men. African chiefs, in conjunction with the chief native commissioner, used evidence of interracial relationships as a reason to request the removal of Indian traders.[32] Their shops were at the center of these concerns. As early as 1904, Indian men were accused of paying "lobola," or the bride wealth price, for "Native" women, leading to "springing up a race of bastards who may in the future be a source of trouble and inconvenience."[33] In 1921, a Black woman filed a paternity action against the Indian father of her child for financial support in the Rusape district.[34] Local chiefs in Umtali complained to the governor in 1929 that Asians with stores on farms bordering the native reserves had rooms at the back of their stores to which they would take Black female customers.[35] M. N. Patel's application for a store site in the Bubi district in 1934 was denied because it would "probably be used as a base for a motor lorry service and will encourage a certain amount of undesirable movement from the adjacent Reserve to Bulawayo, particularly of Native females."[36] This case was part of a larger complaint issued by a meeting of "Chiefs and Natives" that "their women-folk left their homes and travelled by moto-lorry to labour centres, where they lived immoral lives, and it is known that the lorries driven by Indians in Matabeleland have been the means of making such degradation of women a thing far too easy of accomplishment."[37] The trope of immoral Black women was deployed to portray them as voiceless victims who were at the mercy of exploitative Indian men. Neither group was consulted about the issue.

The centrality to these complaints of tropes about how Indians lived and worked reflected the state's concerns about an Indian economic presence in African spaces. As a result, the Native Commission inserted themselves between the two groups, attempting to mediate their contact. Officials cast Indian and African interactions on both gendered and class terms, arguing that even though the Indian "standard of living is no better than that of the Native . . . their knowledge of trading is far greater than that of the Native," creating conditions for exploitation.[38] Claiming the protection of African interests, the Native Affairs Department conducted interviews in the Umtali area in 1944 after complaints by chiefs of Indian exploitation of their customers, linking concerns about morality to economic issues. Africans accused Indians of hoarding large supplies of goods and setting higher prices. Ideas about corruption and cheating were linked to the Gujarati system of what was colloquially known as *uplag*, which vaguely referred to Indians hiding income from the tax collector, usually by charging a higher price for goods than the set price and then noting down a lower amount of profit in their accounting books. An African trader named Nyatsanza testified that Indians were a particular problem:

> Q: Do you think Natives could do all the Native trade without any help from European traders or Asiatic traders?
> A: There is nothing wrong with Europeans, but we don't like Indians.[39]

The commission posed similar questions to the Umtali Native Welfare Society:

> Q: What has the Society to say of the way the African people are selling their produce?
> A: Indian storekeepers in the Reserves we feel are cheating us. They are taking more grain than they should.
> Q: Is it the Indian storekeepers in particular, or all storekeepers?
> A: It is the Indians. No European is doing that kind of thing, and the Africans are not doing it or are following the Indian example. . . .
> Q: Do you think the African trader when he gets a license treats you better than the Asiatic?
> A: The African people if they had stores would treat us much better. We have no complaint against the Europeans, they are treating us quite nicely. But we would rather have nothing at all to do with the Indians.[40]

The loaded nature of the questions suggested that the government's goal was to aid Africans in their commercial aspirations, eventually leading to the creation of a trading middle class. But historians of class in Zimbabwe have argued that the settler colonial project was not designed for the rise of an African middle class, instead relying on a fixed racial and class hierarchy that produced a steady supply of Black labor and restricted social mobility. The Native Affairs Department, who conducted these particular interviews, "regarded an African middle class as a bane of colonialism and attempted to frustrate its emergence in ways large and small."[41] Most businesses in African reserves were, in fact, owned by Europeans.

To that end, the commission's goal appeared to be to guide testimony toward supporting their policy of removing Indians from the African reserves rather than from a place of genuine investment in African commercial aspirations. But Black customers were in reality able to negotiate the terms of their demands as drivers of consumer demands. When they went to European stores, they were treated as second-class citizens; they were not allowed in certain places, and most of the time they could not afford to pay the higher prices. Further questioning in the testimony of the Umtali Native Welfare Commission was revealing:

Q: Why don't the Natives all go to the European store and leave the Indians alone?
A: Most of the things sold in the European stores are specially for Europeans and when we go there with small money we cannot get what we want.[42]

According to one Black African scholar, "in white shops, white people were treated first then you."[43] Africans were welcomed in Indian stores, however, where prices were not set and where the process of haggling was the norm. Indian traders would name a price, African customers would counter with their own, and a back-and-forth would eventually establish a price at which the goods in question would be sold. Africans both resented Indians and relied on them at the same time, and it was that dependence that would ensure the survival of Indian shops even after they were closed in rural locations.[44]

The conflation of the social and economic immorality of Indian men resulted in most of them being pushed out of rural areas. Applications for trading licenses were denied, and children born to interracial relationships were labeled Coloured rather than Indian or African, a deliberate erasure of their roots. But the need for an Indian trading class had become evident. Even as they were phased out of rural life, Indians made more permanent spaces for themselves in trading streets. While the interventionist colonial state was omnipresent, white officials and settlers did not live among the populations they were attempting to regulate. Indians, on the other hand, shared the streets of cities with Black Africans. But the boundaries of domesticity were being fixed. The shop counter became a safe site of both negotiation and contestation. Interactions beyond it threatened patriarchal concerns about the identity of their communities, even as Indians and Africans increasingly relied on each other for economic needs.

THE KOPJE AND LOBENGULA STREET

Urbanization in Southern Rhodesia began in earnest after self-governing status was granted in 1923. The first towns in the colony initially developed as military posts. Smaller settlements sprung into being around mines and farming centers. In 1923, Bulawayo was the largest town with a white population of 16,363, followed by Salisbury with 6,462, and then Umtali and Gwelo. Smaller towns included Que Que and Umvuma.[45] As more white women migrated to the territory, and families grew, ramshackle settlements evolved into well-administered urban locales, structured by roads and newly created suburban neighborhoods in which larger houses could be built. Sanitary and municipal boards run by white residents were created to regulate urban life. Electricity and phone lines spread, while hotels, banks, restaurants, and libraries sprung up. Schools were established, and sporting traditions such as cricket became an integral part of a settler lifestyle. But these spaces were meant specifically for white Rhodesians. African workers constructed buildings and railways and worked as domestic servants and laborers. Their presence and movements were strictly regulated, keeping them as invisible as possible.

The most urbanized population groups, according to census data, were whites, Indians, and Coloureds. In 1904, 58 percent of the non-African population lived in urban spaces. By 1974, that number had risen to 88 percent.[46] Black Africans who found employment in urban settlements lived on the outskirts of towns and cities in townships or locations separated from white neighborhoods and pavements. They constructed their own haphazard homes in locations around the market gardens where Indians grew produce. Conditions in the townships were as dire as those of the reserves, if not worse. Overcrowding and a lack of basic resources led to continual outbreaks of disease. But urban life for Black Africans was not only defined by poverty and tough working conditions. Social life thrived in the locations, from the illegal brewing of beer in *shebeens* to a vibrant church life. Indian traders were not absent from these scenes. Some opened what were called "native eating houses," developing a customer base that was denied service in white restaurants and hotels. Indians also rented out their properties to Africans. In 1926, two African owners of a native eating house who were renting their premises from an Indian landlord voiced concerns about the loss of their business and customers. Their landlord had been issued an eviction notice after being convicted for operating without a license.[47] Other Indians set up general trading sites. Their businesses supplied the basics of daily life but also became sites for African social interactions.

Indians had lived among Africans from the early days of their settlement. They set up their businesses on the outskirts of white settlements, the places where they had first tended the market gardens and around which Black townships sprung up. But as with the rural areas, the colonial state was attempting to segregate urban land, albeit in messier and less strategic ways. This included the creation of informal zones allocated for each racial category. The first wide-scale attempt to remove Indians from African locations in Bulawayo was attempted in 1915 but was largely unsuccessful. Fifteen years later, the Bulawayo Municipality called for a further investigation into the conditions in one particular location, spurred by complaints by both Africans and Indians that certain Indian traders were still living and trading there. The location in question was an "ill-defined and unfenced" part of the commonage that had sprung up with no council or governmental control as a result of radical underinvestment in African urban housing.[48] Neither a part of the African township nor a part of Bulawayo proper, it had about 5,500 residents, a group mostly made up of African workers who traveled to the city for work, as well as 46 Indians and 73 Coloureds. The location had an African brewery, several brothels run by Black women, and a venereal hospital. The commission investigating the complaints noted the prevalence of prostitution and other "vices" in the location, including abuse of alcohol.[49]

Some Indian men were deeply entrenched in the location, and their presence was considered part of the greater moral disorder and chaos taking place. They had built their own houses, using hawkers' licenses to "sell a wide variety of goods." The deputation of Indians from the Bulawayo location who represented their views to the commission pointed out that they had lived in the location for several years, while one even claimed to have been living in the area before the location existed. Another said he had been there for the past twenty-five years.[50] At least twenty Indian stands were identified, ranging from brick houses to tin huts to iron sheds of various sizes.[51] But elites across racial lines opposed their presence and proximity to Black residents.

The Bulawayo branch of the British Indian Association in particular disapproved of their own living in such close conditions with Africans, voicing support for their removal. In a letter to the Native Affairs Commission, they objected to an Indian presence in the location "from a point of view of morals," feeling it "a disgrace to the Indian Community that Indian children should be reared and trained amongst Natives." Their greatest fear lay in the "opportunity for and the danger of undue familiarity between Indian males and Native women in cases where men are separated from their wives and families."[52] The "educated" Black Africans who provided evidence to the commission argued that they did not want to bring their own wives to the location "owing to its bad reputation and the class of native residing there."[53]

These concerns were part of gendered colonial ideologies concerning the role that women should play in maintaining segregated and moral homes, keeping wandering men in line. Men across racial lines saw the location as a site of moral decay and articulated once again the idea that Indian men and "disorderly" Black women were the main instigators of interracial improprieties that threatened boundaries of intimacy. The commission's final report called for stricter regulation of all municipal locations in the colony and for their inclusion in the regulations of the Land Apportionment Act. This move included the provision of adequate education and health facilities—as well as the removal of the Indian residents of the location, whose way of living in their trading stands was deemed "unhygienic," creating breeding grounds for disease.[54] Location regulations stipulated that only Black Africans could live in those zones. The municipality compensated those who had constructed their own homes based on inspections of the buildings.[55] Others had their licenses taken away on the grounds that they were serving alcohol to Africans through their eating houses.[56] Some were convicted for violating the Shop Hours Act and for trading after hours.[57] Their persistent presence in African locations showed how the borders of segregation had to be constantly policed and enforced.

Most of those relocated ended up on what had become known as the Asian, or Indian, trading road, Lobengula Street. By this stage, Indian families were now settled on streets allocated specifically for them in their trading licenses. The creation of these trading streets was strategic. After 1930, municipal authorities would only give trading licenses to stands located in these zones.[58] These particular streets would eventually come to be completely dominated by Indian trading stands and backroom homes: Moffat, Charter, Rezende,

Selbourne, Cameron, and Pioneer streets in Salisbury; Railway, Grey, and Lobengula in Bulawayo. In Salisbury, Charter Road was the location of the sanitary lane. Moffat Street held most of the first Indian stores, and the Indian "ghetto" area was known as the space from the railway station in Salisbury across to the Kopje. Behind the shops, boys would gather to play cricket with makeshift bats and balls.[59] The "ghetto" here marked what would become an important geographic division between the commercial "Kopje" and the administrative Causeway Street, an invisible line that signified the racial and class divisions of Salisbury. In Bulawayo, Lobengula Street divided the allocated native location from "European" Bulawayo.[60] By 1930, Lobengula Street was known in town as the Asian trading road, founded by the pioneer families of M. V. Naik, B. K. Patel, I. Seedat, K. M. Naik, and K. R. Vashee.[61]

The storefront was the center of these premises, goods for sale visible through the windows. With the relocation of Indians from haphazard trading sites in African spaces to established trading streets, their shops became

Figure 2. N. B. Stores, run by the N. B. Patel family, on Selbourne Avenue in Salisbury, sometime in the 1940s. The store is now part of a chain known as Enbee, and the main branch is located in the original location on the now renamed Leopold Takawira Street. They remain the main supplier of school uniforms in the city. (HSA BE-0007-3)

Figure 3. Street map of Salisbury, 1959. Indian trading streets were located in the central cluster of streets shown in the map as part of the central business district. (Federal Department of Trigonometrical and Topographical Surveys, Rhodesia and Nyasaland, Special Collections of the University of Cape Town Libraries, ref. islandora:25214)

permanent, settled commercial institutions. Behind the store there would often be some sort of storage room and occasionally an office space for accounting purposes. Most transactions were handled at the counter, the physical barrier set between the Indian salesman and the Black customer. General trading stores sold everything from pots and pans to clothes and food items such as flour and cooking oil, with goods stacked on shelves running across the walls as well as on stands or racks ordered in ramshackle rows across the sales floor. Most of the bookkeeping was done in Gujarati, leading to complaints by tax officials that Indians were hiding income.[62] Behind the storefront, or above it, would be the rooms in which growing families would live.

After 1923, more women migrated from Gujarat as immigration restrictions prevented their husbands from traveling back and forth as frequently as they had done in the past, and adult males could no longer enter. Their presence ensured that men would not seek formal sexual or marital relationships outside of the transnational kinship networks they were expected to maintain.

Figure 4. Street map of Bulawayo, 1959. Lobengula Street was located in the heart of the city, to the west of white suburbs and east of African townships such as Makokoba. (Federal Department of Trigonometrical and Topographical Surveys, Rhodesia and Nyasaland, Special Collections of the University of Cape Town Libraries, ref. islandora:25213)

They took over the running of the domestic side of the shop, maintaining its private spaces as ones centered around family. The settlement of Indian women thus enforced the domestic boundaries of the *dukkan*, enabling its survival. In 1931, there were 1,138 Indian men and 562 women living in Southern Rhodesia. By 1941, there were 1,546 men and 1,001 women.[63] M. V. Naik's wife, Gangaben, arrived in Bulawayo around 1924 and started working for the family business. They had three sons and a daughter, all born in Southern Rhodesia. Their two eldest sons would marry two sisters from the same village in Gujarat, and in the mid-1940s, both women migrated to Bulawayo.[64]

The growth of the family and the business was maintained through marriage, enabling more and more young women to cross the ocean. There was no separation between house and home: Women who married into families would work behind the store counter during the day and return to the kitchen in the evening to prepare meals, starting all over again first thing in the morning. Hasu Patel's mother, who was only fifteen when she married, arrived in Salisbury in 1926. Over the years, her husband acquired five or six properties, renting out the rooms to other Indian families. "She had to learn how to be a socialite and feed these characters," a "brave lady" who had her first daughter when she was twenty-one, and then seven other children over the next decade.[65] Babies were born at home; women raised their children as they worked behind the shop counter.

In between white neighborhoods and Black townships, these shops became "an intermediate space between [African] homesteads and the colonial state."[66] Indian storekeepers strategically placed advertisements in African newspapers. The *African Weekly* and *Bantu Mirror* regularly carried advertisements for stores such as Dayalji's and K. R. Vashee and Co. in Bulawayo, and for Nagarji and Son and Mehta and Co. in Salisbury. Indian trading streets were often within walking distance of African townships, making them physically accessible, and their advertisements dotted African publications in between news articles. They sold basic necessities but also the luxury goods associated with participation in consumer culture. Nagarji and Son claimed to be the "cheapest in town" and specialized in "the largest stock of Rhodesian Bantu gramophone records of all kinds."[67] Mehta and Co. specialized in "general outfitting, silk goods, and groceries."[68] Dayalji and Co. in Bulawayo specifically promoted itself as a departmental store catering to "African hawkers," supplying mobile traders with goods that they took to the rural areas to supply markets located beyond walking distance of the city center.[69]

These advertisements reflected trends in African consumerism as part of a growing colonial modernity in which they were actively participating.[70]

Interactions between Indians and Africans took place across the shop counter—which also served as a barrier that prevented social mingling. Women could run the counter but did not often cross it. Their presence consolidated intimate boundaries of race and class, preventing the miscegenation that had once taken place beyond the boundaries of the trading streets. Indians had been relocated from African spaces to their own zones of home and business, and engagement between the two groups was mediated by their mutual economic dependence. Indians were materially better off than Africans, and their wealth was visible through the windows of their shops. Communities took on the elite patriarchal language that cast them as racially and civilizationally superior to Black Africans, attitudes learned both from the colonial experience as well as discourse about colorism and class from the precolonial period. Indians often communicated across linguistic barriers by using the pidgin *chilapalapa*, a language created by Boers in South Africa to communicate with their servants. It combined English, Afrikaans, and words from African languages, creating a patronizing form of communication for those who did not learn how to speak the indigenous languages of their workers. Indians added in Gujarati words, allowing women in particular, many of whom had not learned English in India, to communicate with their customers and their employees. It was a demeaning language of command, and one which reinforced the hierarchy of Indians above Black Africans.

But Indian traders relied on their African customers. Without them, they would have no livelihood. Black consumers were vital to the survival of Indian businesses, paying these families' "wages for us to put food on the table."[71] At the same time, Africans relied on Indian shops for quotidian supplies, from food to clothing to luxury goods, and the streets served as a symbol of Indian centrality to African life in the city. Domestic insularity did not mean that Indians were completely isolated from the spaces they occupied. Educated African traders who "resented the presence of Indian traders, would say Indians are exploiting us." African laborers alleged "being pushed around a lot, being commanded." But Africans were also aware of class politics among Indians, with wealthier Indians regarding themselves as "better than low-class Indians. . . . That aspect of that class of that group of Indians, demeaning other Indians who associated with Africans, led to a tendency where Africans viewed Indians with suspicion."[72] Suspicion was based on rhetoric that was not necessarily antagonistic. The haggling that took place between an Indian trader and an African customer was a well-known practice. That history has led to "rhetoric today about how Indians do their business, 'let's do it the Indian way.' The Indian shop has a price, you tell the shop owner you don't have the money, and that leads to haggling, what we say in Shona as *kupopera*."[73] Africans could haggle over prices and the terms of their demands, giving them agency in their purchasing power.[74]

Indian trading streets were buffers between white neighborhoods and Black townships. The shop was a colonial institution, one which placed Indians directly in between Black and white. The streets their shops collectively constituted helped maintain the segregation of urban locales. At the same time, they became spaces where Black Africans and Indians could negotiate the terms of their occupancy in locales regulated by white municipal authorities. They could find ways to haggle both over the prices of goods and their ability to live side by side, albeit on terms regulated by racial hierarchies. Indian trading streets became places in which Africans could aspire to colonial modernity through consumer culture. They were vibrant spaces of commercial life in towns and cities, and integral centers of urbanity. While Indians were physically removed from rural areas and African townships, the livelihoods they had constructed in these spaces were now transferred to specific zones of contact. But the boundaries of segregation were far from being neat and tidy. Nor did Indians conform to their relegation by the settler state as simply economic middlemen, negotiating the terms of their identities as localized residents of an African space. Their lives on the ground survived in the historical record, revealed in one of the main bureaucratic tools of the colonial project—the census.

LOCATING THE *DUKKAN* IN THE CENSUS

As a buffer population, Indians were separately identified and categorized within colonial bureaucratic structures in various ways. The spatial segregation of urban life was reflected in institutional hierarchies regulated by law. As a colonized "alien" population, imperial ideologies ranked Indians as civilizationally superior to Black Africans, and below white Europeans. But as Indians were an in-between population, their classification was messy, a mirror of their lives on the ground through their shops. The first acts of legislation passed in the colony initially grouped Indians as either European or non-European, defined as "African" when they had specific rights that needed to be restricted but classified as "European" or "non-indigenous" when this inclusion would not have significant political implications.[75] They were also occasionally thrown in with the mixed-race Coloured population. Later, the terms "Asiatic" and "Asian" encompassed anyone originating from the Asian continent as a whole. When it came to the sale of liquor and firearms, Asians were initially subject to the same restrictive conditions as "natives."[76] Colonial officials were especially concerned about Indians selling alcohol to Black Africans through their shops.[77] When it came to education, however, Indians were classed as "European." They were also included in European voter rolls, their numbers being so small that they could not make much of a difference.[78] Many acts did not initially define Indians or Coloureds as a specific category, their numbers being too small to warrant specific distinction. At the same time, their lives on the ground and the ways in which they were remaking their lives in an African context defied categorization under one particular racial label.

Indians were eventually located more specifically in the census, a colonial creation that was meant to order and stratify complex intersectional forms of identity into clear and concise categories.[79] As Indian trading streets developed, so did their relegation to a specific racial identity unfold. The first census was conducted in 1897. Indians were tabulated as part of the "European" or "white" group, set against a "native" population. Still a small proportion of the population, Indian migrants were collated as part of the general migration of non-African settler groups to the territory. An Indian identity was initially assigned to those who had been born in India; Indians were not defined as racial group per se. By 1911, Indians were identified as part of a wider racial group of "Asiatics," and their individual household schedules were collated as part of the "C2" collection. Enumerators would fill out census forms based on interviews with the heads of households. That information was later verified, and often "corrected" by district supervisors based on colonial readings of how Indian families functioned. As the next generation of children was born in the colony, they were identified specifically as "British Indians."

Reading against the grain of the official census statistics listing the number of residents per racial group, Mohammed Bhika can be found in the somewhat haphazard collection of individual Asiatic census schedules for

Salisbury. In 1926, Bhika was listed as living with eight-year-old Suleman, a son from his first wife who had been born in Southern Rhodesia, at "34 Garden, Makabusi." He noted his nationality as British Indian, his religion as Muhammedan, and his birthplace as Bombay, India. He noted his profession as "Gardens" and that he was a widower.[80] Ten years later, his family had grown. In the 1936 census schedules, "Mahmed Bhikha," a fruit and vegetable gardener, still lived in the "Garden Plots" of Salisbury, but this time with three sons, Ebrahim, Esmail, and Ahmad, and three daughters, Isa, Katesha, and Uhie.[81] All had been born in Southern Rhodesia.

The location of even the earliest iteration of the *dukkan* in the form of market garden plots in the census reveals how Indians consolidated their homes and businesses. Households would list the names of all residents on their schedules. Each schedule revealed how the household was structured, with several generations often living together in the same space.[82] Under the category of "profession," Indian men either listed themselves as general traders, "employs others," or listed the name of the store they worked for. Most adult married women listed their profession as "household duties," a vague and all-encompassing term for the work they did both at home and in the store. Later census forms also listed the number of rooms in a building. Many Indian families included their business areas in the tabulation of the number of rooms in a home, figures which again were later struck through by census officials who saw the home and the business as separate spaces. Branches of extended families who owned the same business would sometimes fill out separate forms; only by putting the different forms together would their relationship be revealed. The centrality of the store revealed wider familial connections centered around the trading stand that the neat tables of census categories could not always reveal from surface-level readings of an individual family's form and the collective collation of their homes as part of generalized statistics.

Legislation, particularly when it came to immigration, marked Indians as "foreign" and "alien," a lens which defined them as perpetual strangers and migrants. But Indians saw themselves as distinctly colonial subjects who, like European settlers, had made new homes in Africa. In 1926, dozens of families noted their nationality in census schedules as "British" or "British Subject," although the number of schedules with that notation had lessened by the 1936 and 1941 censuses. Those who had children born in the African colony rather than in India noted their nationality as "Rhodesian," which was later crossed out and replaced with "British Indian," creating a racialized distinction of imperial subjecthood.[83] There was, in fact, no such nationality or formal status as "British Indian" outside the subcontinent. One was either British, according to colonial jurisdiction in the Raj or Southern Rhodesia, or a subject of one of the independent princely states, and hence a British Protected Person.[84] An "Indian" nationality did not exist before 1947. With further generations being born in Southern Rhodesia, members of some Indian families in fact had no "Asiatic" place of birth. Rhodesian Indians instead attempted to mark themselves as part of a transnational collective, and some even began to see their children as being disconnected from a subcontinental identity.

Most Indian homes and shops were located on known Indian trading streets, their trading stand number given as their specific address. On the surface, these addresses suggested that Indians were a simple physical buffer between Black and white in segregated towns and cities. But the neat categories of the census masked the chaotic and complex ways that boundaries were being contested. This was especially true for Coloured Rhodesians, who typically claimed European and African descent. Colonial officials referred to the products of miscegenation as "half-breeds" and enumerated them separately from Black Africans in the census.[85] As an in-between population, like Indians, they often found themselves marginalized by "black-white binaries" of both history and the colonial experience.[86] But a Coloured identity was not confined in southern Africa to the products of relationships between Black and white. Indian men also took part in miscegenation, and their families defied easy definition. In reading only official statistics of the numbers of population categorized by race, their presence would be erased. In the schedules, however, their anomalous experiences were revealed, despite the efforts of patriarchs across racial lines to prevent intermixing.

Indian families were thus often found beyond the C2 schedules that were meant to mark their place in society. Mixed-race families classified themselves as "European" or "Asiatic" by filling out the relevant racial schedule. Occasionally, schedules would be half filled out, suggesting the family had requested a C2 schedule, a census official had begun filling it in for them, and upon realizing the "mistake," crossed out or "canceled" the original schedule and filled out a Coloured C3 form instead. In Gwelo in 1941, a Muslim family residing at 59 Third Street initially filled out an Asiatic schedule; Mahomed Abdul Rahaman, listed as the head of the household, with his wife, Elizabeth Rahaman, their children Joseph Abdul and Cadija, and Mahomed's brother-in-law. A census officer later crossed out the names of everyone except Mahomed, noting that they had been transferred to form C3, reflecting how a "Coloured identity and politics were negotiated within the realm of day-to-day politics" even as they were erased from official records of Indian homes.[87] Mahomed would have been counted as Indian in the census, and the rest of his family as Coloured, despite the fact that they lived together among other Indian families.[88] The erasure of the ties that bound them was part of the larger "inaccuracy of colonial censuses and racial categories."[89] This sort of incident occurred several times throughout the census schedules for that year and for 1936. Many of the Indians of Tamil and Madrasi origin who could be found in the first censuses were not seen again in future counts. This was due to a lack of subcontinental diversity in sustained immigration from India to Rhodesia, but it also suggested that they had intermarried with Coloureds and Black Africans, eventually leading to an eradication of the Indian roots of future generations in official statistics.

The census was meant to impose scientific order on a messy society through the collation of lives into simple statistics. In turn, the hierarchical stratification of the census would eventually shape society itself.[90] But labels and figures of race and nationality never managed to encapsulate quotidian experiences or prevent Indians from transgressing the bounds of a colonial middleman identity. The census schedules in their original form in fact revealed the identities that Indians were making and remaking for themselves on the ground. In 1921, of the 1,250 listed as "Asiatic" in the census, 60 listed Bengal as their birthplace, 419 as Bombay (which included the villages of Gujarat), and 118 as Madras. In terms of religion, 812 listed Hinduism as their practicing faith, and 231 listed "Mahammadan."[91] These categories, however, erased the complex and nuanced distinctions that would begin to matter more as the population of Indians grew—caste, wealth, occupation, village of origin. In the C2 schedules, many noted their caste identity in place of their religion. A few gave their specific villages of origin rather than simply the state or region. Others identified their nationality as "British Hindoo," creating a specific colonial identity where religion was more significant than belonging to the imperial construction of "India." Class, religion, and caste were all deeply embedded in their everyday lives, and neither colonial racial categories nor the borders of urban segregation could show the relationships that Indians had with each other, as well as with Black Africans and

Coloureds. As future generations were born in the colony, however, these identities would come to the fore, with conflicts over where they belonged rendering them visible within the colonial archive.

Colonial ideologies and institutions rendered invisible the ways in which Indians were becoming African. Policies of segregation did not mean that Indians were an insular population. Even as their families and their businesses expanded, Indians had to negotiate their lives on the ground with other groups they encountered both behind and beyond the shop counter. The *dukkan* was central to the relationships Indians were making with Black Africans as well as part of a developing Coloured identity. But the anxieties over the protection of racial identities and domestic structures that had led to urban segregation and the development of Indian trading streets simmered in the background. The next generations of Indian children were now being born in Southern Rhodesia rather than spending their early lives across an ocean. Elite Indian patriarchs shifted from concerns about immoral men to the future of their children. They created institutions which metaphorically extended the *dukkan* beyond its physical space, consolidating distinctions not only of race but also of caste, class, and religion. Through their communal organizations, they envisioned how the next generation should live in an African context. Indian elites served as the interlocutors and transmitters of colonial ideas regarding caste and religion from across the Indian Ocean to racial hierarchies in Africa. But it was the voices of those whose lives had once been relegated to the census, whose daily experiences transgressed the boundaries imposed on them by Indian elites and colonial authorities, that would come to the forefront over a critical point of contention—the education of their children.

THREE
PURITY SCHOOLS AND HINDU DAUGHTERS

―

Indian Education, 1930–1950

> Serious strife over site of new Government Indian School: Salisbury Hindoos almost Nazi-like in desire for racial purity.
>
> —MR. COWIE, Department of Education, Southern Rhodesia, 20 February 1939

Taraben Naik arrived in Southern Rhodesia in the early 1950s. She grew up in a village near Mumbai and married an Indian man from Salisbury when she was only sixteen years old. Her husband returned to Africa without her; she waited six months for her immigration papers to be processed. When she finally arrived, she moved into the rooms behind his store on Sinoia Street. The day after she arrived, she went into the shop, the central space of the Indian family in Southern Rhodesia, to help behind the counter. The role of a woman in the "traditional family," according to a report by the Bulawayo Ramakrishna Youth League, was that she "is expected to be subservient to her husband as well as her in-laws. A typical Hindu woman runs the affairs of the home from the time she gets up to the time she goes to bed."[1] Taraben's husband often traveled for work to find suppliers for goods, leaving her to run both the business and the home. She was alone when the first three of her four sons were born.[2] She became the backbone of the family as well as its livelihood, managing the shop when her husband was away.

Taraben's story was a typical one for the women from India who joined their husbands across an ocean. Her labor was critical in the raising of children as well as behind the shop counter. By bringing their wives back with them, Indian men chose to make their lives permanent in Southern Rhodesia, transplanting institutions of kinship rather than going back and forth across an ocean to maintain them. Their numbers gradually increased with the migration of women. Like white Rhodesians, Indians had arrived as settlers, participating in the displacement of Black Africans from their lands. As they became an urbanized trading population, however, Indians found themselves sharing intimate spaces in towns and cities with their African and Coloured customers across the shop counter. Upper-caste politics in India were predicated on the erasure and oppression of lower and Dalit castes, and in maintaining "purity" when it came to marriage and domesticity.[3] As on the subcontinent, marriage between Hindus and Muslims was regarded as deeply forbidden. But in an African context, caste boundaries also had to be set in racial terms against Black and Coloured populations instead. Those who breached the divide of the shop counter and deviated from upper-caste conceptions of endogamous structures were cast as "deviants" by civilizational language which otherized those who transgressed moral and "normative boundaries."[4] Miscegenation with African and Coloured women was regarded as taboo and became associated with Muslim and lower-caste Hindu men.

Elite Indians began organizing along communal lines of caste and religion in order to protect endogamous structures that kept bloodlines and families "pure," reconstructing South Asian traditions in an African colonial context. The first generation of Indian women, most of whom came from outside Southern Rhodesia, were already protected by the boundaries of marriage through their roles in the home and the shop. Fears of intimacy between Indian women and Black men were not as deeply rooted a fear as they were at the same time in other colonial spaces.[5] But a new generation of children was now being born outside of India, their lives fully enmeshed in an African settler colonial space. As they grew older, the question of their education arose. Hindu religious organizations created what were known as "purity schools," funded by the colonial state but run by Hindu patriarchs and intended only for children with two Indian parents. Unlike those of their mothers, the lives of Indian children raised in Africa extended beyond the confines of the *dukkan*.

Purity schools expanded the domestic boundaries of the shop to control the futures of Indian children, providing an education based on colonial curricula as well as Indian vernaculars and religious texts. In their conflicts with other Hindu and Muslim families who objected to admissions clauses based on "purity," Indians transitioned from being a diasporic population to becoming one grounded in local dynamics and contexts. Communal tensions and divisions were less about the nationalist politics of Partition on the subcontinent than they were about generational conflicts over the boundaries of domesticity and debates about morality in an African space.

Caste and class were reframed in an African setting, as generations being born in Rhodesia disrupted the chains of continuity of tradition their parents had maintained with the subcontinent. Conflicts within the community were centered around gendered notions of what the lives of women should look like in colonial urban spaces. What these debates boiled down to was the protection of *daughters* in particular.[6] Sons were expected to maintain the boundaries of home life by marrying women in their own groups. But it was daughters who would bear children and sustain both home and business, creating ties of kinship and community through marriage. By sending female children for their education outside the home and the shop, the men who controlled them risked their "corruption" and exposed them to the potential for "sexual deviancy" through social engagement with those outside their caste and religion. The aspirations of Hindu patriarchs both intersected with and challenged colonial policy over the futures of their daughters, who were critical for the maintenance of familial "purity," enabling continued patriarchal authority through their sons.

Gender and generation are key to understanding how South Asian traditions became localized in African settings. Indian families became "agents of change" of colonial policy through the formation of these communal associations and schools, which ideologically extended the family structures of the shop.[7] Male leaders informed education policy by arguing for the maintenance of the racial boundaries being constructed by the colonial state and consolidated behind the store counter. Their ideas about gender, caste, and religion were no longer solely informed by Brahminic interpretations and colonial ideologies but were instead reframed by local interlocutors in a specifically African context. Just as Black elites were critical to the codification of customary law that reinforced patriarchal control over their families and their communities, so too did Hindu elites take advantage of colonial gaps in knowledge to influence educational policy through the construction of their caste and religious institutions.[8] Here we see a breakdown in a "long precedent in colonial knowledge about India," where Orientalist and liberal ideas concerning caste and religion were not transferred through colonial administrations across imperial spaces but rather by colonized migrants to make sense in their new homes.[9]

THE HOME AND THE WORLD

Women like Taraben Naik were responsible for the melding of business and family structures. At this time, home and store were one in terms of physical space. The integration of women in business meant that they became the invisible backbone of both the rooms in the back and the shop counter in the front, replacing the male labor that was in short supply because of sustained immigration restrictions. Male children continued to live with their parents after marriage, and wives were expected to take care of their in-laws. Daughters left their natal home after marriage, becoming part of a new family and a new commercial enterprise. Women usually married men of their family's choosing, members of the same caste if they were Hindu. If a family could not find a suitable wife for a son from Southern Rhodesia, they turned to their networks in East or South Africa as well as India to find a woman from the same caste. Women were the binding ties of extended networks of family and kin. A joint family structure in Bulawayo, for example, usually consisted of "the parents and the unmarried children, their married sons and their wives and children." The married brothers typically took on the responsibility of taking care of other members of the family. "Ideally, the joint family is supposed to be joint in residence, worship, business and property and where the ultimate power in decision-making lies with the eldest male member of the family," read one report on the history of the Indian family structure in Bulawayo by a Hindu youth group.[10] Within the home, social hierarchies were determined by both gender and generation.

Women mostly stayed confined to the home, but as the community grew, they began to find social lives outside of the shop. Taraben Naik had one African domestic worker, and together they took care of most of the household chores. Men did not help their wives with the housework. She would buy her

Indian groceries, such as spices and specific vegetables, from Patel & Mehta, who imported them from India. Later, Black African market gardeners supplied Indian homes with the special vegetables used in Gujarati cuisine. She wore a sari every day. In the presence of men, she covered her head with her *palav*. She would feed them first, before sitting down to eat herself. Even today, she still has her meals last. Outside the home, she visited the temple in Salisbury on Cameron Street and formed friendships with other women who had arrived in the country as very young brides. She recalled Hindus and Muslims living together "harmoniously like family" in these early years of settlement, despite growing tensions over education and the separation between their networks of endogamy. She spoke some English, but it took her a while to adapt until she learned how to speak the pidgin *chilapalapa*, enabling her to communicate with her servants and the customers at the shop.[11] Women born in Rhodesia led similar social lives. Jasuben Bhagat, who was the same age as Taraben but grew up in Salisbury in the 1940s, "never knew the life of Europeans." Her life revolved around going to school, helping in the home, and attending social activities such as *garba* dancing at the *mandir*.[12]

The public religious institutes that dominated social life were built around the intimate domestic structure of the family. In the late 1920s, soon after Southern Rhodesia attained self-governing status, both Hindu and Muslim communities laid the foundation stones for the societies that were meant to sustain the traditions they were enforcing at home. In 1926, the Hindoo Society was formed, meant to serve the twenty-five Hindu families living in Salisbury at the time. Its goal was to bring the community together through Hindu culture and religion. The male heads of families who became the founders of the society managed to obtain the leases for three stands in Cameron Street, located in the business district where most Indians lived and traded. Membership fees contributed to the construction of the buildings, and in 1929, the foundation stone for the temple was laid.[13] In Bulawayo, the community built the K. R. Vashee Hall, initiated by the patriarch of one of the largest families in the city, Khandubhai Vashee. While he was the biggest donor, most of the Hindu families in the town donated money for the construction of the hall.[14] It was not technically a temple, but it did serve as a site for prayer and gatherings and later became the site of a school for Indian children.

These institutions were built by Indian families themselves with the wealth they were acquiring from their trading businesses. Their profits allowed them to donate money to the construction of community organizations, making them physical outlets of the *dukkan* as well as metaphorical ones. The Islamic Society built the colony's first mosque in 1928, which was mostly financed by three individuals: Hoosein Kassim, Ali Bin Mahomed, and Hajee Esat.[15] Rather than applying for city land from municipal authorities, they bought the land for the mosque from the Transvaal and Rhodesia Estates and then donated it to the Islamic Society.[16] The mosque was constructed at the corner of Charter Road and Kingsway Avenue, a meeting place for the five hundred or so Muslims who lived in Salisbury at the time. Most Muslims who migrated from Gujarat to Southern Rhodesia were Sunnis, and the community always came together for the important religious festivals, including Eid, Bakr-Eid, and the Prophet's birthday.[17] Their mosques were also open to anyone who was Muslim, including Coloureds and Black Africans. Religion served as a bridge between social and racial divides rather than a boundary as it did for Hindu institutions. By the 1950s, the Islamic Society had begun plans to construct a mosque at the "native settlement" in the Highfield area of Salisbury for the growing African Muslim community, most of whom were migrant laborers from Northern Rhodesia and Nyasaland, identifying themselves as part of the Yao ethnic group and known locally as the "Machawa."[18]

As the number of Indians in urban spaces grew, the gender and social norms of the *dukkan* expanded to encompass the idea of community as well. Gujaratis identified their caste through endogamous *jati* origins and identities, a reflection of trade or profession within the *varna*, or class-based, categories of society. These *jati* identities were ranked according to their *varna* classification. How a family lived inside the home dictated how they would interact with others outside of it. Upper-caste notions of purity, conceived by the religious caste of Brahmins, or priests, during the colonial period in India, dictated what was considered "pure" or "impure" according to both the professions and lifestyles associated with each caste. Eating meat, or handling animal carcasses, was considered unclean. Castes associated with meat-eating or professions that involved handling leather, such as shoemakers, or engaging in pastoral farming, were considered lower caste or untouchable. Reproduction with someone from a lower caste led to the loss of caste purity for their descendants over generations. For Hindus, caste identity regulated whom they married, leading to the creation of caste *mandals*, or formally organized communities, as a form of social organization, such as the Rajput *mandal* that extended to South Africa. The self-stated goal of these groups was "the upliftment" of the caste community "socially, culturally, and educationally."[19] Their primary function was to provide a formal network for practices of endogamy.

In a community where most families took part in some form of trading, it was these practices that differentiated caste identity rather than profession. Taraben's son did not recall being conscious of caste until he was older. The Hindu children who grew up in the 1940s and 1950s were aware of the caste system, a "strong but subtle" influence and pressure from families that only came out in full force, as he put it, "when starting to look at girls." While his family did not limit whom he could bring home with him from school, there was a sense that some of his friends came from another caste—and more visibly, from less wealthy homes, with caste and class intersecting in quotidian ways. As a member of an *anavil* family, typically seen as higher caste, one of his uncles would ask the children who came home, especially the lower-ranked *dhobis*, whether they had eaten chicken for lunch. If they had, they would have to sit outside rather than coming inside to watch television. As a result, all the children would say they had eaten *moong*, or lentils.[20]

For South Asian diasporic populations, caste has been evoked in the popular imagination as the central foundation of Indian society, even as its visibility as a modern phenomenon was a specific product of the encounter between India and the West during the colonial period.[21] Colonial ideologies of caste and its associated hierarchies were transplanted across the Indian Ocean but remade to make sense in an African context, "reproduced through social and economic practices."[22] Local interlocutors of South Asian traditions argued that "caste in India and caste in modern Bulawayo are very different phenomena" because of transformations associated with the migration process.[23] The most common caste identities claimed in Southern Rhodesia were that of *patidars*, or Patels, *anavils*, *khumbars*, *mochis*, *khatris*, *dhobis*, and *brahmins*. *Patidars*, or the landowners, were the dominant peasant caste, with local conditions giving them a higher social and economic position than their counterparts in the rest of India.[24] This caste was associated with the name Patel, but as many high-caste *patidars* were known to complain, a large number of *kolis*, or the landless laboring caste, Hindu and Muslim alike, took on the name when migrating to Southern Rhodesia.

Caste offered a way for migrants to remake themselves in a new colonial space, and therefore find upward social mobility in a community where most families who ran shops were accorded "middleman" status in both racial and class hierarchies. Members of the *anavil* caste often claimed *brahmin* status; they were not priests but were instead descended from officials, landowners, and civil servants during the Mughal era.[25] In South Asia, this distinction was understood. In Africa, however, they used these origins to claim a higher-caste status—one they did not have in South Asia—when it came to social hierarchies within communities. Caste sometimes took on the same professional associations it had in Gujarat; some Indians in Bulawayo, for example, originated from south Gujarat, where they belonged to the *mochi* or shoemaker caste, an occupation they continued by setting up leatherworking and shoe stores.[26] In Bulawayo, however, in order to claim upper-caste status, the *mochi mandal,* founded in September 1918, identified themselves as families with warrior origins and as "soldiers in the armies of the many rajahs" whose descendants later took to farming, labor, and craftmanship. In claiming a precolonial myth of lineage, they attempted to take on identities predicated on upper-class notions of hygiene and cleanliness as a way of raising their status in a colonial context outside India. The founders of the group "were inspired with thoughts and ideas about progress, reform, knowledge and understanding," attempting to fight the stigma associated with their almost "untouchable" origins that came from working with tainted leather.[27]

Caste, class, and capitalism were intertwined in the formation of complex hierarchies. Their intersection in the creation of communal divides was most visible when it came to the role of gender and marriage in creating families. Members of the Islamic community were more disposed toward social integration with the Coloured and African populations around them, using religion as a bridge between racial divides where Hindus used caste to justify domestic insularity. For Muslim families, whose religion did not formally recognize any castes, marriage outside the confines of caste—and therefore race—was more acceptable and widely practiced, as seen in census returns as well as when it came to the classification of children with Muslim fathers.[28] In 1949, in correspondence relating to the education of "Indo-African" children, the Department of Education found that "Moslems were allowed 'mixed' marriages" in a way that "Hindoos" were not—but that the products of these marriages could not be classified as "Coloured" because of their "Asiatic ancestry."[29] Even though colonial classifications of race designated Indians as "foreign," those who took part in intermarriage assimilated themselves with other urbanized groups. Muhamod Ebrahim-Patel, who was born in Salisbury in 1944, "converged" with Coloured children "for the first time" at school. He married a Coloured woman in 1971 but had already integrated himself socially with the Coloured communities of the city as a renowned football player for Arcadia United, Salisbury's Coloured team.[30] Upper-caste Hindu elites looked down upon Muslims and lower-caste Hindus who participated in miscegenation, as was seen in the removal of Indian families from the African location in Bulawayo in 1930.[31] Mixed families were seen as less "pure," anomalies to the boundaries of tradition being consolidated through the *dukkan*.

Debates over racial purity took on a more public stage when it came to the expansion of colonial education for nonwhite children—and therefore who would regulate their lives outside the *dukkan*. The first generation of female migrants were largely controlled by the patriarchs of the families they married into, and their behavior was governed by the rules of family structure and endogamy articulated by group leaders and the *mandals* they created. Their children who were born in Africa, however, attended colonial schools outside the home. It was the regulation of their behavior and ideas of what their future should look like that became the focus of negotiation between elite Hindu patriarchs, the colonial state, and those who did not conform to imagined upper-caste Hindu ideals of family. Here, religion, caste, and class all intersected in the production of complex hierarchies that were not reflected in official colonial racial pyramids but that were critical to the construction of the colony's education policy. Children, more than wives, became a central focus of communal notions of identity and tradition as Indian fathers—both Hindu and Muslim—publicly negotiated the terms of their education with the colonial state and another "in-between" group: Coloureds.

PURITY SCHOOLS AND PUBLIC CONFLICTS

Between the 1930s and 1950s, the Southern Rhodesian government developed its educational system.[32] The first Education Ordinance in 1899 provided for European and African schools but did not create separate facilities for Asian and Coloured children, with the former being educated at home and the latter attending mission schools. In 1930, education became compulsory for all non-African children in the colony.[33] The Education Act recognized three classes of children—European, Native, and non-European, "which embraces both Asiatic and Coloured."[34] European and African education systems were separated administratively; European education was maintained by the Department of Education, whereas African Education was dealt with by the Native Affairs Department.[35] Within the Department of Education, schools were categorized according to race, separated between European, and Asian and Coloured. Over the next decade, the colonial state undertook to provide educational facilities for all racial groups, gradually replacing mission schools with government facilities.

Initially, there were not enough schools for the growing population of Indian children. In 1934, 883 children were attending the eight Coloured and Asians schools in the territory, and it was estimated that an equal number of children in the territory were not receiving a formal education.[36] By 1935, Indians numbered approximately 1,300; 700 were noted as Hindu, 400 Muslim, and 200 Goanese from the Portuguese territories in India, most of whom were Roman Catholics. In Salisbury, there were 225 Indian children, 125 of whom were of school age.[37] Leaders of both Hindu and Islamic communities thus constructed their religious institutions with the goal of educating their children as well. By extending the *dukkan*, Indian families could prepare their children for the responsibilities of adulthood and participation in colonial society while maintaining the traditional values that were foundational to the family and the business. The Hindoo Society's prime mandate was education; the principles of social responsibility would follow from that.[38] The first Islamic school was initially housed at a building on Pioneer Street, not far from the Hindoo School, with instruction in Urdu and reading of the Koran in Arabic. There was no formal teaching of Gujarati in the Islamic school, but it was used as medium of instruction because it was the language spoken in the home.[39]

Education became key to the maintenance of imagined concepts of Hindu religion and upper-caste constructs of purity and hierarchy. Their institutions were built on public land and therefore could be considered public facilities. Islamic societies were located on private land, and while they were open to all Muslims across racial boundaries, their schools remained privately controlled.[40] The main goal of the Hindoo Society was to construct a vernacular Gujarati school, which included some instruction in English and arithmetic. But realizing that lessons in vernacular languages would not prepare their children to enter colonial society, the Hindu communities of Southern Rhodesia

Figure 5. Group photograph of the Hindoo Society Salisbury Gujarati School, including the president, secretary, principal, staff, and pupils, 1944. (HSA ED0028)

set up full-fledged schools in the 1930s, subsidized by funds from the colonial government. Citing a lack of government education facilities for their children, the school committees successfully negotiated some measure of colonial support, allocated grants by the Department of Education to cover teachers' salaries. The Bulawayo Indian School, which opened in 1933, was partly funded by government subsidies, a temporary arrangement that was meant to last until a public school for Asians was constructed. The government agreed to supply teaching staff, while funds for the erection of the school came from the estate of the late Charelick Solomon (a Jewish man who had died in 1931), "European merchants of this Colony and the Union," and the Indian community itself, altogether totaling 2,500 pounds in donations.[41]

Admission to these schools was based on racial identity. Hindu committees permitted Muslim children to attend Hindoo Society schools to further their education according to the colonial curriculum, as their local *madrasas*, or religious schools, remained privately run and focused solely on Quranic instruction in Urdu. But the issue of what to do with children who only had one Indian parent arose. In response to applications for admission for those children, the same Hindu elites who had created and sustained caste-based *mandals* within the Hindu community developed what became known as an admissions policy based on "purity." They applied their upper-caste conceptualizations of gradations of "pollution" that were used to rank *jati* identities to racialized conditions for admission. "Purity" meant that both parents of an admitted child should be of Indian descent or origin, based on the assumption that children who had a non-Indian parent had less "pure" origins or ancestry and were not living in households that adhered to proper conceptions of morality. Mixed-race children were thus denied access.

The status of these children had always been contested. White colonial officials historically discouraged interracial relationships as threats to a "colonial social order."[42] Elite Hindu ideas about race, civilization, and purity intersected with these concerns, and purity school leaders appropriated colonial language to justify exclusive admissions policies. They argued that if white schools were allowed to be racially exclusive, then so should theirs. In 1934, an Indian deputation to the government maintained "that as neither Indians nor Europeans are indigenous to this country the conditions in their cases should be similar, particularly as they are both races whose civilisation and culture are superior to those of the Coloured and Native races."[43] Members of the Hindoo Society in Salisbury justified the "purity" principle by referencing "the same objections which Europeans feel to children of mixed European and Native descent attending European schools," arguing that "daily intercourse between children of mixed marriages and those of pure descent" would break down the "ordinary barriers to further race impurity"; as a result, "Indian culture and ideas will be seriously impaired."[44] Instead, they insisted that these children should attend schools meant for Coloureds or Black Africans.

In setting these standards for admission, Hindu elites used colonial legal definitions of race which conflated racial identity with a "way of life" at home. They extended the standards they argued should be maintained in the *dukkan* to their public institutions. Education policy designated children as Coloured or "Native" depending on where and how they lived. For example, the definition of a "Native" child was based on two criteria. The first was being "any member of the aboriginal tribes or races of Africa"; the second was being "any person having the blood of such tribes and races living among them and after the manner thereof." For the children of Indian and African parents, the department recommended that if "an Asiatic provides a home and the native mother no longer lives among the relatives and after the manner thereof, it is reasonable to suggest that the children of the union should attend the Asiatic School. The same reasoning is applicable if the father is a native who provides a suitable home for an Asiatic mother."[45] The justification was that in some cases, children with an African parent were "brought up in native reserves and according to native customs."[46] Later, this policy was applied to the case of Kenneth Nakwa, a boy who had an Indian father but an African mother, and who was considered "native" in terms of the Native Status Determination Act because he had "lived all his life in an African reserve area in the care of various African relatives."[47] Where the committees of the Hindu schools went a step further from colonial policy was to argue for the exclusion of any children of mixed parentage, even if they did live with their Indian relatives. They defined an Indian identity not just as being tied to the *dukkan* but as one that was compatible with upper-caste definitions of purity and morality. For Hindu elites, an Indian "way of life" was predicated on racial purity and structures of endogamy rather than simply where and how one lived. By expanding the principles of the home and the shop to the outside world, they could protect their children and ensure the replication of their "traditions" across generations.

Gendered and racialized ideas about childhood could "shape interventions in the lives of children," not only by colonial authorities but by the parents for whom the stakes were about larger conflicts over race, class, and caste.[48] In 1935, the Bulawayo Indian School advisory committee defended the implementation of a "purity" clause due to the dangers of miscegenation:

> The question of mixed marriages is responsible for the whole of the difficulty that has arisen between the Indians of pure blood and those who have contracted alliances with Coloured and Native women. It is the unanimous opinion of responsible Indian leaders that in the Colonies where there is any danger of mixture of blood, the very greatest care should be taken that the children of Indian descent should be of good stock and pure blood. Some Indians have unfortunately contracted alliances with Native and Coloured women and the Indians of pure blood have the greatest objection to their children, especially their daughters the mothers of future generations, associating with children of mixed blood during their educational career, and we contend that there is a moral and sacred obligation, no matter where we

live and what vocation we follow, to rigidly maintain our purity of blood. It is therefore incumbent upon us to discourage and protest against any matrimonial alliances with persons of an altogether different race, otherwise there is the great danger of the Indian Race being contaminated.[49]

The language of purity of caste and of blood, of gendered sanctity and contamination, collided here with white supremacist language of morality against miscegenation in a multiracial society through the dangers of exposure of daughters, "the mothers of future generations," to sexual alliances outside of racial and religious bounds. Many Indians in Bulawayo articulated their desire to discourage "mixed marriages" in the future in "advocating an exclusive policy."[50] They used language that Rhodesian colonial officials would understand to make their argument for racial and religious purity that would in turn sustain the caste hierarchies they had constructed and which they used to justify their own continuing authority.

But their dominance was challenged by Hindu, Muslim, and Coloured men who contested the admissions clauses. Their arguments were not just about where their children would go to school but also about who was considered a part of an "Indian" community and could claim that heritage and identity. Debates between Hindus and Muslims specifically were about local dynamics and contexts rather than the politicized communal divides of the subcontinent that would eventually result in Partition and the separation of a Muslim state from a secular Indian nation.[51] The debate had become about whether Indians should adhere to ideas about racial and caste purity gleaned from their experience on the subcontinent, or whether localized contexts and experiences necessitated change and flexibility in the definition of who belonged. Leaders of contingents who challenged the Hindoo Society schools pressed for the inclusion of children of mixed-race families in Indian schools based on standards of morality and civilization. In 1935, a leader of the Rhodesian Born Indian Association argued for the inclusion of the children of mixed marriages within the category of "Asian" or "Indian": "Among our members are many who have married respectable coloured women. Our wives have lived up to the traditions of Indian women, and we have brought up our children in a completely Indian atmosphere, and in all respects as though they were pure-blooded Indian children, and we can confidently say that there is no difference in any way between these children and pure Indian children."[52] A "completely Indian atmosphere" suggested a life centered around the *dukkan*, structured by gender and generation, where Indian traditions such as diet and religion were adhered to. Islamic societies similarly challenged Hindu dominance of Indian education. In Bulawayo, the Hindoo School had received not only governmental grants when taking on a colonial curriculum but donations from Muslim families as well. Now, however, Muslims accused Hindus of taking control and preventing Muslim children of mixed race from attending, which they argued was discriminatory against all Muslims.[53] They insisted that those from their community who married non-Indians "have committed no breach against their religion or the established law of this country to merit degradation and humiliation" and were "not bound like Hindus to marry within their own caste."[54] They also pointed out that there was no example of such a "purity" school anywhere else within the British Empire.[55]

Their arguments suggested that as "Rhodesian-born" generations, their children deserved the education that was being provided to "racially pure" families. The conflict between those who led the purity schools and those who opposed their restrictive admission policies was more than just a religious debate over marriage practices and the traditions that constituted their domestic lives. It was also articulated as a difference between firstcomers and newcomers. "Firstcomers" claimed longer roots in the colony, seeing themselves as more willing to integrate with Coloured and Black African communities, having resided in the colony "since the Pioneering days." They accused the leaders of the Hindu schools of being "comparative new comers," sons or younger relatives of those who had already settled in Africa, men who later founded their own families and refreshed ideas about caste and purity from Gujarat when taking over the leadership of community institutions.[56] The complexities of age and generation came into play in their conflicts. The vanguards of Hindu religious and caste institutions were older men, many of whom had been born in India and come over as young adults. Those who contested their authority were from a more liberal, younger generation who had been born in Southern Rhodesia or brought over as young children, knowing only Rhodesia as home.[57] Rather than challenging the colonial state, which funded these institutions, they requested state intervention in their internal generational conflicts over morality, religion, and belonging. But when the state intervened in their domestic lives, fathers directly contested education policy, revealing their main concern: control of their children's lives—and, more specifically, those of their daughters.

FATHERS AND DAUGHTERS

By 1939, purity schools had become a persistent point of contention between different factions of both Hindu and Muslim communities. In Salisbury, the conflict boiled over and resulted in accusations of physical violence against Indian daughters, symbols of domestic purity for their potential for the transmission of tradition over generations. The Hindoo School was staffed by three teachers; A. J. Naik from Surat, P. Lalloo from Pietermaritzburg, and a Miss M. Remedios, who was Goan. The headmaster was Mr. Bitshoo, a teacher from Natal who was appointed in 1941.[58] They were all seen as "outsiders" by local communities. They came as professionals, usually on temporary contracts, and did not set up trading businesses. In 1939, N. M. Patel, a parent, complained that Mr. Lalloo had disciplined his daughter with violence. An inspector from the Department of Education visited the school after Patel complained, demanding that Lalloo pay medical expenses. The child had marks on her arms, legs, and hips that indicated "quite unnecessary violence." Lalloo admitted to caning the girl "but did not appear to realise its violence," claiming that he "had been given authority by [her] mother and uncle to punish [the] child when necessary." Bitshoo supported him, saying that when children were sent to school, "a common Hindoo formula is 'The skin is yours, the bones are ours.'"[59] Physical punishment was a common mode of discipline in schools at the time but was usually reserved for male children. Girls were seen as more physically delicate, but there were also concerns about male teachers initiating any kind of physical contact with a young unmarried girl. According to Patel, his daughter was "in such a hysterical state that he feels it desirable not to compel her to return to school."[60]

Challengers to the purity schools highlighted the treatment of female children and potential for their sexual corruption in their reports to the state. Complaints of violence and abuse by the staff of the school continued, particularly against the headmaster, Mr. Bitshoo. In 1941, J. P. Naik's daughter was "beaten by him . . . so that her ears were bleeding and her earrings knocked out." Other parents also noted severe beatings of their children. Parents also reported that Bitshoo summoned "girls into his office to make tea and asks them for similar small personal services as a result of which girls are afraid of him. This is particularly resented on moral and religious grounds as he is a bachelor and such practices are, in the eyes of the community, likely to cast reflections on the character of the girls."[61] In 1943, N. D. Mehta, one of the trustees of the Hindoo Society and a member of the school council, led a group of parents in protesting Bitshoo's actions at an annual general meeting, calling for Bitshoo's resignation. The meeting erupted in "quarrels," and "violence was threatened," leading to Mehta and his group of friends walking out of the meeting "in order to avoid violence actually taking place." Of the eighty-six parents in attendance, forty were part of this latter group.[62] Mehta was far from innocent, however. He allegedly "organised an attack on Bitshoo by a gang of Coloured 'roughs' as he was catching a train at Salisbury Station." Bitshoo reported the incident to the police, but he began staying indoors as much as possible after being ousted from his position.[63]

The real "crux of the matter" behind the rumors and violence, however, was "factional recrimination by the teachers against the children of parents" who were against the purity clauses.[64] A group of parents, both Hindu and Muslim and led by Mehta, protested the very existence of the school through complaints about the behavior of the staff toward their daughters. On the other side were those members of the Hindu community who continued to safeguard the school and its interests in racial purity, a faction led by a Patel family, more recent arrivals to Salisbury. In March 1943, twenty-two of those parents signed a petition in which they stated that they would withdraw their children from the school if Bitshoo were fired.[65] Despite these conflicts, the purity schools continued to receive government funding. Education authorities were reluctant to get involved in the conflicts, seeing them as a "domestic matter."[66] They could not admonish these schools while they continued to impose the same rules of racial admission to European schools—an irony acknowledged by the chief education officer, where he noted that it seemed "most illogical" that the government "should deny to others the right that we claim so unequivocally for ourselves."[67] In 1940, the school committee requested that the government take it over until a public school in Salisbury was constructed, a request that was ironically denied as "it would not be in accordance with Government policy to administer a school with religious restrictions such as the Hindoo Society would desire to retain."[68] Until the construction of government schools for Indians, these institutions were allowed to continue their racially based admissions policies, revealing the ability of Hindu elites to co-opt colonial language regarding "way of life" and "racial purity" to advocate for their own concerns.

The conflict eventually died down as the government began to provide public schools. The Hindoo Schools continued to operate, but as vernacular and religious institutions that only Hindu children attended during afternoons and weekends. Even after the government fully took over the education of Indian children, however, clashes between Indians and Coloureds over the separation of schools according to race—and even gender—continued. Indians were permitted to attend public schools allocated for Coloured children, which included Moffat School in Salisbury and McKeurtan in Bulawayo. Tensions between the two groups reached a breaking point in 1945, when some of the Indian parents suggested to colonial authorities that Moffat should be physically fenced off to separate the two groups. The government seriously considered the physical separation, as well as handing over the school to the Indian community and building another for the Coloured community. After this, the idea would be to use the physical division of the school to allow for the separation of boys and girls in school, another request being made by some Indian parents based on concerns about the sexual purity of their daughters.[69] In 1949, Coloured parents petitioned for the removal of "Asiatic children" from Moffat, wishing to avoid the drama taking place at the Hindoo School over concerns about racial purity and intermixing.[70]

The government eventually opened a separate school for Indians in Salisbury, caving to their demands. Named after Louis Mountbatten, the school was opened on the site west of the Kopje in 1946, allowing children who lived in the trading district to walk to school every day. Authorities insisted that the school was not meant to be for children "of pure Indian descent only" and that admission to the school would be at the discretion of the government.[71] But most Coloured children lived in Arcadia, the location of Moffat School, and did not enroll in the new school. In Bulawayo, where the purity schools had not caused as much chaos, the Robert Tredgold School was set up for both Indian and Coloured children. In the 1950s, Morgan High School and Founders High School were established in Salisbury and Bulawayo respectively, the smaller number of both Indian and Coloured students who made it through for a secondary education justifying combined schools.

The lives of the children in Southern Rhodesia in the 1940s were heavily shaped by and subject to the debates over their future by their parents, their teachers, and the colonial state. Beneath the surface of these public contestations over the status of purity schools and colonial education lay the heart of Indian patriarchal and generational concerns about the future of their children—and in particular, that of their daughters, many of whom did not stay in school long after they reached puberty. Sons did not face any such concerns about their physical eligibility for marriage and were mostly allowed to remain in school and complete their education. The *dukkan* as a social space was at the center of ideas about what the role of girl children should be when they grew up and how they should best be prepared to take on those duties. Men needed an education to be able to run the business. Women, on the other hand, were not expected to need advanced skills in literacy to run the home. Taraben Naik was the eldest child in her family, but while her brothers went on to become qualified professionals in India, she left school at the age of fifteen—and was married a year later.[72] Her generation expected the same for their daughters, in a world across the Indian Ocean. Their fathers' desire to control their daughters came down to protecting their sexual and reproductive "purity" as the future bearers of children who would uphold the institutions that were central to their lives and their identity in Africa.

Because of their centrality to the future of communities, Indian daughters unwittingly became the catalyst for their fathers to directly challenge the colonial state. As Indian children transitioned to lives outside the home and the *dukkan*, these patriarchal elites articulated their insecurity regarding interracial social intimacy in African urban spaces by claiming the right to control when their daughters would attend school, what they should learn, who they should interact with—and when they should leave. In the shadow of the more visible conflicts over purity clauses and admissions, Indian fathers were fighting the state over their rights to withdraw their daughters from school. After education for all non-African children was made mandatory, Indian parents began requesting the withdrawal of their daughters from school before they turned fifteen, when they were legally allowed to drop out. Girls were expected to learn the necessary domestic chores and help with the business, typically by running the shop counters. Men regarded the education of the first generation of daughters born in Southern Rhodesia as largely unnecessary for the place they were expected to take in the joint family social and economic structure. After marriage, women joined the social and economic network of their husbands' families. Very rarely did a daughter's husband join the business or home of her father and brothers.

Fathers requested exemptions to education rules about when children could drop out, arguing that their daughters needed to prepare for marriage or, at the very least, that their domestic labor was required in the service of their families. One of the most notable cases was that of Shantiben Naik, whose father withdrew her from school at the age of fourteen, wanting her to be "trained for a year in preparation for her marriage."⁷³ The case was taken to the High Court after government authorities refused Naik's request, who was subsequently charged with contravening the Education Act and convicted and sentenced to a fine of one pound, or three weeks' imprisonment. Naik appealed the conviction, arguing that the government and the Hindoo School did "not offer suitable educational facilities" that would prepare his daughter for marriage. In the judgment regarding the appeal, the sitting judge summarized the following evidence in support of Naik's case:

> The appellant is a Hindoo of high caste, and as such must observe strictly the rules governing the Hindoo religion. According to such rules his daughter should not attend the Hindoo school. If she did she would be compelled to mix freely in class with Hindoo boys of her own or of greater age. As she has arrived at the age of puberty and is a well developed girl, the Hindoo religion forbids her to consort with males. Another objection based on Hindoo rules is that the teachers under whose instruction she would come at school are males.⁷⁴

Shantiben Naik unwittingly became the focal point for conservative Indian debates regarding gender roles and the sexual virtue of women that was inextricably linked with the "purity" of the Indian race. Indian girls' virginity was critical for their marriage prospects and therefore for their potential to further the traditions that were critical to the preservation of the *dukkan* and communal boundaries. The concerns of the home and the shop came first, the institutions which had allowed them to call Southern Rhodesia home.

Naik's appeal was dismissed, but similar cases were instigated over the next few years by both Hindu and Muslim fathers. In 1945, Amina Ismail was withdrawn from school at the age of thirteen. Her parents argued that Amina, who had "attained the age of puberty," was "in danger if she attends a mixed school or is taught by a male teacher."⁷⁵ The family's lawyers argued that being of the Muslim religion, "daughters after attaining the age of puberty, should live permanently with their parents until they are married . . . in the event of any misfortune overtaking a daughter who is compelled to go to a mixed age school, after attaining this age, the parents are also degraded in the Indian community; and the misfortune reflects on the family," a reflection of growing stigma against mixed-race families.⁷⁶ In 1947, Mariam Esat's father requested that she be withdrawn from school at the age of fourteen;

his eyesight was failing, and he required "his daughter's help in the house."[77] All of these requests for exemption used "religion" as the primary justification for the withdrawal of their daughters, and in every case, the girls had "attained the age of puberty," a critical age in the regulation of women's sexuality and reproductive capabilities.[78] These requests were supported by the various institutions tasked with safeguarding cultural and religious values, including the Bulawayo Hindoo Society, Salisbury Hindoo Society, and the Bulawayo Indian Muslim Society.[79]

Colonized subjects from India attempted to inform policy across the Indian Ocean, challenging not only who their daughters would go to school with but their patriarchal right to withdraw the girls from school when they reached puberty. State power was being tested here. In their conflicts over purity schools, Indians had requested colonial intervention in internal disputes. When it came to direct control of their daughters' education, however, they challenged education authorities. While white officials could find some sympathy with the Hindoo Schools' principles of racial purity, these court cases called into question "whether the laws of the Colony shall apply to the Indian community." The secretary for the Department of Internal Affairs was firm in his condemnation of the Indian population, writing in response to the case of Amina Ismail that "from an educational point of view there is no doubt that the Indians take comparatively little interest in the education of their girls." From the state's point of view, it was "most desirable that this education should be continued to at least the minimum age of fifteen years," seeing requests for exemption as "passive resistance [*sic*]."[80] A compromise was eventually attempted: The law would not be relaxed, but the government and the Indian community would work together to make necessary changes to the Domestic Arts curriculum that would take into account skills in cooking and housekeeping that Indian wives were meant to be versed in. But the Indian community never responded with suggestions.[81] The status quo continued: The colonial state required all girls to attend school, and some of their fathers persisted in withdrawing them early. The debate had become one over which moral order would prevail: that of providing all children with a colonial education; or safeguarding their virginity and therefore their prospects for marriage.[82]

While Taraben's sons socialized across communal boundaries, they all married women from the same caste. The men who chose to live with Black

African and Coloured partners lived on the fringes of Indian society, floating between Indian and Coloured spaces and institutions. Indians remade South Asian traditions to demarcate the boundaries of belonging in African urban settings, their social and community lives centered around their shops and the institutions they created to extend the traditions of domesticity to a wider colonial world. Caste and religion deeply shaped their home lives, creating class differences between those who adhered to elite, upper-caste conceptions of purity and morality, and those who continued to transgress those lines. The men who debated the terms of their children's education became local interlocutors of Indian ideologies in colonial African spaces, reframing what schools should look like and who they should serve. Within Indian populations, Hindus and Muslims contested what it meant to be "Indian" in Southern Rhodesia, and who belonged to the community. Centered around ideas of both gender and generation, they eventually came to an uneasy truce, learning to exist side by side with the Coloured communities with whom they had been relegated to in-between social and political categories in colonial bureaucracies.

But Indians also began challenging the colonial state when it intervened in their private lives. In the past, they had mostly adhered to immigration regulations and segregationist restrictions. Court cases regarding Indian daughters' futures revealed an Indian presence in the court system, bringing the state into intimate conversation with domesticity in a public space. Rather than simply conforming to colonial laws and regulations, Indian men were challenging the state directly when it restricted the kinship and economic structures of the *dukkan,* and eventually, where and how they could live their public identities outside of it. As further generations were born outside of India, the stakes for claiming a colonial African identity were critical to their rights as local residents. When they extended their institutions beyond the confines of their shops, Indians publicly engaged with segregationist legislation in a way they had not done in the past when relegated to urban spaces and specific trading streets. In so doing, they became more and more visible in white colonial spaces, defying white settler definitions of who could be considered "Rhodesian."

FOUR

THE *DUKKAN* AND THE COURTROOM

—

Indian Legal Challenges, 1950–1965

Applicant's case was that he wished to make use of the Central Baths for the purpose of swimming and also as a spectator, and that Respondent's decision to exclude him from this bath was grossly insulting to him by reason of the implication that, purely because he was an Asian, he was unfit to associate with the other inhabitants of Salisbury in a swimming bath. He alleged that the actions of the Respondent were grossly unreasonable, discriminatory, unlawful and in breach of his rights.

—S. N. MEHTA V. CITY OF SALISBURY, 1961

One day, Suman Mehta came home to find the head of a pig spiked on his front gate. His white neighbors were waiting cautiously outside the house, watching his reaction. Assuming he was Muslim, they had left the pig head on his gate at 36 St. Dominic Road in the neighborhood of Milton Park; a sign of hostility toward his presence in "their" space. According to the stories told in the years after the incident, including by his son, Deepak, who was with him at the time, Mehta simply laughed and took down the head.[1] Mehta had a reputation for being a "troublemaking chap."[2]

Like his father before him, who had challenged the racist policies of the Hindoo School in Salisbury, he was actively involved in local Indian politics. He was a founding member of the Asian Association, which aimed to breach the communal divides that had plagued his father's generation. He was also a member of the National Democratic Party, an offshoot of the Southern Rhodesia African National Congress. When he moved into the neighborhood of Milton Park in 1969, his neighbors responded not only with the crude gesture of the spiked pig head but also by throwing stones onto the roof of his house at night, or with open and unreserved hostility. "We weren't harassed physically," his son recalled. "It was more psychological abuse."[3]

Before he moved in, Mehta was already notorious in the neighborhood for publicly flouting the rules. In 1961, he challenged the city's municipal council in the High Court over access to a public swimming bath, questioning the regulations which prevented him as an Indian man from accessing what had been unofficially designated a white space. But that was not his family's first experience with the legal system. When his father died in 1950, the state argued that his mother would have to pay succession duty on her inheritance because their marriage was deemed polygamous by Southern Rhodesian law, despite her being the only wife. The family brought suit against the state in the Supreme Court and won their case. Immigration restrictions not only prevented the entry of adult males but regulated the entry and rights of women according to their marital status. State intervention in domestic concerns led to Indian interlocutors challenging segregationist legislation that treated Indian migrant families differently from white settlers in the courts. That experience gave them the confidence to challenge the rules that governed their lives outside of the *dukkan*.

Indian legal confrontation took two forms. The first was through the use of the court system as an intermediary between the state and families when it came to the negotiation of their rights that structured relationships inside the *dukkan*. Centered around the home and the shop, immigration and family law regulated the domestic networks of kinship and labor that sustained both household and business. Because many Indian couples had been married in India before migrating to Southern Rhodesia, the legal terms of their relationships were mediated through the application of colonial personal law in India, as well as Roman-Dutch law in Southern Rhodesia.[4] Indian homes were structured according to gender and generation, and the terms of marriage, divorce, and inheritance were complicated by the previous status of these relationships across the Indian Ocean. As a result, the state treated them in law as transient immigrant populations. But when the state interfered with domestic structures, their children challenged the law in colonial courts, making a case for their rights as permanent residents.

The second form of Indian participation in the legal system was seen in cases against segregation. While federal law did not officially segregate urban spaces as was the case in apartheid South Africa, local municipal authorities regulated where nonwhite populations could live and participate in public forms of socialization outside the *dukkan*. Men like Mehta were not lawyers but, with the help of white counsel, challenged the concept of segregation as a whole. Before the infamous 1961 swimming pool case, Yashwantrai Desai used the court system to obtain a trader's license in a predominantly white town that the local council had denied. Nine years later, Mehta defied those who restricted the terms of his access to public amenities outside of the shop and Indian trading zones. These challenges by ordinary citizens—neither politicians nor lawyers—were part of a "new history of colonial lawyering" by legally fluent members of colonized populations "as cultural intermediaries trading in colonial forms of knowledge."[5] Mehta's challenge was part of a longer history of Africans using the courtroom dock as a political platform to challenge the state and, "in effect, place it on trial."[6] Rather than turning only to legal reports from South Africa, the justices overseeing the case turned across the Atlantic to judgments made by the Supreme Court of the United States to consider the intangible effects of segregation. Their questioning of the ambiguity of definitions of race and urban segregation policies reflected the ambiguity of how Indians fit in the legal system. Indian interlocutors used this legal haziness to press for their rights to expand their family shops outside of designated Indian streets, as well as where they could find space as individuals outside of them. In so doing, they advocated for their rights to belonging as full citizens of Southern Rhodesia.[7]

Mehta was not the first to contest the authority of local councils, but his case became a seminal one for future challenges to segregation. Segregation played out in complex ways on the ground. The desires and experiences of ordinary people often defined official policy in the intermediary space of the courtroom, which brought the state into intimate contact with its residents in a way that would have real implications for Rhodesia's future.[8] Race as a concept in Southern Rhodesia was not just implemented from the top but built up from the bottom, as the insidious forms of segregation based on ambiguous racial legislation proved to be deeply entrenched in the everyday experiences of ordinary citizens making claims to public spaces and the right to define how they lived their private lives. The spaces of the home and the shop were key to understanding how and where Indians would attempt to find belonging outside their communities and the zones to which they had traditionally been confined.

Rather than the *dukkan* existing as a space insulated from the outside world, it instead became a tool with which to challenge segregation and contribute to legal contestations against both local and federal authorities. Mehta was part of a generation transitioning to a form of politics that went beyond their community. Political solidarity between Black Africans and Indians was not always about presenting a synchronous, united front but was often found in the mutual modeling, invoking, and borrowing of ideas and strategies. As a result of contestations over the invisible boundaries of race and class, white settler nationalism in Rhodesia intensified. This led to local authorities gaining more power when it came to their ability to enforce segregation and, with it, the rise to power of the overtly racist Rhodesian Front.

LEGISLATING THE *DUKKAN*

Nagarji Dahyabhai Mehta, infamous for his role in the disputes over Hindu purity schools in the 1930s, died in Salisbury in 1950. In his will, he left a total of £58,863 to his wife, Ichhaben Mehta, the sole beneficiary. His business was left to his eldest son to run, as was the tradition for most Indian families. The master of the High Court, who executed wills, asserted that Mrs. Mehta was "a stranger in blood to the testator" because Southern Rhodesian law characterized their marriage as polygamous and therefore invalid. According to the Death Duties Act, an heir who was not related to the testator by blood or marriage was required to pay succession duty on the inheritance, which in this case came to the amount of £7,292. The main issue here was a mismatch between the legal systems applied in India and Southern Rhodesia. The couple had married in 1913 or 1914 in Bombay Province in India, and according to the laws in place at the time, Mehta would technically have been permitted to take a second wife. The family's lawyer countered that while Mehta would have been allowed to marry again, he did not do so. Instead, "the marriage subsisted until the testator's death and throughout the period of its subsistence Ichhaben Mehta remained the sole wife of the testator" and was therefore the "surviving spouse" within the terms of the Death Duties Act. Even though Nagarji Mehta had remained monogamous throughout their marriage, the presiding judges ruled in his widow's favor because polygamous marriages were still recognized by law as valid for the purposes of succession, and "in the present case the wife was a surviving spouse within the meaning of the Death Duties Act."[9]

Ichhaben and her children benefited greatly from the declaration of the marriage as valid, saved from paying a hefty sum in succession duty. Their eldest son, and the one who ultimately took over the family business, was none other than Suman Mehta. Born in 1932 in Salisbury, he was one of the few who went abroad at the time to the United Kingdom for secondary school. There, he dreamed of becoming a doctor, but after his father's death, he came home to manage the retail and property business.[10] Many aspects of his life, and those of his generation, came to be defined by their positionality at the intersection between civil law in Rhodesia and personal law in India. Their lives were influenced by the concept of legal pluralism, whereby the laws that regulated their homes and their businesses did not originate solely from the colonial state but from a diversity of "normative orders," methods of enforcement, and institutions for the resolution of conflicts, decentering the state as a hegemonic force.[11] The Mehta family's futures were determined by several orders: the domestic and economic space of the *dukkan*, the colonial state, the city council of Salisbury, the Hindoo Society, and personal law in India.

Legal systems in Southern Rhodesia were defined by the bifurcation between civil and customary law through British indirect rule: the former for citizens, who were white and urbanized; and the latter for Black African subjects, who were instead regulated by colonial institutions of traditional leadership.[12] English law determined criminal procedure, whereas Roman-Dutch law was applied to the regulation of property, persons, succession, and contracts, following South African traditions of legal practice. Rather than being a one-way imposition of legal codes based on colonial forms of knowledge concerning African "tradition," however, customary law was shaped by both Africans and Europeans. "Conquest did not destroy indigenous systems of law" but rather "subordinated them to metropolitan legal traditions" and altered their relation to political authority and modes of production.[13] Nor was the legal divide between citizen and subject necessarily a strict one, either.

Africans were still subject to civil law and systems of justice while living in the cities. Scholars of colonialism in South Asia in particular have considered the claims that colonized subjects were able to make to imperial citizenship, both in and beyond the subcontinent.[14] Indians were neither white citizens nor Black subjects in an African legal context. In India, their domestic lives had been regulated by personal law, regulations codified by elite conceptions of Hindu and *sharia* traditions. In Southern Rhodesia, however, Indians were subject to civil law rather than customary legal systems, complicating the bifurcation between colonizing citizens and colonized subjects.

Even though they were subject to colonial legal orders aimed at white citizenry, immigration legislation often targeted Indians as a separate group, regulating the transnational mobility that sustained the growth of their families and their businesses through marriage and labor. These laws, while not coded as part of customary legal systems for Black African subjects, relegated Indians to a form of second-class citizenship. In 1953, Southern Rhodesia became part of the Federation of Rhodesia and Nyasaland, a primarily economic union that had been in the works for decades with the goal of forming a buffer against South African hegemony in the region. The Federation was predicated on the lofty imperial goal of "multiracialism," which envisioned a "partnership" between Europeans and Africans in the governing of all three countries.[15] But the rhetoric of "multiracialism" masked growing racial discrimination. In 1954, the Federal government passed its first piece of comprehensive legislation: an Immigration Act that replaced the individual immigration regulations of the three separate territories of the Federation, which had all to some degree or another restricted Asiatic immigration. Southern Rhodesia, as a self-governing colony, had been given the most leeway when it came to restricting Indian immigration, to the extent that "it was at an almost negligible level" by the time of Federation.[16] When the three territories were joined together under the Federal umbrella, the northern territories—Nyasaland as a protectorate, and Northern Rhodesia as a Crown colony—took on the policies and legislation of Southern Rhodesia, part of a larger extension of Southern Rhodesian dominance over the region.

The catalyst for reinforced immigration restrictions across all three territories was an increase in Indian migration to Northern Rhodesia and Nyasaland. The government's goal was to curb Indian migration to the northern colonies through the barriers that had already been erected in Southern Rhodesia.[17] Linked to the Immigration Act was the Inter-Territorial Movement of

Persons (Control) Act. While the Immigration Act continued to restrict the entry of those migrants deemed "on economic grounds, or on account of standard or habits of life, to be undesirable inhabitants or to be unsuited to the requirements of the Federation," restricting further Indian immigration to wives and minor children of those already resident, the Control Act went one step further to prohibit the migration of Indians between Nyasaland, Northern Rhodesia, and Southern Rhodesia.[18] The law prevented the mobility of previously fluid family and business networks across Central Africa, restricting the migration of Indians from the northern territories to Southern Rhodesia. The Control Act did not specifically refer to "Asians" but prevented voluntary migration to Southern Rhodesia of "any person who is born or resident in Northern Rhodesia or Nyasaland and who is not a European or a native or a coloured person having the blood only of a European and of a native, is prohibited from entering the Colony after the date of commencement, unless he is in possession of a permit."[19] By process of elimination, that meant Indians.

Following in his father's political footsteps, Suman Mehta became a leader of the Asian Association, an organization which aimed to unite a younger generation of Hindus and Muslims in Southern Rhodesia after their fathers' disputes over their children's education.[20] Formed in 1952, the association's goal was to protect Indian rights in the political transition. Protest against the Control Act galvanized individual Indian societies across all three territories of the Federation, who became "more vocal and consistent in thinking."[21] Together, they formed the Central African Asian Conference, headed by the Nyasaland Asian Delegation.[22] These individual organizations initially protested the formation of the Federation, which would lead to the restriction of Indian movement throughout the region, the spread of racial discrimination from Southern Rhodesia to the northern territories, and the "strangulation of the development of Asians," both politically and economically, allowing white settlers in Southern Rhodesia to take over economic interests in Northern Rhodesia and Nyasaland.[23] Their protests echoed those of African political groups, particularly in the northern territories, who feared the northward extension of Southern Rhodesia's segregationist policies.

At this stage, however, Indian community concerns in Southern Rhodesia mostly centered around domestic issues. The growth of family networks was critical to the maintenance of Indian family structures in the *dukkan*, sustaining their presence in the territory. Restrictive immigration laws interfered with the internal domestic structures that were the foundation of business and community, which allowed Indians to make a living and stay in the colony. Immigration restrictions in turn intersected with civil law procedure when it came to conflicts over issues such as divorce and inheritance. While the migration of adult males from India was restricted, accommodations were made for the wives and minor children of men already resident in the Federation, based on the "accepted principle" (which one immigration official argued was founded on "biblical authority") "that the husband is normally the breadwinner and that the wife will normally take up her domicile with his."[24] According to the Immigration Act, Indians resident in the Federation could only bring over one wife each, and could not bring over a second wife if a first wife was currently residing in any of the three territories. In turn, only the children of one wife could enter with their mother.[25] Marriages that had taken place in India became the subject of legal disputes between Indian families and the state as questions of polygamy and the validity of these marriages arose.

The implication was that marriages not regulated by Western legal standards were subject to dissolution at any moment and that men were the sole form of domestic authority. Indian marital relationships were subject to extra scrutiny as a result, both when it came to immigration applications as well as questions of inheritance. Colonial assumptions, which conflated Hindu and Muslim customs, stemmed from the idea that there was "much stricter control over the marriage and divorce of Europeans." Indians often did not register their marriages with the Federation, meaning that divorce could "take place more or less at will with no formality at all and without the intervention of an impartial third party."[26] Immigration authorities argued that the arranged nature of Indian marriages meant that the "sentimental considerations which arise in similar circumstances with Europeans are not in any way involved," and that all Indian marriages were "marriages of convenience."[27] The colonial view was that it was "not possible to judge Hindu marriages and divorces by European standards. Although the procedure is slightly different in the case of Hindus and Muslims, any Indian can, in effect, discard one wife and take another whenever he feels inclined to do so."[28]

Indian relationships were denigrated as traditional, and out of sync with Western customs. Authorities justified these assumptions based on cases such as that of a man from the Parmar family of Ingutsheni, a small locality located east of Bulawayo. The man allegedly divorced his first wife, citing "insanity" as a cause. He then took his first wife back to India after removing her from a mental institution into which he had placed her, and "brought back another woman in her place" in an example of what was described as "Indian 'jiggery pokery.'"[29] The Parmar case was cited throughout the following years as an example of the chaos brought about by the nonregistration of Indian marriages; without the necessary paperwork, problems "arising from marriages and divorces carried out merely in accordance with ancient custom" led to instability when it came to both marriage and immigration.[30]

The authorities' interpretations were deeply gendered, based on colonial assumptions about the patriarchal structures of the *dukkan*. Men could bring their wives from outside Southern Rhodesia to live with them, but women who married outside the colony would not be allowed to return with their husbands. There were exceptions to this policy, such as the Shingadia family in Marandellas. After several members of the family were involved in a serious car crash, resulting in one death and severe injuries to the rest, a son-in-law of the family was allowed to enter Southern Rhodesia to act as the breadwinner for the broken family and take over the family business.[31] Similarly, the state regulated the migration of older relatives. While official policy as stated by the Ministry of Home Affairs was that "applications by Asians to introduce aged dependants [sic] should be considered on the same basis as applications by Europeans," with no differentiation between a parent or parent-in-law, the assumption was that "the sponsor is the husband or son, rather than the wife or daughter of the dependant."[32] Sons could apply to bring their parents over to live with them, but applications made by daughters were often denied, the implication being that in Indian familial structures, it was the son's duty to take care of his parents.

After India gained independence, the postcolonial government amended key personal laws, making Indian marriages more compatible with Western standards. In 1955, India passed the Hindu Marriage Act. The law provided for the civil registration of marriages conducted according to Hindu marriage rites and outlawed polygamy as a condition for this registration.[33] It applied to any person who was Hindu, Buddhist, Jain, or Sikh but exempted Muslims, Christians, Parsis, and Jews.[34] Theoretically, the act should have simplified the immigration process for Hindu wives migrating outside of India, as well as for their rights when it came to divorce and inheritance. Immigration authorities, however, argued that the "legislation seems to be of no significance whatsoever insofar as the Federation is concerned since Federal citizens who go to India to marry are not domiciled there and are not subject to the laws of that country." Further, the act "leaves the door wide open to divorce in accordance with Hindu custom ... vitiating the value of the registration of marriages."[35] Officials continued to scrutinize whether another spouse was present in the Federation before allowing a wife from India to enter, arguing that the Hindu Marriages Act did not apply to any marriages that took place outside of India. Muslim immigrants continued to face the same bureaucratic challenges as the act did not apply to marriages conducted under Islamic rites. "Indeed," the author of an immigration memorandum concluded, "our Asian population seems to enjoy the best of both worlds ... being resident outside India."[36]

Conflicts over the interpretation of immigration law and the validity of marriages often made their way into the court system, rendering the private domestic sphere visible in a public space. In 1953, two cases concerning the validity of polygamous marriage came before the High Court of Southern Rhodesia.[37] In the first case, a Muslim man by the name of Karimshah had died leaving his estate to his second wife and all his children. The executor of the will held it was not null and void despite the second Islamic marriage being deemed potentially polygamous according to colonial marriage laws. Judges often considered African customary regulations as well as Indian personal law in these cases. While polygamous marriages were not recognized according to Southern Rhodesian civil law, the children of these marriages could be, leading to complications when it came to the execution of wills and the inheritance of personal and business estates.[38] The judge overseeing the case considered the Native Marriages Act of 1950 but acknowledged that it was only applicable if "both parties to any such marriage are natives." Immigration laws, on the other hand, recognized the wife of a polygamous marriage, but only if no other wife was present in the colony.[39] While Karimshah's case was dismissed due to a technicality, the complexity of the case and the inability of the judge to make a conclusive decision demonstrated the legal ambiguity that surrounded polygamous marriages conducted by non-Africans.

While most Indian homes were regulated according to gender and generation, and polygamy did sometimes occur, colonial laws regulating domestic spaces did not always reflect reality. A second case that year involving considerations of marriage and polygamy concerned a Patel family. In 1931, the couple were married in India according to Hindu rites. The man, Vallabhbhai Patel, lived in Southern Rhodesia; after the marriage, his wife, Ambaben Patel, returned with him. In 1950, Vallabhbhai wrote a will, appointing his wife as the sole heiress of the home and their business. In 1953, the couple registered their marriage officially according to the Southern Rhodesia Marriage Act, possibly having been advised to do so with immigration and inheritance cases being complicated by the lack of civil marriage records at the time. Three months later, Vallabhbhai died, but the master of the High Court, who was the default executor of wills, took the position that the wedding ceremony in 1953 rendered the will of 1950 null and void. The logic behind this argument was that the second marriage invalidated the first, making the foreign marriage polygamous—despite the fact that the man remained married to the same and only woman during this entire time. The judge in this case considered the Native Marriages Act and immigration laws concerning polygamy but also turned to the word "marriage" as it was defined in law. He concluded that Southern Rhodesian legislation recognized Christian marriages as being essentially monogamous, while Islamic and Hindu marriages could always be considered as being potentially polygamous, even if the person in question did not marry more than once. The justice found in favor of the decision of the master of the High Court, stating that until 1953, the couple's marriage was not one recognized according to Southern Rhodesian law. Because the will had not been revalidated after the second wedding had taken place, it was no longer applicable, and the widow was not recognized as the sole heiress to her husband's estate.[40] The estate would then have gone to the next legally recognized heir, which in this case would be the couple's adult children.

The premise that all Hindu and Muslim marriages had the potential to be polygamous not only complicated immigration cases but also called into question the validity of the family relationships that were central to the growth of the *dukkan* and problematized processes of inheritance. Women, whose labor was key to the maintenance of home and business, were recognized by their families when their husbands died. Even if they did not take over the family businesses, their husbands left them significant assets in their wills. But Indians held an ambiguous place in colonial legal systems, leaving their homes at the mercy of regulations that did not always make sense. In debating whether Indian polygamous marriages could be recognized under civil law, the Federation government acknowledged that Indians were definitively not African and therefore subject to the same legal codes as Europeans. At the same time, immigration authorities denied rights to Indians because their standards of living and customs of marriage were *not* European. In between legal codes for white Rhodesians and Black Africans, Indians were left in limbo. In Nagarji

Mehta's case, Ichhaben Mehta was successful in claiming her rights as the sole surviving wife. Ambaben Patel's marriage, however, was deemed inherently polygamous, her rights to inherit her husband's estate and business denied by a patriarchal legal code that would instead hand over her husband's assets directly to her sons according to the intersection between Hindu personal law and Southern Rhodesian civil law.

But individuals were beginning to challenge state intervention in their family lives. Suman Mehta used his family's past experience in the courtroom to his advantage more than a decade later. He, and others like him, were learning how to navigate the Rhodesian legal system. Indians' ambiguous position in the country's legal codes was reflected in the messiness of regulations governing urban segregation, which were not as clear-cut as the rules for division of rural land. When Indians faced resistance to their movements, where they could set up their shops outside of Indian trading zones, and their access to public amenities, they used the courtroom and existing laws to challenge restrictions. Despite being relegated as in-between populations when it came to their legal status and presence in Southern Rhodesia, they began to make public claims to their rights as Rhodesian citizens, not transient diasporic subjects who were at the whims and mercy of immigration regulations. In so doing, they contributed to the radical argument that all residents of Southern Rhodesia had claims to the full rights of citizenship.

THE INTANGIBLE EFFECTS OF SEGREGATION

In 1961, Mehta took the City of Salisbury to court after municipal authorities denied him admission to the Central Baths of the city, typically reserved for Europeans. He followed in the footsteps of Yashwantrai Desai, who had challenged restrictions to his trading license in 1952, a notable case that would be referred to in future challenges to segregation. But the 1961 case was a seminal challenge against segregation as a whole in Southern Rhodesia and would form the basis for future African contestations over access to public spaces and amenities. Mehta went beyond the shop to argue that Indians belonged outside its confines, too. Indian legal challenges to spatial segregation, while few and far between and initiated by individuals rather than communities, were significant. They led to growing calls by conservative white settler residents for increased power for local authorities through wider enforcement mechanisms of segregation. Two cases raised by Indian individuals bookended this history of legal resistance to segregation in Southern Rhodesia. The first contested restrictions against a man's ability to trade. The second contested restrictions against another man's ability to swim.

Segregation in towns and cities was often regulated and restricted by local authorities on a case-by-case basis, similar to the enforcement of Jim Crow laws in the Southern United States. While Indians could theoretically apply for a trading license in any part of a town or city, municipal boards run by white residents often denied applications on the basis that the race of the business owner would depreciate the price of properties in the surrounding area. In January 1952, a man named Yashwantrai Desai requested a general dealer's license in the town of Bindura, a center for nickel and copper mining. The Town Management Board denied his application, arguing that "the value of the surrounding premises or property would be depreciated by the granting of the license."[41] White residents had made similar claims about the depreciative value of their properties when Indians bought homes in their neighborhoods.[42] Desai took the case to the High Court, asking that the proceedings of the meeting that denied his application be set aside and that the Board reconsider his application. The presiding judge, Justice Robert Tredgold, argued that the Town Board's decision was based on the race of the applicant, pointing out that, "in the absence of express statutory authority," it was "not lawful for a local authority to introduce into its administration considerations involving racial discrimination." The board's justification for denial would make sense if it was based on the nature of the trade being applied for; "for example there might be several fishmongers in a street, but to allow another to open next door to premises built to house a superior type of restaurant might be unfair." However, the personality of the applicant (in this case, their race), was not grounds for rejecting an application for a general dealer's license. Even if a board were allowed to consider "personal characteristics . . . it is not entitled (as was done in this case) to assume that, simply because an applicant belongs to a particular race, the grant of a license to him will depreciate the surrounding premises."[43]

The decision nullified the argument by local councils that the race of a particular person in applying for trading licenses or purchasing property would depreciate the value of the surrounding premises, threatening their ability to protect "white" spaces. In July of that year, the Gatooma Town Council had attempted to deny a general dealer's license to Keshav Kala based on those very same grounds. The local government officer stationed in Gatooma notified the municipality that there were no grounds for a refusal and ordered that a license be issued to Mr. Kala.[44] White residents feared an influx of Indians into "their" spaces through expansion of their shops and businesses outside of traditional Indian trading zones. Later that year, the Town Management Board of the town of Gwanda near Bulawayo resigned en masse in protest against the alleged "encroachment" of Indians, a direct result of the decision made in the Bindura case. At a meeting in August to elect a new board at which thirty Europeans and four Indians were present, not one person would accept a nomination in protest. The incident led to a national conversation about the powers given to local town management boards, and, under pressure from white voters and local representatives, the government suggested that new legislation in the future would give these institutions wider powers.[45]

In September 1952, Parliament amended the License and Stamp Act to give local authorities more discretionary powers when it came to issuing licenses and regulating the sale of properties, making it more difficult to challenge the decisions of municipal boards in higher courts. While these amendments were still grounded on a "non-racial basis," the new legislation gave town boards wider jurisdiction when it came to the management of towns and cities, which they could—and would—use as legal justification to keep Indians out of white areas.[46] Public spaces could be designated to serve a particular community, especially those in residential areas. Everything from restaurants to post offices had unofficial discriminatory admissions policies, covered by the "admission reserved" clause. Nonwhite populations began to face discrimination in subtle, underhanded ways. Some European stores served Africans "through a hole in the wall," or only allowed Africans to be served by African employees.[47] Africans could not use sanitary lanes, roads, and footpaths. Federal employment policy was nonracial in practice, but several high-ranking officials in the government admitted "misgivings about the future prospects of Africans in the Federal service," and there were large numbers of complaints during the first year of the Federation of non-Europeans' job applications being rejected.[48]

Outside their shops, Indian access to public amenities was heavily restricted. Their experiences intersected with those of other racial groups, creating a collective identity of oppression. Certain spaces were distinctly reserved for certain races, even if they were not allowed to be labeled as such.[49] Municipal bylaws prohibited Europeans from using the same "sanitary conveniences as Asiatics, Natives and/or Coloured people," who in turn were not allowed to use toilets reserved for Europeans.[50] When Indians and Coloureds attempted to book first-class rail travel, they were often told that "the trains are full," while seats were allocated by race in second and third class.[51] Even in death, the population was segregated, with cemeteries dividing their burial grounds according to race and religion.[52] In the past, Indian families had faced discrimination when it came to regulations governing their family lives. As they earned more wealth and moved out of the rooms behind their shops, purchasing property in white neighborhoods in their desires for upward class mobility, their social lives were restricted too. In turn, they found themselves facing similar racial stereotypes that restricted the mobility and legal rights of Black Africans on a quotidian basis that went beyond their immigration experience.[53]

Segregation was insidious, pervading both the public and private lives of Southern Rhodesia's nonwhite populations through policies that accorded rights depending on race. In 1952, the Municipal Act created space for a number of public swimming baths to be constructed from public funds in certain neighborhoods in the city, opening up the elite recreational activity to ordinary residents who could not afford to have pools in their own backyards. Public swimming pools had a contested history as community spaces that allowed "visual and physical intimacy" of scantily clad bodies. In the United States, pools systemically denied access to Black Americans because of stereotypes of disease and fears of miscegenation and interracial sexual relations. Pools were also "emblems of a new, distinctly modern version of the good life" that reshaped cultural standards of middle-class life.[54] Similarly, in a world across the Atlantic Ocean, public facilities like swimming baths became spaces where different racial and class groups fought over how they would share common social amenities.

The Salisbury municipal board initially aimed to keep these amenities segregated. Three baths were placed in areas occupied predominantly by Europeans, one in a Coloured part of town, and another in an African township in the Salisbury area. The municipal board also approved the construction of a bath for the Asian community of the city, which had yet to be built. Most Indians, however, still lived in the trading streets downtown across the Kopje. When the baths were opened, a few Black Africans and Asians who were resident near the Central Baths, which was located in a predominantly white neighborhood, were admitted to the pool, causing consternation on the part of some of the white residents. On 5 September 1961, the municipal council officially restricted the Central, Cranborne, and McDonald Park Baths, all located in mainly European areas, for the "exclusive use of Europeans." The Arcadia Bath, located in the Coloured neighborhood of the city, was restricted "for all sections other than European and African," while the Geo Hartley swimming bath was located in an "African Township and has been used exclusively by Africans." The very next day, Suman Mehta, who owned property and was enrolled on the city municipal voter roll, deliberately went to the Central Baths, paid the admission fare, and asked that he be allowed to use the pool. The attendant of the baths denied him entry.[55]

The swimming pool case was part of a larger form of protest against segregation led by a group which called themselves the "Citizens Against the Colour Bar," whose members included faculty members at the University of Rhodesia such as Hasu Patel and Terence Ranger. When the swimming baths restrictions were introduced, they selected Mehta as a rate payer in Salisbury to make a claim against the city.[56] Mehta took the City of Salisbury to the High Court of Southern Rhodesia later that month. His case was "that he wished to make use of the Central Baths for the purpose of swimming and also as a spectator," and that the city's "decision to exclude him from this bath was grossly insulting to him by reason of the implication that, purely because he was an Asian, he was unfit to associate with the other inhabitants of Salisbury in a swimming bath." He stated that the city's actions "were grossly unreasonable, discriminatory, unlawful and in breach of his rights," and asked that the order passed by local authorities on 5 September be declared illegal.[57] Here, Mehta challenged the restrictions that prevented him, as a nonwhite citizen, from accessing white spaces, rather than simply requesting resources for his own community by demanding the allocation of a bath exclusively for Asians in their neighborhood. In an interview a decade later, he saw the case as part of a larger shift in Asian thinking where they were "not confined to their own nutshell."[58] In response, the City of Salisbury argued that Europeans were subject to the same restrictions when it came to the use of the African baths, and therefore that no discrimination was taking place.[59]

Mehta's history with the court system was both personal and political. The legal conflict over his father's inheritance, which suggested that his parents' marriage was invalid and that their children were illegitimate, was an issue to which he "took great exception." As his politics evolved, he used his identity to fight for the rights of all taxpayers across racial lines when it came to access to public amenities.[60] Unlike his political predecessors, however, he did not use this battle to argue for Indian social parity with the white settler population. Instead, he saw the issue as one that transcended race and made the claim that all citizens of Southern Rhodesia, which his case defined as being any resident who paid taxes, had claim to its public spaces, a radical form of thinking for both his time and his community. While the regulation of home life inside the *dukkan* led to his first interaction with the legal system, it was the rules governing how and where he could find space outside of it that inspired his actions in 1961. Later, when he purchased his home in Milton Park instead of in the new neighborhood of Ridgeview allocated for Indians, he argued that he had the right to purchase a home anywhere in the city rather than being relegated to a specific neighborhood as a "second-class citizen."[61] In both cases, Indians argued for their rights as permanent residents rather than as immigrants.

Mehta's actions led to a shift in legal considerations of how segregation impacted people on the ground. Unlike the family cases which concerned affairs of the home, and even the Desai case which centered around the shop, the swimming pool case saw Indians and Black Africans as sharing a collective identity that was being systemically oppressed. Chief Justice Hugh Beadle oversaw the case. In his ruling, he considered whether racial "differentiation" in this case also amounted to racial "discrimination," accounting for the psychological as well as the physical impacts of segregation and its validity within the framework of a colonial constitution as it applied to all non-European populations. He turned to the decisions of his contemporaries across the Atlantic rather than the ones south of the border; South Africa's courts had not questioned the psychological implications of segregation in the same way that the Supreme Court in the United States had.[62] The High Court judgment thus included references to notable cases in the United States, including *Brown v. Board of Education of Topeka* (1954), *Dawson v. Baltimore City* (1955), and *Holmes v. Atlanta* (1955). Like Mehta's case, *Dawson v. Baltimore City* involved access to public beaches and bathhouses maintained by the City of Baltimore. The judgment contended that "segregation cannot be justified as a means to preserve the public peace merely because the tangible facilities furnished to one race are equal to those furnished to the other," and that the Supreme Court had to "take into account the psychological factors . . . including the feeling of inferiority generated" when people were separated "solely because of their race."[63] In *Holmes v. Atlanta*, a challenge to the city's regulations over golf courses, the judges similarly found that the City of Atlanta "may not deny to a Negro, because he is a Negro, his individual, his personal right as a citizen to use and enjoy the facility furnished at public expense, while permitting a white man, because he is white, to use and enjoy it." Importantly, the judgment also recognized that there were not "two classes of citizens, a first and second, but one class, with all of equal rank in respect of their rights and privileges to use and enjoy facilities provided at public expense for public use."[64]

The unstated premise of Mehta's case was that Indians—as well as Black Africans—who paid taxes were citizens deserving of the same legal rights accorded the white settler population. The Southern Rhodesian High Court combined analysis of these precedents with notable local cases, including Desai's past case, in considering whether it was lawful for a local authority to make administrative decisions based on racial discrimination. Beadle distinguished between "tangible" and "intangible" factors of discrimination. The "tangible" factor of discrimination in this case was that the Arcadia Bath was two miles away from the area in which most Asians in Salisbury lived, whereas the Central Bath was only one mile away. But the "intangible" factors of discrimination were more important in his consideration. He drew from the decision in *Brown v. Board* that although the "'tangible' factors may be equal" when it came to schools provided for Black Americans and Europeans, segregation in schools violated the Fourteenth Amendment and was illegal based on consideration of the "intangible factors" involved.[65] Specifically, in the Mehta case, these "intangible" factors induced "amongst Asians feelings of humiliation, insult and of inferiority."[66] In response to the city's argument that Europeans were not allowed to use the Coloured and African baths, Beadle argued that it would "be fanciful to suggest that Europeans have suffered any comparable injury. The fact that Europeans are not allowed to bathe in the Harare and Arcadia baths when the reason for the prohibition is the Europeans' prejudice against the mixed bathing of the races can hardly be said to be insulting to Europeans, though it may cause some of them to become indignant."[67]

Mehta's case was notable as one that did not differentiate between Indian and African; he instead deployed his Asian identity as a challenge to segregation in general rather than specifically for his own community. The Rhodesian press picked up on the significance of the suit: If Mehta's challenge succeeded, the preservation of public amenities for the exclusive use of races would be compromised. The chief justice's second consideration was based on whether the Municipal Act allowed the city to maintain separate swimming baths for different racial groups. Beadle's analysis of the case in turn had significant implications for the gap that existed between Federal and municipal legislation when it came to the implementation of segregation in urban spaces. He concluded that the relevant sections of the Municipal Act did not give the city the authority to "differentiate" between different races when it came to the use of swimming baths.[68] Nor, he argued, was the Land Apportionment Act that had segregated rural land and relegated Indians to urban spaces relevant. While he acknowledged that the case concerned "Asians" and not "Natives," he interpreted the legislation here as distinguishing between "Europeans" and "non-Europeans." Therefore, if the court allowed Asians to use the bath, that would mean that Africans were also allowed to make use of the facility. The Land Apportionment Act, which restricted Africans from "leasing, using, or occupying" land reserved for Europeans, was not applicable in this case in the original sense of the language used.[69]

Mehta's challenge to segregation used Southern Rhodesia's existing legal system to contest rules that affected not only where and how his family could live, but what their rights were beyond their shops. The city appealed the decision in the Federal Supreme Court.[70] All three justices concurred that without a bylaw that allowed city authorities to exclude Mehta as a nonwhite resident from the swimming bath, the decision made by the High Court stood. Justice Clayden pointed out that while the Fourteenth Amendment in the United States enabled "equal protection of the laws" to all citizens, there was not as yet any provision in the Federation that declared that racial discrimination was invalid. The Supreme Court, he argued, did not have the power to set aside any legislation that did create racial discrimination. What they could do was decide whether the legislation invoked was originally intended to discriminate. He referred to cases that had taken place in South Africa and argued that the language in the Municipal Act did not allow regulation of admissions to public spaces in the absence of any specific bylaw granting them that power. Salisbury's bylaws allowed the reservation of a bath or portion of a bath according to gender, but not to race. The appeal was dismissed.[71]

The systemic discriminations Indians faced intersected with legal restrictions against all nonwhite populations, and the swimming bath case made that clear. The next year, a Black man by the name of Chamboko took the Mabelreign Town Management Board of Salisbury to the High Court for denying him access to the swimming bath in that particular neighborhood. The board argued that it was not denying him entry because he was African but because he was an African who was not an "inhabitant" of the location. After the Mehta case, the board had added a clause to their own bylaws stipulating that non-Europeans who were not "inhabitants" of the area would not be permitted to enter—based on the assumption that in a white neighborhood, there was less danger of having any nonwhites use the pool. But Chamboko was a domestic servant working for a family in the neighborhood. Both the High and Supreme Courts found in favor of Chamboko, arguing that as an "inhabitant" of the neighborhood, based on the fact that he lived on the premises of the family he was working for, he was entitled to use the pool.[72] However, while Justice Beadle based his judgment once again on the "intangible discrimination" that Chamboko had experienced, Justice Clayden argued in the appeal judgment that "intangible discrimination does not affect the legality of what was done," contending that mechanisms in the constitution of Southern Rhodesia allowed for special provisions to be made for the treatment of Africans. Instead, he based his dismissal of the Town Board's appeal on the fact that noninhabitants could not be refused entry to the pool on the grounds of race, and that the bylaw in question was contradictory and therefore null.[73] Ultimately, the implication was that properly constructed bylaws could allow discrimination.

Both Mehta and Chamboko were represented by the same law firm, de Villiers and Brighton. In 1960, there were only three African lawyers in Southern Rhodesia.[74] For cases involving their domestic affairs, Indians had to rely on white lawyers as well. African lawyers would eventually make a name for themselves after 1965, led by the formidable Herbert Chitepo, defenders of members of the nationalist movement against an increasingly repressive state. Their forces would be joined by Indian lawyers such as Ali Adam. Until then, however, those like Mehta and Chamboko had to rely on liberal white lawyers to take on their politically charged cases, working within the legal system and the "stipulations of Rhodesian law" and "the niceties of the Rhodesian courts."[75] The courts did not always find in their favor. Mehta and Chamboko's segregation cases were successful, and Mehta's family had won their case a decade earlier over the issue of N. D. Mehta's will. But many families, Indian and African, were at the mercy of colonial regulations that did not account for the complicated workings of their home lives, or the rights that they claimed outside their domestic spaces. The nationalist movement of which Mehta became a member would eventually go beyond these institutional structures in order to challenge the state from outside rather than from within. But legal challenges to the government persisted as "sites of public performance" of resistance.[76] Segregation was ultimately upheld from the bottom up by ordinary citizens, who formed local councils and who enforced discrimination on the ground. In turn, it was challenges by ordinary citizens like Mehta and Chamboko that became the biggest institutional threat to segregationist policies.

Legal cases concerning marriage, immigration, and inheritance were forerunners to Indian challenges against segregation. They introduced Indian families to the legal system but also provided a forum for individuals to challenge the state when it intervened in their lives both in and beyond the *dukkan*. In both forms of confrontation, a new generation of Rhodesian Indians made claims to local forms of citizenship rather than to imperial subjecthood as members of a colonial diaspora as their fathers had once done. Through these cases, the family life of the shop was made visible in the courtroom. While many of these cases critically affected the lives of women, the public space of the courtroom became a site of male political performativity. Indian men became more visible in the legal system, while women were confined to the insular domesticity of the home and the shop, even as their lives were heavily regulated by the colonial state. But individual challenges to discrimination and segregation in the courts marked a generational shift, as a certain faction of Indian men transitioned from insular concerns to larger forms of resistance to white minority rule. Indians were also starting to separate home and shop in critical ways. Wealthier families began to move out of the rooms behind their stores, purchasing homes in white spaces and challenging the foundational principles of a segregated society. Both young Indian men and women began to compartmentalize their lives, upholding Indian traditions within the *dukkan* but finding belonging outside of it as members of Rhodesian—and African—society.

Their presence outside the confines of the *dukkan* threatened the principles on which white Rhodesia was founded. Segregation in Southern Rhodesia was less about the overtness of discriminatory legislation as it was about how it actually played out on the ground in the lives of ordinary folk in their day-to-day lives. Mehta and Chamboko's success in the courts, represented by white lawyers and overseen by white judges, prompted letters from conservative white residents to the editor of the *Rhodesia Herald* arguing for the right of residents to decide whether they wanted to socialize "inter-racially."[77] Their influence as voters as well as members of local boards ultimately prevailed. The right-wing Rhodesian Front party won general elections in 1962, leading to the eventual dissolution of the Federation and Southern Rhodesia's Unilateral Declaration of Independence (UDI). But the idea of Rhodesia as a state exclusively maintained for the benefit of a white minority continued to face resistance. After its formation in 1960, Mehta became a member of the National Democratic Party, a revolutionary act for both the Indian community and Salisbury at the time, where elite white liberal circles chose to continue the charade of multiracialism rather than recognize its impending doom. In the lead-up to UDI, Mehta would find camaraderie with Indian nationalists farther south, in Bulawayo. His peers in Salisbury, however, continued what he had begun with the swimming baths case by running for local office, seeking representation and belonging within Rhodesian society rather than against it. In so doing, they challenged the notion that Rhodesians could only be white.

FIVE
"RHODESIANS FIRST, ASIANS SECOND"

Politics, Modernity, and War in Salisbury, 1965–1980

> A lot of Europeans are transients: their hearts are still in England or South Africa. But for us, Rhodesia is our home—our only one.
>
> —DR. HASU PATEL, quoted in "Twilight Citizens," *Illustrated Life Rhodesia,* 18 October 1972

Bhanabhai Dahyabhai Patel was known as a rather eccentric character in the small township of Shabani.[1] Born in 1897 in the Surat district of Gujarat, he migrated to Southern Rhodesia in 1913. He was one of the first men in their family to leave rural India in search of better opportunities. He was of the *koli* caste, a descendant of generations of farmers. He was the only son of a second son; whether he had any sisters is unknown.[2] His family owned land in the small village of Mandir, located near the town of Navsari. But he was of the generation of restless young men who had heard about a place across the Indian Ocean where gold could be mined. He also ended up becoming one of the men who realized that these riches were not meant for them. He settled in Shabani, a small town in the Midlands Province that had grown around a mine which opened in 1916 to supply asbestos during the First World War. Bhanabhai first worked in the mines but later set out on his own as a trader and became the storekeeper of a general dealership. He was married but had left his wife and property, including farmland, back in India. He rented his trading stand from the municipality, for which he paid five pounds per month in rent in 1941. He lived in a room in the back of his store, alone.[3]

Bhanabhai traveled to and from India after settling in Southern Rhodesia, fathering three sons: Haribhai, Ramanbhai, and Manibhai. All three would eventually migrate to Southern Rhodesia themselves when they reached the age of sixteen. His eldest son, Haribhai, arrived in 1937 and worked for various Indian families, spending time in Bulawayo working in stores as an assistant. He eventually moved to Salisbury, setting up a retail business of his own. There, his two younger brothers eventually joined him. At some point, he returned to India, marrying Dahiben Patel, who came from the neighboring village of Hansapur. The family shop began as a general dealership in the business district of Salisbury. Later, Haribhai decided to specialize in men's clothing and called the store Smartwear Outfitters. It attracted the "more urbane Black clientele, who were made to dress in the European Western fashion," according to his son. It was known in those days as a "gentleman's outfitters," with a "reputation for being a shop for the smart middle-aged Black man."[4] It was here in Salisbury that the family set down roots.

Many Indian families today in Harare, once known as Salisbury, are descended from a more recent generation of migrants to Southern Rhodesia, those who settled in the years up to and during the Second World War and

Figure 6. Haribhai Patel and Dahiben Patel, Salisbury. (Author's family collection)

maintained ties of property and kinship in India, families who "kept their feet on both sides of the ocean."[5] By the 1970s, they were also some of the wealthier families in the country. Bharat Patel, Haribhai's only child, recalled living "relatively comfortably"; as he grew up in the 1950s and 1960s, he "wanted for nothing." When he was about five years old, his mother took him to India for a few years to stay with her in-laws in the village of Mandir, the family maintaining physical connections with an Indian homeland.[6] But they increasingly transferred those roots to African urban settings. In addition to Smartwear Outfitters, the family acquired property all over Salisbury, gradually selling off their land in India. By the late 1970s, most of the extended family had moved into a large residence in Ridgeview, the unofficially designated Indian neighborhood.

Bharat Patel's generation found themselves at the crossroads of an intersecting Indian identity defined by their lives inside and beyond the shop. They were a generation who had been born in Rhodesia, one whose domestic lives were still dominated by their parents' conceptions of Indian tradition and morality. But in their social lives as young people, they started to find belonging as members of a society defined by Western values and forms of modernity outside the *dukkan*. Men like Suman Mehta challenged the white gatekeepers who determined the rules of access to public forms of socialization in Salisbury.[7] This new generation compartmentalized their identities to find belonging in white Rhodesia but, at the end of the day, returned to the safety net of the shop and traditional forms of domesticity. They reinforced their fluid and multiple senses of belonging by participating in Western forms of modernity through their education, the clothes they wore in public, the music they listened to, and the movies they watched. But they always retreated to the safe space of the *dukkan*, reinforcing gendered roles and Indian traditions through the prayers they said, the food they ate, the labor they performed, and the languages they spoke at home. Their participation in the outside world was in turn gendered. Men were allowed to perform their Westernized identities publicly, while women had to be more covert so as not to ruin their chances at a good marriage, upholding the kinship networks that were the foundation of the *dukkan*. But for their generation, both men and women, being Indian and being Rhodesian were not mutually exclusive.[8]

Social participation in Western forms of modernity led to increased participation in local politics. As Indian families acquired more wealth, they began to separate home and shop. They purchased properties in the Indian suburb of Ridgeview, located west of the Kopje. But white residents continued to push against Indian expansion outside of the *dukkan*. Mehta's victory against segregation in the courts led to municipal councils gaining increased powers to keep certain urban spaces reserved for white Rhodesians only. After the Rhodesian Front's rise to power and its Unilateral Declaration of Independence (UDI) from Britain, legislators introduced the Property Owners (Residential Protection) Bill, or the POP bill, as it was colloquially known, in 1967. Its main goal was to extend the racial classifications of the rural Land Tenure Act to towns and cities, explicitly preventing nonwhite populations from buying or renting property in reserved European neighborhoods, threatening Indian visions of upward class mobility. But past investment in the judicial system now meant that Indians had the tools and the experience to resist. Some men collaborated with local Coloured leaders to prevent the bill from being passed by running for local offices in town councils and municipal authorities. They developed political slogans based on the premise that they were "Rhodesians first, Asians second." For the first time, Indians were seen as significant players in local politics. Through the wealth they had acquired from their shops, they had earned the means to claim rights of full localized citizenship as Rhodesians. They aimed to participate in the system by reforming it from within. The shop was no longer a living space but was still critical to family livelihoods, supporting their transition to wealthier forms of urban modernity.

The traditional argument that Rhodesians could only be white erases the new generation of Indians born in Rhodesia who demonstrated that "belonging" was multifaceted and not bound to a singular culture or racial identity.[9] This chapter considers what it meant for those who were not white to belong to a nation held together by white power. But Indian claims to a Rhodesian identity were complicated when they were forced to participate in the conflict between Black and white. Their financial security was threatened when the Indian men who were meant to take over the family businesses were recruited to the Rhodesian army to take part in a war they did not believe was theirs to fight. After UDI, African nationalists' struggle to take back their country led to a guerrilla war with the white state, colloquially known as the "Bush War." In 1977, Indians and Coloureds were drafted into the Rhodesian army. Before then, the war could largely be ignored by a politically ambivalent Indian community in Salisbury who did not see beyond their own needs, disregarding the calls for Black majority rule that were swirling around them. But as administrative and transport personnel, Indians used their role as indirect soldiers to create connections with rural Africans caught up in the battle between Black and white, delivering food and essential goods to secure their own safety as they crossed battle lines. Their ambivalence in the war called into question Indian claims to being "Rhodesian" in the sense of the identity claimed by the white settlers who refused to give up their hold on power. In turn, the history of Indian participation in the "Bush War" complicates postcolonial narratives of the conflict between white Rhodesians and Black Africans. Those who fell into the "in-between" groups of the battle explicitly avoided taking sides and, in so doing, found themselves lost in mainstream narratives of the past as Rhodesia became Zimbabwe.

MODERNITY AND TRADITION, MINISKIRTS AND SARIS

By the 1970s, Haribhai and his brothers owned property across the city, transitioning from retail trade to becoming part of an upper-middle class of real estate developers in a space of suburban and commercial development. Unlike their father, who lived a largely rural existence, they invested in their families' futures in Salisbury. While Bulawayo farther south was a city first founded by an African king, Salisbury was a fort founded by Cecil Rhodes's Pioneer Column in 1890. The city was constructed around the Kopje, a hill that would later divide white, commercial Salisbury from the Indian business and trading district. The Kopje was once the lookout spot for the Rozvi peoples who lived in the area. In colonial narratives, the hill was the spot where the Shona people saw the approach of the "fierce Matabele warriors" and fled from their attackers. Their chief was killed, an act predicted by the Shona spirit medium Chaminuka. The chief was succeeded by Neharawa, a lesser chief, whose name would nonetheless provide the inspiration for the city's postcolonial renaming to "Harare," the city that never slept. After years of warring and conflict between the different chiefs and "tribes" who lived in the region, or so the colonial history went, the Pioneers arrived in September 1890.[10] They named the settlement Fort Salisbury, a tribute to the then prime minister of the United Kingdom, the third Marquess of Salisbury. The name of the settlement also evoked a sense of nostalgia for the cathedral city in the south of England. It erased centuries of African history in the region, and the city was remembered as one with only a white past, central to the foundational legends of the Pioneer Column and the Rhodesian nation. G. H. Tanser's history of the first ten years of the city is a story of hardship and of development, of malaria and dysentery and a lack of food supplies, but also of cricket games, the building of roads and homes, and of the creation of the first administrative structures that were a beacon of pioneer "civilization."[11]

The fort attained municipality status in 1897; in 1935, it officially became a city, formalized as the capital city of Southern Rhodesia. Later, it became the capital of the Federation of Rhodesia and Nyasaland, and by 1965, it was the center of the "new" Rhodesian nation. With the dissolution of the Federation of Rhodesia and Nyasaland, all three territories experienced "independence" of some sort. Nyasaland became Malawi; Northern Rhodesia changed its name to Zambia on 24 May 1964. That day, government institutions and businesses in Southern Rhodesia dropped the "Southern" from the name. "Residents had already been doing this for years, speaking as if 'Northern Rhodesia' were a branch, not the real Rhodesia," wrote one historian of Rhodesia.[12] Led by Ian Smith as prime minister, the new government attempted to negotiate for its own independence from the metropole but under continued white minority leadership. When talks failed, the Rhodesian cabinet adopted a statement titled the Unilateral Declaration of Independence, or UDI. At 11:00 a.m. on 11 November 1965, Smith announced that Rhodesia was an independent and sovereign state, no longer under the jurisdiction of the British Empire.

By now, most of the Indian population had been born in Rhodesia rather than in India. At UDI, all Indian residents automatically became Rhodesian citizens.[13] In 1965, the Asian Association amended and ratified a new constitution, defining the term "Asian" as "any person the original home of whose ancestors was on the continent of Asia."[14] The key difference between this definition and that used in state legislation lay in the use of the word "ancestors." Indians retained their ancestral ties and cultural identity to the subcontinent through their "pioneering" grandparents, but those born in Rhodesia grounded themselves in a localized form of a transnational Indian identity. Memorandums and petitions produced by the Asian Association after 1965 emphasized that "it is the very basis of the Asians' life in Rhodesia that they consider themselves, and wish to be considered firstly as Rhodesians, and only secondly as Asians": "Except for some elderly folk, and a small minority of immigrants from Zambia and Malawi in Federal days, Asian Rhodesians were born in Rhodesia, were educated here, were brought up on English as their vernacular language, and against the Western, English–South African background of Rhodesian civilisation. They do not regard India or Pakistan as their home; are rapidly losing touch with these countries, and would now be completely out of place and unassimilable in India or Pakistan."[15] They stressed their birthright as Rhodesians and their assimilation with a world outside of the *dukkan*.

"Rhodesia" was marked as modern, "India" as traditional. They associated "modernity" or "being modern" with cultural forms of consumption of "Western" clothing, music, and behavior. It was this world to which they claimed belonging. A younger generation of Indians, born in Rhodesia and educated at Rhodesian schools, articulated their desire to take part in a lifestyle their parents would have seen as taboo—socializing with and "dating" the opposite sex, attending dances and socials, wearing miniskirts and wide-legged trousers, listening to British and American music. This was a world separate from the *dukkan*, and yet one that had historically been enabled through the shop, the economic and social space that, over time, allowed them to call Rhodesia "home." In 1972, the Bulawayo Ramakrishna Youth League published a magazine on its history that also surveyed the cultural landscape of the Indian community in the city. In an article titled "The Younger Generation," the author articulated this generational shift in values and norms: "Almost every Hindu youth is Rhodesian born and bred. Consequently, all through his life, he has been influenced by the Western type of culture. On the other hand, unless he is one of the few, he has never been to India. Thus the classic identity and loyalty which his father feels towards his family and relations in the Indian village has no significance for the typical Hindu youth. It is so remote from his world of experience, that he feels little sympathy towards the basic values promoted by it."[16] India had become a distant and metaphorical homeland rather than a physical one, even with ties of assets and family. Whereas their parents and grandparents had extended the *dukkan* into colonial society in order to protect Indian values and traditions, their children now saw both spaces as completely separate.

Ironically, the Rhodesian state banned many of the cultural exports that Indians were beginning to take part in for being "subversive" and encouraging a culture of resistance. The state censored everything from novels such as *Lady Chatterley's Lover* to the writings of Karl Marx and Che Guevara to the music of both local and international artists. But even as Rhodesia isolated itself, cultural borders were porous, seen in local producers such as the African rock band Wells Fargo, who were inspired by the music of Jimi Hendrix to produce a style of music they called "Zim heavy," which fused Western rock with elements of disco, reggae, and funk.[17] At the same time, the country was subject to sanctions, led by countries like India in the United Nations, becoming a pariah in the international world along with South Africa. By participating in "subversive" forms of culture that transcended borders and sanctions, Indians were finding their place as modern young Rhodesians.

One group that participated in this form of counterculture as a way of locating themselves as "Rhodesian" was the Hindu Youth Movement in Salisbury, formed in 1966 by a group of young Hindu men. Eventually, the group opened up to let women join. Their parents were initially against the idea of men and women intermixing—one of the first female members of the group said that her mother in particular was concerned about "what type of girls were there, that I wouldn't get into trouble with boys, afraid I would mix badly with boys," concerns about female sexual purity still dominating conversations around control of daughters. But the founders argued that it would be important to give the girls of their community, who "were shy and always lagging behind" and who "didn't have an opportunity to advance," the same sort of opportunities they had for social engagement. Members of the club were all between the ages of twelve and twenty-five.[18] While its main goal was to organize social events, such as dances and debates, the social integration of unmarried men and women for the first time reflected a generational shift in thinking about morality and community outside of the traditional strictures established by the *dukkan*.

This generation in particular associated being "modern" with being "Western," and therefore, with conforming to the "way of life" lived by white Rhodesians and increasingly by educated Black Africans. The founders of the club had different views about arranged marriages and dating but agreed that they were overall "more modernized" than they had been a decade before: "The older generation is dying out, those who came from India originally.

Younger parents are coming in, they're brought up here, have a more liberal outlook." They even saw the *dukkan* as a space that was "modernizing." They cited changes in the home, the fact that dating was now more accepted, the clothes they wore, and the changing role and education of women as evidence of this shift. Television programs that showed "Westernized life," for example, led to increased demands by young adults for a more "English way" of life, with a different "way of living in the house." For example, one of the founders pointed out that "in India, men ate first, and then the females. Here you find they're all eating together."[19] Middle-class families saw growing parity between men and women, with "the trend now . . . for the wife to gain more or less equal status as her husband," while more and more young girls were finding employment outside family businesses, gaining "higher educational qualifications."[20]

Just because they were outside the *dukkan*, however, did not mean that women escaped its strictures. Rhetoric about gender equality did not translate to radical changes in the roles women were expected to take in the home and the shop, even with an education or a career. Men more than women were able to publicly perform this compartmentalization of their identities between being Rhodesian outside the home and Indian inside of it. In their outside lives, women were still keenly aware of the image they had to maintain in order to conform to their parents' expectations regarding marriage. Ratna Bardolia, for example, stated that she was both a Rhodesian and a Hindu and that for her, being Rhodesian meant she was "born here, brought up here, know nothing else but Rhodesian life"—but still "linked with Indian culture" in terms of "respect to my parents, religious thinking, some of my social activities." She wore miniskirts when out with her friends at dances but would wear saris at wedding ceremonies or to the temple. Her male peers agreed that while they could get away with "dating" women before marriage, a single girl who was seen in the company of a boy who was not her husband would have her "reputation" ruined and her prospects for marriage diminished.[21]

Participation in "modernity" did not mean an erasure of the customs of the *dukkan*. Instead, women had to adjust in order to maintain their lives between home and the outside world. Haribhai Patel's wife, Dahiben, was a registered nurse in India before she married.[22] She had to give up her career when she moved to Salisbury, expected to devote her time to the home and the shop as the wife of the eldest son of the family. "She was a very strong

Figure 7. Wedding of Bharat Patel and Hansa Naik in Bulawayo, 4 July 1976. (Author's family collection)

woman, and she ran the shop on her own," maintaining both home and business after her husband died in 1981.²³ When Bharat Patel married, his wife, Hansa, had to wear a sari every day, cover her head with her *palav* in the presence of men, and wear anklets around her feet. But both their families compromised on their expectations that their children would marry within their respective caste groups: While Bharat's family was part of the *koli* caste, Hansa came from a higher-ranked *anavil* family. Hansa was also trained as a teacher and persuaded her mother-in-law to let her continue her career after marriage rather than work behind the shop counter. She was even allowed to wear long dresses instead of saris to work as a compromise. She was still expected to conform to certain traditions within the home, however, including helping with the cooking and taking care of the men's needs.²⁴

Instead of the anxieties of caste, class, and religion abating, with young Indians departing completely from the generation before them, modernization here became a means for a select group of educated Indian youths to perform a more "liberal" identity by publicly castigating endogamous structures of caste and marriage even as they continued to uphold them.[25] Some men argued that the Indian youth "rejects the diverse features of all traditional beliefs and practices, and finds them outmoded. The Caste System is also rejected by him and he finds it very 'undemocratic.'"[26] At the end of the day, however, young Indians still participated in these practices behind the private doors of their homes and religious institutions, a form of "modernity" that did not disrupt the core tenets of their parents' "traditions." The Bulawayo Ramakrishna Youth League magazine surveyed fifty women and twenty-five men in the community, asking questions about their religious beliefs, generational gaps, arranged marriages and the caste system, the education of women, use of drugs and alcohol, music, sex before marriage and sex education, and clothing. An analysis of the results suggested that while a "very liberal attitude" was "predominating" in the responses, "this liberalism has not been used as an excuse to usurp our culture, religion and traditions." The conclusion was that "today's youth have a more liberal and open outlook than their predecessors but are still prepared to accept most of the traditional norms albeit from a modified viewpoint."[27]

What marked this generation from the previous one was that they were able to reconcile their national and cultural identities by compartmentalizing them—performing a Western way of life associated with a Rhodesian identity in a more visible, public realm but retaining an Indian identity in the home, eating Gujarati food, speaking the Gujarati language, marrying within caste and religion, and living with their parents and grandparents. While Bharat Patel attended private high schools dominated by white students and teachers, the food his mother and aunts cooked at home was Gujarati, the family listened to Hindi music, and they all spoke Gujarati in the home. The women of the household performed all the domestic labor, as well as continued to run the shop counter. When he started attending the University of Rhodesia as a law student, Bharat returned to Smartwear Outfitters every weekend to work in the shop. Even after he moved to London for graduate studies, he returned to Harare in 1982 after his father died.[28] While he was making a life for himself outside of the *dukkan*, he still always came back to it.

The idea of a compartmentalized form of belonging was demonstrated in an article published in 1972 in the magazine *Illustrated Life Rhodesia*, the cover of which showed a group of Rhodesian Indians with the men dressed in suits and ties, one woman wearing a red sari, another woman a red, long-sleeved Western blouse with black pants and a black scarf, and a small female

Figure 8. Cover of *Illustrated Life Rhodesia*, October 1972. (HSA HIS0010)

child wearing a yellow dress over a white blouse. The author described Indians as political and social inhabitants of a "twilight zone," classed as European for the purposes of the vote but discriminated against in most aspects of their daily lives. The Indians interviewed by the writer, however, stressed the idea that they were "cultured" and "better educated than the Europeans of Rhodesia," "naturally progressive" and "urbanised, Westernised residents" of the "sophisticated" neighborhood of Ridgeview that hid the community's "peasant agricultural" origins.[29] The contributors to the Hindu Youth League magazine articulated similar sentiments, pointing out that over the past two years, "Hindu families have bought homes in hitherto exclusively European suburbs," suggesting that "these new recent ventures indicate a change in economic perspective and life-style."[30] The *Illustrated* article was an opportunity for the various Indians interviewed, most of whom were educated professionals, to perform a Westernized identity for a white Rhodesian audience based on the wealth they had acquired through "clean money" and trade through the shop rather than being precluded from it by a "traditional" identity.[31]

This performance of a modern identity was part of a larger "reworking of the signs and symbols of the global mass culture industries" for younger generations across the African continent, complicating conceptions of Western modernity as being intrinsically oppositional to a "traditional" way of life of the colonized subject.[32] But their claims to a cultural identity as Rhodesians were threatened as the white settler government made moves to keep Indians segregated to specific zones, formally legislating the unofficial policies of urban division that dated back to the 1930s. White Rhodesians saw Indians as "invaders" and "aliens," ironically ignoring their own recent history of migration to the continent. They argued that Indians did not belong; while they largely ignored and dismissed Black Africans as laborers and servants, they described Indians as intruders to their spaces and way of life.[33] In response, Indian men began running for local office, staking political claims to the localized cultural identities they were now making their own.

POP GOES THE NEW BILL

With UDI, the country's legislative foundations as a British settler colony did not entirely disappear. The Immigration Act of 1966 replaced the Federal Immigration Act of 1954 and continued to restrict entry on economic grounds.[34] But where the Southern Rhodesian government had used the language of economics to restrict Indian migration, the Rhodesian government openly used the criterion of race in order to restrict the rights of not only Black Africans but Indians and Coloureds as well. The Land Tenure Act of 1969 repealed the Land Apportionment Act of 1930, classifying land by European, African, and National areas with the regulation of Tribal Trust Land.[35] Significantly, however, the act allowed for the regulation of urban land in what were designated European areas, which did not permit the use of land by any other racial group unless it was specifically designated a nonracial commercial or industrial area.[36] This act drew from South Africa's apartheid-era land tenure legislation, giving municipal authorities the legal basis to maintain exclusive sections of white land.

By 1969, more and more Indians had begun moving out of their shops, transferring the domestic space of the *dukkan* to the neighborhood of Ridgeview, the former site of an aerodrome that had been unofficially allocated as the Asian neighborhood. Families paid for the construction of about approximately 375 homes in Ridgeview.[37] Eventually, they built mosques and a temple in the neighborhood, shifting from the religious institutions located in Salisbury's trading streets to ones closer to their homes. In 1969, the community's Orientals cricket team set up their own sports club, Sunrise, in Ridgeview as well. Muslim sportsmen created their own club in the neighborhood, named Universals.[38] By separating home and shop, they articulated a desire to assimilate with "modern" society as well as set down further roots in Rhodesia through the purchase of more assets. Asians still only numbered 8,965 as compared to 228,296 Europeans out of a total population of 4,846,930 in 1969.[39] But as more and more Indians could afford to build and buy homes and move out their shops in the trading district, the space of Ridgeview was no longer sufficient, and their visibility outside Indian "zones" in the city was increasing. Those who desired to purchase property outside the boundaries of Ridgeview were generally families who had expanded their trade beyond the single general dealer's store, venturing into investment in industry, property, mining, or stocks in Rhodesian trade.[40] While caste was still associated with a hierarchy of trading activities and way of life at home, acquired wealth began to matter more in practical terms, creating class divides within the community.

As in the past, Indian families in white spaces were met with hostility. White voters used the language of "infiltration" to continue their efforts to evict nonwhites from white suburbs.[41] Complaints came specifically from the residents of the neighborhood of Belvedere in Salisbury. While traditionally viewed as a "white neighborhood," more and more Indian families were buying houses there, expanding from the adjacent suburb of Ridgeview. As a result, Dennis Divaris, a businessman who both lived and ran supermarkets in Belvedere and was the government chief whip in Parliament, led a call to introduce legislation that kept nonwhites out of white spaces in Salisbury. Similarly in Bulawayo, one member of Parliament, John Newington, alleged that the Asians in Rhodesia had "resorted over the years to the importation of foreign brides to increase their numbers and their economic and political influence." Asians across Africa had, he argued, "sucked the economies dry," using language of "infiltration" and "alien presence."[42]

As a result, the Rhodesian government made further moves toward the creation of apartheid-like statutory structures with the introduction of the Property Owners (Residential Protection) Bill, otherwise referred to as the POP bill. The proposed bill would use the Land Tenure Act as the basis for racial classification of residential areas in urban spaces.[43] Its main goal was to protect the areas defined as European in the Land Tenure Act, preventing "non-African races" from renting or owning property. The segregationist measures that white residents and municipal authorities had been enforcing ad hoc for the past four decades through local bylaws would now be uniformly enshrined in state law. While the 1969 Rhodesian constitution continued the Federation policy of including Asians and Coloureds in the European voting bloc, that was a categorization intended only for the voter roll, based on the assumption that these populations were not numerically strong enough to have a significant political impact and elect their own representatives.[44]

The POP bill specifically targeted Indians and Coloureds, in-between groups in racial and class hierarchies, but Black Africans publicly condemned it as well. African and European reverends and church leaders penned a statement of condemnation, arguing that the vague language of "denominations" used to describe populations did not do much to mask the fact that this was, indeed, "a Racial Segregation Bill, designed ultimately to enforce the complete exclusion of persons of Asian and Coloured descent from areas of predominantly European occupation" based on the "the fact that they are of an alien race." Thirteen denominational heads from across Rhodesia, including the Roman Catholic Church, the Anglican Church, the United Methodist Church, and the Evangelical Lutheran Church, among others signed the letter to the minister of local government and housing, which stated, "As individuals and families make progress in wealth or social standing, they have a right to move into areas more suitable to their new stage of development." The POP bill, they argued, would "deny Asian and Coloured citizens the means of such advancement," condemning them to "live in racial ghettos."[45] Africans also opposed the bill because it was "another step towards complete racial segregation . . . one in a series" which included the Urban Areas Accommodation and Registration Act, which prevented African children from living with a parent who was a domestic servant in a white household; the Municipal Amendment Act, which allowed for the exclusion of certain races from using a public amenity; and the Land Tenure Act, which limited "the human rights of an African to residence in a tribal reserve."[46] The denominational heads who opposed the bill articulated the fears of a growing class of urban African professionals who saw the POP bill as another constraint to their ambitions of finding a space for themselves beyond the roles of invisible laborers who maintained urban spaces for white residents.

If the bill passed, Suman Mehta's victory against segregation of public amenities in the courts less than a decade before would be virtually erased. His actions, however, had inspired a new generation of budding Indian politicians. Asian associations across the country condemned Newington's statements, accusing him of "climbing on to the Idi Amin bandwagon."[47] Individuals began to campaign for local positions, running on the platform of representing their own communities, rather than electing white officials. These men advertised themselves as specifically Rhodesian citizens, demonstrating their birthright and their desire to assimilate. Even before the introduction of the POP bill, Indians had been using this language in their political campaigns since the early 1960s. In 1963, Chhagun Kidia became the first Asian alderman and local councilor in Rhodesia for the town of Gatooma. "I laughed when I was approached to stand" by the Indian residents of the town, he told the press a decade later. "What chance did I have as an Asian?" "The blunt answer was rubbish," he went on. "I was told that I was a Rhodesian." While he scoffed at that reasoning, he was elected for a further three terms. "Rhodesia is my home," he said at the conclusion of his interview. "India does not really mean much to me."[48]

This sort of language indicated a public supersession of a Rhodesian identity over an Indian cultural identity. Mahomed Ali Adam, an advocate who ran for the position of ward councilor in the Salisbury municipal elections of 1963, highlighted his education in Rhodesia and at Oxford in England. "As a born Rhodesian," one of his campaign pamphlets read, "I have always been proud of Salisbury, and am offering myself for election as to me it would be an honour to perform my civic duties in the service of my fellow-citizens," emphasizing that he had been "born in Salisbury, and have never known any other place as my home."[49] While he lost the election, his candidacy inspired others like G. Ismail, who was also the president of the Asian Association, to run in local council elections in 1971, with the threat of the POP bill looming. Like Adam, Ismail emphasized his commitment to Rhodesian society, including his appointment as a commissioner of oaths in 1961 and his involvement in social work at the Salisbury Central Hospital, the Rhodesia Red Cross, the Salisbury Council of Social Services, and the

Prisoners' Aid Society.[50] In so doing, he highlighted his work as a responsible and civic-minded member of Rhodesian society, as well as his participation in local Indian politics.

Once again, it was men who performed this identity publicly. While younger women were also starting to see themselves as more Rhodesian than Indian in certain aspects of their lives, it was their fathers, brothers, and husbands who spoke on their behalf and represented them outside of the *dukkan*. Indian women had historically been denied the right to vote in the first place. In 1919, married white women were granted the franchise in Southern Rhodesia. Indian men, along with Black African men, attained their right to vote in 1923, dependent on assets, income, and literacy. Indian women, however, were not allowed to vote because their marriages were deemed inherently polygamous according to Southern Rhodesian law, an issue that had led to contestations over inheritance when their husbands died.[51] The Rhodesian government had argued that the terms of the municipal act extended "the municipal franchise to married women over twenty-one years of age, other than a woman married under any system permitting polygamy. This is in conformity with the Electoral Law of the Colony. Generally, women married under such a system are not familiar with political questions and are not, therefore regarded as capable of exercising the vote in an intelligent manner."[52] Women who married later in Rhodesia, whose legal status would have been recognized by the state, did not always register to vote, leaving concerns outside the home for their husbands to consider.[53] As a result, their views were erased when it came to the election of local political candidates.

Indian men did, however, collaborate with a group with which they had historically been at odds, particularly when it came to miscegenation and the education of their children.[54] The POP bill united Asian and Coloured voters and communities for the first time, despite tensions between them that were the result of both class and racial prejudices. "Coloureds looked at the Indians as rich, too close to authority, not really fighters in the physical sense—all things which Coloureds prided themselves on," said the son of Gerald Raftopoulos, one of the political leaders of the Coloured community in the 1970s. Coloured peoples integrated more with the poorer Muslims who did not live with the rest of the wealthier Indians, he argued, developing a kind of "social hooliganism" and "kind of combativity" that came with being Coloured and less privileged than Indians.[55] Whereas most Indians were traders or businessmen, the Coloured identity was confined to what another informant saw as a class position based on a working-class status.[56] In 1967, at a joint meeting organized by representatives of Coloured and Asian groups attended by nearly two thousand people, it became clear that while "at the top official level between the two communities" there was "cordial" dialogue, "at the level of the general public there definitely is a mutual feeling of distrust," which was "an impediment for joint action."[57]

But the POP bill, because it targeted both Asians and Coloureds specifically, served as the impetus for the first formal efforts at public and political collaboration. The 1969 constitution which made Rhodesia a republic divided voter rolls between Europeans and Africans, with Europeans granted fifty seats in the assembly and Africans eight. Indians and Coloureds were once again included in the European voter roll, and voting qualification depended on the payment of a certain amount of income tax.[58] Local elections in urban municipalities were based on a universal franchise of qualified European voter roll residents, which effectively ensured the dominance of white representatives and the political silencing of Black Africans living within the boundaries of municipalities. This dominance was threatened, however, when Indians and Coloureds united to put up a joint candidate who could speak to both communities' shared goals. The Rhodesian Asian Association and the National Association of Coloured People banded together in 1971 to arrange "financial backing" for legal challenges to the bill, should it be passed.[59] In 1970, Mussa Essof Hassan ran for Parliament in Salisbury, hoping to attract both the Indian and Coloured vote as a Muslim man who was well known in both communities.

Hassan won the election—not due to the overwhelming turnout that he and Joseph Thornicroft, a leader in the Coloured community, had hoped for after campaigning and canvassing both populations but because the Rhodesian Front had put up a weak candidate, not expecting to win in an area mostly occupied by Asian and Coloured residents.[60] But their victory was still meaningful. With the election of an Asian representative, the Salisbury City Council as a whole rejected the POP bill. It ended up being shelved indefinitely, after going through fifteen drafts, with several clauses facing "watering down" that was unacceptable to members of Parliament for the Rhodesian Front.[61] The Reverend R. Elliott Kendall, a British Methodist missionary, pointed out that "Hard liners want the full rigours of racial apartheid, while others are content with the existing racial separation and discrimination."[62] Facing opposition from all sides, and ultimately unable to garner the votes it needed in Parliament to pass, the bill was quietly shelved.[63]

By participating in the system, the power of Asian and Coloured communities to affect legislation through participation in local politics was becoming clear to the Rhodesian Front. A few years after the failure of the POP bill, Ian Smith allegedly reached out to leaders in Asian and Coloured organizations, offering each community a Senate seat. The event, while not formally documented in the archives, was widely discussed and reported in the press through hearsay, narratives which form part of "rumored archives" that cannot be officially verified but which were passed around by enough people to suggest that some sort of meeting did take place. In 1974, the press reported that Smith had held secret meetings with Coloured and Asian leaders during the election season, with the Coloured and Asian vote being a "crucial factor" in a vote for a seat for Salisbury City. Smith had reportedly offered five seats in total to these communities, in what was described as "an attempt to buy off the Asian and Coloured vote."[64] According to stories told after the meeting, the Indian community eventually decided to turn down the offer, saying, "no, we're not for sale," a retrospective analysis which highlighted "resistance" to the white state in postcolonial Zimbabwe.[65]

Indians fought the POP bill because it directly threatened their own interests, not because they were advocating for Black majority rule. But one faction of the African nationalist movement did issue a public statement in support of Indian refusal for separate representation, seeing their rejection as a critical act of defiance to the Rhodesian Front's attempts to justify minority rule. According to Abel Muzorewa, then president of the African National Council:

> The ANC welcomes the stand taken by the Southern Rhodesian Asian Association in refusing to accept the Rhodesia Front's offer of a seat in the Senate to the Asians, on the grounds that this offer is an attempt to buy the Asian Community as a political bloc. In the present political structure of Rhodesia, the ANC is of the view that the Senate is not the most important part of the legislature and therefore an additional seat in the Senate does not improve the political status of the Asian Community. On the contrary it segregates them from the rest of the European voters of which they are constitutionally a part.[66]

While Asians argued that they were Rhodesian first, they also made sure to distance themselves politically from the Rhodesian Front, refusing to be "bought" when it became clear that their vote was more important than the government had anticipated in including them in the European franchise in 1969. Their compliance and their association with a Rhodesian identity further came into question as the guerrilla war against the white state intensified. When called to battle, Indian men questioned their loyalties, unwilling to risk their lives and their livelihoods for the idea of Rhodesia.

THE SECOND CHIMURENGA

Despite the hostility and resentment they faced, many Indians had voted for the Rhodesian Front. Their communal insecurity stemmed from fears of the population's future under Black majority rule, particularly after the expulsion of Asians from Uganda in 1972. They feared the loss of their assets, their homes, and their shops, which sustained their presence as they became further disconnected over generations from India. Suman Mehta argued in 1970 that "first and foremost the Asian here tends to pay much more attention to his own means, because he's engrossed in business, business comes to him first. Politics and other things come to him second."[67] Mussa Essof Hassan voiced an even stronger condemnation of Indian politics: "Another point in the political apathy of our people is that 'the anchors haven't really been put onto us yet,' situation is materially 'too good' for a lot of our people.... [O]ur problem has been 'bapna gharma mota thaya, bapna gharma kaam karyu' therefore little opportunity for responsibility and self-reliance.... Therefore in both Asian and Coloured communities there is a 'middle-class mentality' where values are placed on material goods than on other things."[68] Rather than challenging the system as a whole, Mehta and Hassan argued that Indians looked for a place for themselves within its structures in order to secure their interests.

That security was threatened in a very real way when the war in the "bush" finally directly affected young Indian men, taking them away from the *dukkan* and disrupting generational continuities when it came to the running of the business, inheritance, and family structures. The "Rhodesian Bush War"—known to the nationalist movement and in postcolonial

Zimbabwe as the Second Chimurenga—took place from 1964 to 1979 between the military wings of the country's main nationalist parties, the Zimbabwe People's Revolutionary Army and the Zimbabwe African National Liberation Army, against the Rhodesian army.[69] The war took place mostly in the "bush," with the African "tribal" reserves in the borderlands serving as a front line between the Rhodesian forces and the nationalist guerrillas, many of whom were stationed in the neighboring countries of Botswana, Zambia, and Mozambique. By 1977, the war had spread throughout the country.

Most Indians who lived in the cities could not escape the war's effects. In 1977, the government announced that it would be drafting all eligible Indian and Coloured men into the Rhodesian army. They were mostly employed in transport duties, tasked with taking supplies to units stationed at outposts across the country. They largely remained in the barracks located in urban spaces. European, African, and Coloured and Asian units were separated, with the Ministry of Defense justifying the division by arguing that "the problems of integration (colour/creed and other factors)" made any propositions to abolish segregation in the army "impractical."[70] They were offered lower salaries than white conscripts, with no opportunities for promotion. Some, like Bharat Patel, whose family could afford it, were able to escape the draft; after graduating from the University of Rhodesia in 1975, he left to pursue his legal studies in London.[71] Some were allowed to attend a shortened period of six months of training if they committed to studying law and becoming a military prosecutor. Others stayed and defied their orders publicly; in August 1978, three Indian and three Coloured men faced charges for failing to report for training after receiving call-up papers. Three of those men were members of the Zimbabwe African People's Union (ZAPU) and so resisted on grounds of principle. Another one of the men, Krupal Shingadia, stated in court that he refused to attend national service because of the "inferior facilities" offered at the Lewellyn Barracks in Bulawayo to Indians and Coloureds, after his application for a job with the air force was turned down because the position was only available to Europeans.[72]

Those who were recruited had no choice in their conscription but were able to resist in more quotidian ways, translating the kinship networks of the *dukkan* and the community to the barracks. Hemant Naik, who enlisted straight out of high school, joined the army on 19 January 1977. He was supposed to go in for only nine months but was retained for three years. The role of the Indian and Coloured recruits, he said, was more about "protection" than it was about "fighting in a war," and most of them did not go into "the bush" for actual combat. The Rhodesian state did not put them in the field, concerned about their loyalties to a war they had not voluntarily signed up for. This was a battle Indian conscripts did not see as their own, either on the side of the Rhodesian army or the guerrillas. The state treated them as such, keeping them to administrative positions or as transport personnel. But as the young men were able to rise through the ranks over those three years, they became more organized about protecting their own:

> We were more organized. With our Indian guys, we took them and gave them office jobs and kept them in towns, because we were able to. We made sure they didn't go into the bush and were not exposed to what was going on outside. We were thinking about what are we going to do after the war, after the army. All we thought about was staying alive and getting home, and trying to do normal things.... I don't know any one of our Indian soldiers who thought this was great and wanted to fight a war and kill people. Because we were young, we were all thinking about what happens after.... We felt it wasn't our war, not going to risk friends and life for a cause we don't believe in.

If someone they knew was being stationed in another town, they would use their contacts to make sure he was taken care of. They learned how to "buck every system in the army to make it better for our own people," in Naik's words, such as forging signatures of their white superiors in requisition books to get better weapons, and finding better food, just to make things "more comfortable."[73]

The language of "our people" versus "their war" called into question Indian claims to a Rhodesian national identity. Their material and class aspirations did not necessarily translate to giving their lives for the idea of the "nation," even as their ancestors had claimed rights of imperial citizenship through their participation in the world wars fighting for Britain. With the escalation of the war the next year, however, several of their stations were attacked. In the end, ambivalence was not sustainable. They found themselves creating practical alliances on the ground with people they had previously encountered as customers and servants:

Whenever we could take advantage of our positions, we did, we had to, I think. Also in the bush we were friendly with the locals. Used to go to the villages and take the medic with us and treat them. That time, they used to ration mealie meal to the villages. We used to give them stuff like that. If we made friends with them we wouldn't be attacked so often. Like at the village at Vumba where I was, I used to offer them lifts to Mutare. If they didn't come, we didn't go, because we knew we would be attacked. Give and take, that was part of the war.[74]

Those with whom they created these practical alliances were also caught up in a war not of their making.[75] In return, the guerrillas and liberation fighters deliberately did not target Indian and Coloured soldiers.[76] The rumor was that ZANLA forces, or the military wing of the Zimbabwe African National Union (ZANU), would warn Asian and Coloured soldiers to leave areas about to be attacked.[77] The idea of Indian and Black affinity in the war was corroborated by previous statements of the National Democratic Party, which advocated for alliances with Indians and a boycott of white "imperial" commercial institutions.[78] Any documentary evidence of a deliberate policy to avoid targeting Indians and Coloureds beyond rumors and hearsay, however, is missing.

The "Rhodesian Bush War" was one in which allegiances and loyalties were blurred and unclear. Those on the margins of the war, including the nonwhite conscripts and the rural residents of the villages, did what they could to survive.[79] The history of Indian participation in the war, even if coerced, complicates postcolonial narratives of a civil war between Black and white that is now being even further complicated by historians of Rhodesia.[80] With ZANU attempting to mobilize political support in the villages, and the Rhodesian Front defending the white populations in towns and on their farms, the Indian and Coloured soldiers served as a bridge between the two spaces in the war. They did not explicitly take sides, suggesting that their claims to a Rhodesian identity did not extend to defending its continued existence. When they faced violence and death, however, they took on the language of white Rhodesians to condemn Black African guerrillas. Because of their relative marginalization in the army, young Indian men were able to avoid being killed. But five men, according to one informant, did not survive the war, shot by the "terrorists," an invocation of the same language used by white Rhodesians as a racist dismissal of nationalist aspirations.[81] They may not have had a burning desire to protect white Rhodesia, but they had still become a part of it, imbibing political and social biases against the majority population on whom they depended for their livelihoods. That meant that when Rhodesia became Zimbabwe, and a Black majority government took over, many Indians in Salisbury felt lost in a world to which they had not yet staked a clear claim. As a result, they had to reorient their identities to make sense in a new postcolonial reality.

If the war proved that Indians were not truly "Rhodesian," then who were they? The shop had helped them become a vital part of colonial economies, and their maintenance of Indian traditions connected them to wider collectives of transnational diasporas as well as a sense of being part of a British Empire. As Rhodesia broke away from the constraints of an imperial metropole, Indians attempted to relocate themselves in a localized decolonial modernity that still upheld the principles of white supremacy. Once again, it was men who created a public persona of being "Rhodesian," expecting young women to continue to maintain the structures of domesticity of the *dukkan*. As Rhodesia began to crumble, unable to sustain a war in the "bush" as well as a battle with the outside world for recognition, the Indians in Salisbury who had linked themselves to the renegade nation faced uncertainty in the transition to a postcolonial order.

Farther south, however, a cohort of men used the shop to fight for the idea of an independent Zimbabwe. Like Suman Mehta, they became members of the nationalist movement and used the wealth of the *dukkan* to help sustain the battle against white minority rule. Indian families in Salisbury were mostly descended from more recent migrants to Rhodesia. They had more physical ties to India through property and could afford to send their children to England for education. Many Indian voters in the country had helped the Rhodesian Front's rise to power in the first place, fearing their future in African-led countries even as they displayed reluctance toward giving their lives for the white cause. Indian families in Bulawayo, however, saw themselves as the "original pioneers" who had settled more than a century before. Bearing the brunt of racial segregation right from the beginning, they became more politically active with future generations.[82] The history of labor activism in Bulawayo meant that it was a nationalist center, and Indian members of African political parties engaged with Black ideologies of resistance. As descendants of migrants from South Africa in the 1890s, rather than eastward directly from India, Indian families in Bulawayo had firmer roots in urban spaces through their relationships with their Black laborers and customers. It was here that they began to imagine a future for themselves that went beyond the limited perceptions of both the larger Indian community as well as white Rhodesians.

SIX

THE *KUMALOS* OF LOBENGULA STREET

Anticolonialism in Bulawayo, 1950–1980

Naik is one of us, but he has his own way of life.

—JOSHUA NKOMO REFERRING TO RAMANBHAI NAIK
DURING THEIR TIME IN DETENTION IN THE 1960S

Manibhai Vasanji Naik was born in the village of Kadoli in the Bombay Province in 1900. In 1921, while working in South Africa, he was invited to join the family business in Bulawayo by his maternal uncle, Khandoobhai Vashee. In 1924, just as immigration regulations were closing the borders to single, unattached males, he brought over his wife, Gangaben, from India. A year later, their first son, Hari, was born, the first of the family to be born in Africa. Initially, the extended family lived together at Stand 881 on Lobengula Street, along with Manibhai's uncle and his cousin and their families.[1] All three male adults were part of a larger firm of extended family members conducting business on Lobengula Street.[2] K. R. Vashee and Company went on to become one of the largest trading corporations on Lobengula Street, but it would eventually dissolve as each partner went on to found their own venture. In 1930, Manibhai started his own general dealer's store, M. V. Naik's. As the family grew, it would be called M. V. Naik and Sons, and the store catered to Black African customers by selling clothing and "pots

Figure 9. Manibhai Vasanji Naik, Bulawayo. (Author's family collection)

and pans and things like that."[3] Haribhai Naik began working in the family business at the age of sixteen. Fluent speakers of Ndebele, Manibhai and Haribhai were given the title *kumalo* by their customers, who knew both men to be generous and benevolent. The business of M. V. Naik was better known by its customers as "Kumalo Bazaar."[4] It was this relationship with their customers that led to Haribhai's involvement in the nationalist movement in Bulawayo, a cause to which he would devote most of his energy and finances.

M. V. Naik and Sons, like other businesses on Lobengula Street, transitioned from an economic and social space to forming part of underground resistance networks, the facade of the shop window masking the political activity taking place within. As a population, Indians were not involved en masse in the resistance politics of the country, which had intensified as the conflict shifted from a political arena to the civil war between Rhodesian forces and nationalist guerrillas. In Salisbury, particularly after Rhodesia's Unilateral Declaration of Independence, Indians chose to work within the system of white minority rule to protest increasing segregation and restrictions. But in Bulawayo, even before the rise of the Rhodesian Front, a select group of Indian men who had been born in Africa used their economic middleman status to become political intermediaries between nationalist elites

Figure 10. Gangaben Naik, Bulawayo. (Author's family collection)

and their customer base, using their shops as a front to recruit customers and secretly raise funds from the rest of the Indian community. Their participation was critical to the quotidian activities of the Zimbabwe African People's Union, or ZAPU, which was based in Bulawayo. The *dukkan* was a social space at the heart of Indian families but also allowed a generation of Indian men who knew only Rhodesia as their home to engage with Black Africans, enabling Indian participation in the anticolonial movement.

But Black African and Indian elites did not believe that social intermingling was necessary for political collaboration. Both groups had historically constructed patriarchal boundaries against interracial mixing that were both informed by and transgressed colonial ideas about racial segregation.[5] Debates and ideas concerning the need for Black African and Indian collaboration were articulated through the *Lotus* magazine, a publication created in the 1950s by a group of Indian and Black men responsible for small-scale protests against segregation. The first issue of the magazine was printed in an outbuilding at the back of M. V. Naik's property, which housed both the shop and the family home. Intended for a local Indian audience, the publication took an editorial stance aimed at convincing Indians that their belonging in the country was as much at stake as that of Black Africans in the anticolonial struggle against the Rhodesian Front government. The notable Black politicians and scholars who contributed writings stressed that solidarity did not have to mean sexual intimacy but could instead be found through increased social contact and political collaboration. Indian writers stressed that while India was an important part of their past, Zimbabwe would be their future.

This meant that Indians became integral members of the nationalist movement, going beyond the political organizations which had once focused only on their interests. Rather than their foreign origins precluding them from participation, Indians drew from nationalist ideologies on the subcontinent to find inclusion. More than that, however, their shops, local institutions that were a core part of the fabric of urban life, became key political spaces. They were eventually detained with their Black peers in the 1960s at a camp called Gonakudzingwa, located in a remote corner of the country. Even in prison, Indians and Black Africans continued to collaborate politically while acknowledging and respecting that they had different lifestyles and traditions. Nationalist historiography in Zimbabwe tends to focus on the ethnic and ideological split between ZAPU and the split-off faction of the Zimbabwe African National Union, or ZANU, which took place in 1963. Indian involvement reveals that another key difference between the two parties was the ability of ZAPU to include both ideas and people beyond indigenous imaginings of self-rule in postcolonial Zimbabwe. Through the *dukkan*, which enabled their participation in ZAPU, Indians were reimagined as African citizens who had every right to belong to the postcolonial nation.

But this was primarily a story of the men who led that movement; the history of Haribhai Naik told through the eyes of his daughter was one in which she and the other female members of the family existed on the sidelines of the greater cause. Once again, it was men who decided what the boundaries of their political involvement would be. Men risked their families' financial—and sometimes even physical—security. Men penned articles and petitions, became members of the nationalist movement, took on leadership roles, and were detained by the Rhodesian state. Women supported men, silently, from behind the shop counter.[6] The shop maintained structures of endogamy and tradition in the "protection" of women, who remained confined to the insularity of their domestic roles while facing significant upending of their lives. The wives and daughters who were left behind kept families together, their labor sustaining the shop while their husbands and fathers risked their safety. Their historic relegation to the domestic space reinforced the patriarchal nature of the pioneer narratives that told the story of how Indians arrived in Rhodesia.[7]

If the history of Indians in Rhodesia began with the pioneers, it ended with the nationalists who helped the country become Zimbabwe. Even though the Indians were a minority, their stories of daily collaboration exist beneath the surface of the glorification of the Bandung moment of Afro-Asian anticolonial solidarity, the first transnational conference which laid the foundations for the Non-Aligned Movement defined by alliances in the Global South.[8] It is often difficult to escape the rose-tinted view of hagiographic oral histories and memoirs which romanticized Indian participation in the nationalist movement, highlighted as part of a glorious struggle for freedom from white oppressors. This chapter attempts to parse these accounts for daily acts of resistance, exploring the small deeds of defiance and statements of support which collectively contributed to the end of white minority rule. It is less a story of fraternity versus friction than it is of the quotidian participation of a group of Indian men and their families in the resistance movement against white minority rule. Their involvement folded into a larger Black nationalism rather than forming a separate element.[9] Their story is that of an active attempt on the part of both Brown and Black peoples in Zimbabwe to stress the inclusion of Indian nationalists, even as they lived a separate "way of life" grounded in the social and endogamous spaces of the *dukkan*. Despite their colonial origins, Indians in Bulawayo demonstrated that their shops and their family lines would survive the demise of white settler rule in Zimbabwe. In between the conflict between guerrillas and Rhodesian forces, and between ZAPU and ZANU, were the lives of the families who lived on Lobengula Street in Bulawayo, which became a borderland, a frontier, between their identities as the descendants of Indian ancestors and migrants, and their claim to belonging in an African future.

LOBENGULA STREET

Bulawayo was the city founded by the Ndebele king Lobengula when he settled in the region that would later be named Matabeleland.[10] "White man's Bulawayo" first began as a shanty settlement located three miles away from the original settlement. The street set along the western border of the town was named Lobengula Street, dividing the allocated native location from "European" Bulawayo.[11] The city was haunted by the specter of its violent past throughout its colonial history. While Salisbury would become a flashier town, a city of gold and wealth, colonial Bulawayo would become a quieter, humbler "town whose business was commerce and the railway."[12] The link between the railway and urban political consciousness was key to the city's role in the nationalist movement. Nationalist politics in Bulawayo were also defined by "Ndebele consciousness," a subthread of "black resentment" that was being felt by rural and urban workers alike in the years after World War II.[13] Union politics fermented through the development of worker solidarity. In 1947, laborers in Bulawayo were the first to strike in protest against food rations led by the Bulawayo Municipal African Employees Association. From there, the strikes spread and continued throughout the next year to Salisbury and other towns including Umtali, Gwelo, and Gatooma.[14]

In the postcolonial period, a Shona-dominated government marginalized Bulawayo's history in narratives of resistance to colonialism because of its centrality to a Ndebele ethnopolitical identity. The colonial state originally created a unified "indigenous" Shona identity set against the trope of an invading alien Ndebele state led by Lobengula's father, Mzilikazi. But it was the leaders of various factions within the nationalist movement who solidified an ethnic division as a political one. In the years after World War II, Black resistance had been largely driven by trade unions organizing mass workers' strikes against low wages, poor working conditions, and police harassment, which later evolved into demands for "one man, one vote," which became the rallying cry for student protests and continued strikes.[15] The nationalist movement, led by the Southern Rhodesia African National Congress party, later emerged as the National Democratic Party (NDP), which was re-formed as the Zimbabwe African People's Union (ZAPU), with trade-union leader Joshua Nkomo as president and the revolutionary Pan-Africanist Robert Mugabe as information and publicity secretary. ZAPU was banned in 1962 but continued to operate underground. In August 1963, Mugabe and several other ZAPU leaders decided to split off and form their own party, the Zimbabwe African National Union (ZANU). Urban activism continued but was overshadowed by the shift to a guerrilla war in rural territories.

The differences between ZAPU and ZANU were initially negligible. Both advocated for majority rule; both continued to seek external support; and both set up bases outside Rhodesia to coordinate foreign activities, guerrilla training, and recruitment.[16] But the political split between the two was articulated as an ethnic one between Shona domination of ZANU and Ndebele leadership of ZAPU, which would translate into the postcolonial violence against ZAPU insurgents in Matabeleland, known as Gukurahundi, in 1982. Ideologically, ZANU had a more Maoist orientation and aimed at rallying the rural peasantry, based on Pan-African principles and "Nkrumaism" and the cooperative economics of Julius Nyerere's Ujaama, whereas ZAPU embodied principles of Geoism and an ideological alliance with the Soviet Union through urban laborer uprisings. ZANU socialism was an amalgamation of Maoist mobilization tactics combined with a Marxist-Leninist single-party structure that advocated the creation of a socialist public centered not on the urban working class but on the rural peasantry. For this, land redistribution after independence would be critical.

Bulawayo's urban-based nationalism did not always sit well with this objective, and its history was thus contested after independence. Nationalist narratives that invoked the spirits of the ancestors suggested that the souls of the ancestors could only be found in an authentically African countryside and not in the colonial construction of the city.[17] Urban histories came into the spotlight just as the contentious process of land reform was taking place in the country in the twenty-first century. They tested the boundaries of the nation and notions of who belonged, complicating narratives of a single rural-based nationalist trajectory that erased the complexity of multiple African political cultures.[18] The struggle in Bulawayo was not necessarily about land, even though land displacement had created the conditions for urban poverty and restlessness. In mainstream accounts of resistance to white minority rule, however, activism in towns and cities was erased by the guerrilla war to take back land.[19]

The history of Indians in Bulawayo was similarly marginalized because of their affiliation with ZAPU and urban political culture rather than ZANU. As a population, they were primarily based in towns and cities, but they were not laborers. They were traders and landlords. In 1930, municipal authorities forced out a group of "lower-class" Indians from an African township on the outskirts of the city, most of whom were Muslims or lower-caste Hindus who ran "native eating houses" serving meat, anathema to upper-caste vegetarian Hindus.[20] "High-class" Indian Hindu families, however, were "more prosperous in their trading activities," separating them from the

Black migrant laborer communities of Bulawayo.[21] Unlike in Salisbury, however, where Indian families were largely by this time settled in the wealthier neighborhoods, most trading families in Bulawayo continued to live in housing behind or above their stores, on the frontier between white and Black Bulawayo: Lobengula Street, now widely known as the Asian trading road. As nationalist activity increased, Indians and Black Africans engaged daily, sharing ideas and experiences. It was Lobengula Street that would become a critical site for the playing out of quotidian experiences of the nationalist movement, serving as a frontier zone between Black customers and Indian traders.

LOVE, ONENESS, TRUTH, USEFULNESS, AND SERVICE

The 1950s in Southern Rhodesia saw increasing interactions between elites of all racial groups, enabled by an atmosphere of liberal "multiracialism," which called for partnership and friendship across lines of communal identity. This facade of multiracial cooperation masked the insidious and pervasive forms of racial segregation that continued to dominate life on the ground. But in Bulawayo, a group of men transgressed these liberal, white-dominated spaces. They were educated Indians and Black Africans, writers and activists who formed a radical youth league which called itself the Civil Rights League, and who were responsible for small-scale protests against the exclusion of nonwhites from public spaces, infiltrating "whites-only" cinemas or publicly protesting segregated seating at mixed-race events.[22] In 1955, they decided to express their solidarity in print, creating what would be called the *Lotus* magazine. It was named for the lotus flower, a Hindu religious symbol, but also for an acronym that the founders called LOTUS, or "Love, Oneness, Truth, Usefulness and Service."[23] The core group of editors consisted of Ramanbhai Naik, A. V. Desai, Don Naik, Dhirubhai Desai, Natubhai Mooney, and Ibrahim Rahman, who was responsible for the layout and the cartoons, while notable Black names in the city's political scene, such as M. M. Hove, a federal member of Parliament for Matabeleland, and J. W. Vera, a social organizer and sportsman in Bulawayo, regularly contributed articles.[24]

Lotus was produced in Indian shops but could not be found for sale on store shelves. It did, however, reflect the engagement between Black and Indian political elites that took place across the sales counter. The printing press for the magazine was initially run from the house of Manibhai Vasanji Naik.[25] While the women and children lived in the main section of the house located at 47 Lobengula Street, the press was set up in a section attached to the back. Because of its location in a private domestic space, it was able to operate smoothly and without interference or censorship from the government. While it was not marketed as a political journal, the fact that it was being produced by Indians would have been "frowned upon."[26] After Manibhai Naik's death, the magazine was moved to the home of Ramanbhai Naik, who converted an outhouse on his property into a room which housed both the printing press and a library of books donated to the Lotus Group by Nirmal Singh, the second secretary from the India High Commission in Salisbury. Throughout the 1960s, the "Lotus Library" and its reading room were available to nationalist leaders, activists, and teachers, who could use the books for their external degree courses.[27]

Lotus was a local production by Indian and Black elites but was also part of a larger Indian Ocean printing press culture created by diasporic South Asian populations across the landscape of the British Empire, from Mauritius to Durban.[28] It translated transnational activist ideologies for a local audience. As these publications had done in the past, *Lotus* used its forum to expand on the history of Indian nationalism and print biographies of Indian heroes from Rabindranath Tagore to Dr. Radhakrishnan, and reproduce the independent Indian national anthem and even the first postcolonial Indian constitution. But the magazine was also part of a regional Black print culture which included the *Bantu Mirror* in South Africa, and the *African Weekly*, *African Parade*, and *African Home News* in Bulawayo (run by Charlton Cezani Ngcebetsha, a regular contributor to *Lotus*). Until 1956, these publications were the mouthpieces for the views of "Western-educated African middle classes and intelligentsias." While the editors were criticized for being "stooges" of white liberal thought, their productions later became "the voice of the African masses that articulated people's desires for self-rule," which as a result led to their closure by the Rhodesian government.[29]

Lotus was a deeply localized publication that addressed a particular perspective on nationalism. It was entrenched in the facets of life in Southern

Rhodesia and local politics, intended for a local Indian audience, and increasingly took on an editorial stance that advocated for growing connections between Indians and Black Africans and overt support for the activities of the nationalist movement and ZAPU. It demonstrated that Indians were part of a larger nonwhite collective actively resisting continued white minority rule. The stated goal of the magazine was to publish "articles of interest to all" members of the "Indian Community" of Rhodesia and, in so doing, to counter the "misrepresentation of Indians in this country from certain quarters" as foreigners.[30] Its audience reached beyond Bulawayo to East Africa as well as Nyasaland and Northern Rhodesia. Published articles included write-ups on sport, religion, culture, and the biographies and obituaries of Indian "pioneers" in Rhodesia. A typical edition would print an article on an aspect of precolonial Indian culture, such as the history of the art of the Ajanta caves; a summary of sporting events, mostly cricket matches; the history of a local landmark, such as the "discovery" of Victoria Falls; a news piece on the activities of a local Indian organization, such as the Indian Women's Council; a political editorial of the country, usually critical; and finally, a contribution by a Black writer on the history of African oppression or on the need for solidarity between local Indians and Black Africans.

The connecting focal point of these various articles was that Indians belonged not only to colonial society but to a future that transgressed it. While both Black and Indian authors stressed the need for collaboration in order to effect radical political change, however, they also argued that Afro-Indian collaboration did not have to mean social or domestic intimacy, highlighting instead separate "ways of life." In postcolonial African countries, Indians were often criticized for not "allowing" their daughters or sisters to marry African men.[31] Debates over interracial mixing also implied that Indian men abused African women through sexual relations and illicit domestic partnerships while "protecting" their Indian women from African men. Historically, however, both Indian and Black elites had seen interracial intimacies as transgressive.[32] The elites of the Lotus Group reframed these debates to argue that both groups had a right to protect their social and domestic orders but also a duty to overthrow the colonial order which kept Africans and Indians politically separate.[33] Ngcebetsha argued in one issue: "Whilst for obvious reasons it is not desirable, at least in the foreseeable future, to encourage blood admixture through inter-marriage between Africans and Indians I, however, think that most broad-minded

Africans and Indians will readily admit that there is a great need for more and more social contacts between racial groups. . . . I think it is essential to extend them, as far as is feasible, to cultural and political spheres as well."³⁴ Ngcebetsha went on to articulate the view of the *African Home News* that total racial mixing would lead to "mistrust and suspicion," calling instead for more "cordial relations" between the two groups if they were to coexist in peace.³⁵ Although they were breaking down political racial hierarchies, the domestic order of the *dukkan* driven by the anxieties of both Black and Indian patriarchs was left intact.

Lotus reflected the growing involvement of Indians in the nationalist movement, even as the interior intimacies of the *dukkan* were kept separate. The magazine's links with the NDP, and later ZAPU, became clearer over the course of *Lotus*'s publication. The formation of the Lotus Group marked a shift in the political attitudes of Asians in Southern Rhodesia who were rejecting the Federation's principles of "partnership," expressing "views which were quite radical in relation to those of the conservative-minded community leaders."³⁶ By the early 1960s, all the magazine's writers were pressing for African majority rule, calling out the white state as undemocratic.³⁷ They also defended the party's increasing turn to violence.³⁸ In September 1962, the same month that ZAPU was banned, an editorial argued that ZAPU was not responsible for the current "wave of arson and sabotage sweeping though S. Rhodesia" and that these acts were instead "the work of the 'angry young men' who are tired of the apparently fruitless effort of Zapu to gain political advancement for the mass of the people." While defending ZAPU, however, the author denounced the retaliation of Southern Rhodesian security forces: "So long as the Government remains in power against the wishes of the majority of the people, strong-arm methods will utterly fail to restore peace."³⁹ By then, ZAPU had made the decision to smuggle arms into the country as well as recruit cadres for training abroad, primarily in the Soviet Union and Eastern Europe, to take on a more coordinated strategy of sabotage and confrontation. After being banned, the party went underground.

The Lotus Group also made the decision to cease its public-facing work. In 1962, the Rhodesian Front (RF) won national elections in Southern Rhodesia, defeating the United Federal Party led by the then prime minister, Sir Edgar Hughes. In three years, this would lead to the country's Unilateral Declaration of Independence, and the transition of Southern Rhodesia to simply Rhodesia. In response, *Lotus* ceased publication. The editorial for the last issue argued that this was the final shattering of the "myth of partnership preached by the Europeans" and that white politics were thoroughly out of sync with the wishes of the masses: "To the non-white, there is no difference between the two main parties that contested the elections. The RF, though, has been honest about its future plans for S. Rhodesia. Today the Non-European knows exactly where he stands and who his enemies are. Hence, the RF victory has been a blessing in disguise for the Nationalist forces—it will unite the different factions and with unity achieved, their task will be much simpler."[40] While politically disastrous for African nationalism, the RF's election was the catalyst for increased Afro-Asian solidarity on the ground, and Indian involvement in ZAPU transitioned from simply raising funds to also supporting the party's move to more militant tactics. When that happened, even the intimate spaces of the *dukkan* would be breached.

But the editorial board lamented the inability of the larger Asian population to express solidarity with the nationalist movement, even as their Black readership increased. They spoke to the widening gap that was emerging between the few who were involved in the nationalist movement and tied to ZAPU, and the rest of the Indian community:

> It is a matter of regret that right throughout the publication of "Lotus" as a quarterly, support from readers by way of contribution of articles was negligible. It is also significant that Asian leaders failed to use "Lotus" as a medium for expressing and leading Asian opinion. . . . We have evidence, and are proud, that the "Lotus" had tremendous impact and influence on the intelligentsia in Rhodesia. We consider it significant that in later years the non-Asian support for "Lotus" outgrew that of the Asian. Our comment on controversial and political topics may have been unpalatable to a section of our readers (some advertisers even threatened to withdraw their adverts if we did not change our political opinions). Those opinions were the sincere belief of the Lotus Editorial Board; it is regretable [sic] that that section of our readers who found these opinions unpalatable should be so intolerant as to withdraw their support.[41]

As ZAPU went underground, so did the members of the Lotus Group. The end of the publication of *Lotus*, however, did not mean the end of the visions of a postcolonial future it had articulated—nor did it signal the end of the contribution of the Indian community in Bulawayo to the nationalist cause.

RESISTANCE ACROSS THE SHOP COUNTER

Indian involvement in the nationalist movement took place across the shop counter. The *dukkan*, a space that contained the Indian family unit as well as helped ground it in colonial social and economic frameworks, had now become a center for resistance to the white state. Like colonial allegations that Indians hoarded goods and hid profits, the activities of the underground nationalist network took place in the shadows, with the shop becoming a space for the raising of funds, the recruitment of Black customers, and the scene of subterfuge and illicit meetings. Worker strikes and protests took place in a more visible—and therefore more vulnerable—way. The "underground" movement could instead be found behind the vibrant storefronts of Lobengula Street, which served as a smokescreen for ZAPU's underground activities. While they remained a minority, this allowed a faction of Indians to represent their communities as they secured their shops to survive the transition to an imagined postcolonial future.

A metaphorical extension of the *dukkan*, a community center on Lobengula Street was also used as a meeting space for Indians and Africans and came to be a "significant symbol of connection between the Indian community and the emerging Black political community" in the city.[42] The hall was named after K. R. Vashee, the entrepreneur who was responsible for the migration and employment of relatives from his village in the Valsad district of southern Gujarat, many of whom went on to join the NDP and then ZAPU. He was the maternal uncle of Manibhai Vasanji Naik, and the two families initially lived together in one home on Lobengula Street until the 1940s. The hall was erected in 1939, built from donations initiated by Vashee. It was not a temple, and while it was used as a space for prayers and the Hindu and vernacular Gujarati schools, the fact that it was not a religious institution meant that non-Hindus could also use it.[43] Joshua Nkomo, ZAPU's leader, often gave talks and speeches at Vashee Hall, and meetings held there were attended by other prominent members, including Robert Mugabe after one of his trips to Ghana. On his return from a stay in England, Nkomo's first stop on his march across Bulawayo in a series of rallies held to welcome him back was Vashee Hall.[44]

Haribhai Naik, Vashee's great-nephew, was a prominent *kumalo* of Lobengula Street. His shop was a vital link between the Indian trading economy

Figure 11. Haribhai Naik, Bulawayo. (Author's family collection)

and the men he recruited and trained from his customer base for ZAPU. Haribhai completed a basic schooling, but as soon as he was old enough, he began working in the family business, as did his younger brothers. He and his brother Amratlal married two sisters from India, Lilavati and Kusum, and they lived together with their younger brother Gunvantrai, his wife, Niranjana, and his children, in the house on Lobengula Street above M. V. Naik and Sons. In 1951, Haribhai and Lilavati's daughter Anila was born. In 1954, Lilavati gave birth to a second daughter, later named Hansa. Lilavati died at home soon after childbirth, and Haribhai later married another woman from India, Urmila.[45] In 1958, Manibhai, the patriarch of the family and the original *kumalo*, passed away. As the eldest son, Haribhai took over the family and the business. He was a fluent speaker of Ndebele, and his children grew up speaking Ndebele, Gujarati, and English.[46] He could communicate with Black Africans on an intimate and a political level, going beyond the traditional relationship between shopkeeper and customer.

The connections that men like Haribhai fostered across the shop counter allowed them to use their businesses as a front for the nationalist movement's underground activities. ZAPU's goal in the early 1960s, before its split with ZANU, was to "undermine security morale, organize support among the rural population and begin to build an intelligence network."[47] The Lotus Group became a key part of ZAPU's leadership during this time. With Haribhai's background in business and his connections with the Indian

Figure 12. Lilavatiben Naik, Bulawayo. (Author's family collection)

trading community in Bulawayo, he was able to serve as an effective treasurer, backed by underground financial networks.[48] He and the other Indian businessmen who were members of ZAPU became critical to the day-to-day operations as the party began to build up a broader urban base. They used their business and family connections, many of which dated back to the days of partnership under K. R. Vashee, to channel funds and donations from the rest of the Indian community to support ZAPU's growing underground network of operations.[49] They also organized items such as cars and bank accounts, and provided shelter to those who were in hiding. Haribhai Naik's family once harbored a soldier from the Zimbabwe People's Revolutionary Army, or ZIPRA, the military branch of the party, who was being sent to the Soviet Union for training. His daughters had to refer to him as *kaka*, or "uncle," outside of the home so as not to raise suspicions about their visitor.[50] Gujarati, the language of most Indians in Rhodesia, and "which the authorities did not understand . . . became a vehicle for communication between freedom fighters in the three Central African territories and people in the liberation movement in South Africa" through the use of select phrases and words that white secret service agents would not be able to comprehend.[51]

Their involvement took place in the shadows behind their shops, but they became well known to the cause. They would put up visiting African lawyers in their homes, such as the Ghanaian advocate George Commey

Mills-Odoi, who was representing Dr. Hastings Banda during his detention in Southern Rhodesia for his activities in Nyasaland, and an Indian woman by the name of Urmilla Naik worked voluntarily as his secretary during his stay in Bulawayo.[52] Her brother, Dhirubhai Naik, known more widely as "Don," was known for his campaigns and speeches on behalf of the party at rallies in the city, and in 1960, he was part of the working committee that formed to welcome back Joshua Nkomo to Bulawayo after twenty months in exile, along with Jason Moyo, Dumiso Dabengwa, Ethan Moyo, and Pillani Ndebele—all familiar names in the history of the NDP and the nationalist movement in Bulawayo. Less lauded and less known were the names of the Naik men: Haribhai, Don, Ramanbhai, and Amratlal. Others included Prag Naran, who lived in the town of Que Que, and Suman Mehta, the first Indian member of ZAPU based in Salisbury. After the NDP was banned in 1961, Joshua Nkomo's relationship with his Indian colleagues deepened, and "this was the high point of the collaboration between Asians and the African democratic movement."[53]

Their families did not have much of a say, if any, in this participation. While the shop counter became a point of political contact between Indian and Black men, it continued to serve as a barrier of domesticity, as once articulated by the elites of the Lotus Group. Ideas about gender continued to sustain a division in labor, with women now taking on even more of the burden of maintaining the household's finances and family life. The women effectively ran the shops, serving customers, packing goods for delivery, and counting the money at the end of the day. The nationalists' wives mostly came from India, married young with a limited education and no knowledge of English. They fulfilled their roles in the home and the shop unquestioningly, taking for granted the values and the domestic order that structured their lives. Their daughters, born in Rhodesia, received a full education but had to learn how to cook and to work in the shop on weekends, expected to fulfill the roles of wife and mother in the future. Haribhai Naik allowed his daughters to attend university, but with the idea that a degree increased their chances of finding a good husband within the community.[54] As in the past, they were meant to be safeguarded from the outside world, keeping them separate from the Black population with whom their husbands and fathers were finding increasing affinity.

Afro-Asian solidarity in a public forum masked the complex relationship between Indians and Black Africans, with the *dukkan* serving as a space for

Figure 13. Hansa Naik standing in the backyard of M. V. Naik and Sons before her first day of work as a teacher, April 1976, Bulawayo. (Author's family collection)

interactions that were both mutually beneficial but also tense. Indians were employers and business owners; their relationship with their customers was predicated on hierarchical differences of class and race, and on a general racism toward Africans. Older anxieties relating to domestic structures of endogamy and caste centered around the protection of female sexual purity were translated into comments to Haribhai Naik by other members of his upper-caste *anavil* group, who suggested he was willing to threaten the family and the community by allowing his daughters to marry Black men.[55] Colonial tropes of Indians as exploiters of Black Africans continued to pop up from time to time in African publications. Contributing to a decades-old debate over the exploitative role of Indian traders, the *African Daily News* published an article in 1956 accusing Indians of cheating their customers and preventing African trade in the reserves.[56] In 1958, J. Z. Moyo, a leader of the Southern Rhodesia African National Congress, told the *Daily News* that several Indian-owned butcheries in Bulawayo were enacting a "colour bar" by keeping one counter to serve Europeans and Asians, and another counter for African customers. He also said that "Africans could not be served with meals in some of the Indian owned Cafes there because they were Black." "To any thinking person," he wrote, "the Asians had accepted the evil system of racial segregation based on the philosophy of racial superiority," accusing them of double standards when they complained about the discrimination they faced while enacting it themselves on Africans.[57]

Zimbabwean scholars have since articulated these connections as what they term an "ambiguous situation."[58] Indians were seen as "predominantly fighting on the side of the Blacks" during the colonial period, alliances which were translated into collaborative race relations between Indians and Blacks after independence.[59] By 1965, prominent ZANU member Nathan Shamuyarira expressed his belief that "Indians and coloureds are gradually being absorbed into, and identifying themselves with the African people."[60] African publications were well aware of these complexities. They relied on Indian sponsorship of advertisements from businesses in Salisbury and Bulawayo such as Dayalji's, K. R. Vashee and Co., Nagarji and Son, Moffat Tailors, Mehta and Co., Ashabhai and Co., M. Laxman and Co., and, notably, Hajee Ismail Saleji Islamic Butchery. Because of this sponsorship, Black reporters interviewed Asian businessmen about allegations of racism in butcheries, covering both perspectives. Khalpey Butchery on Lobengula Avenue denied the "partition" of counters and said that "his policy was that of first come first served," pointing out that most of his customers were in fact Black. The reporter of the article also interviewed "some Asian leading personalities" who "were shocked" at the generalizations, "because there was plenty good will between most Africans and Asians."[61]

That "good will" never translated into full social integration between Black Africans and Indians, prevented by the economic inequalities that existed between the two groups and general Indian racism and domestic insularity. But Indians in Bulawayo reworked this privilege to contribute to the nationalist movement. "There were people who didn't take care of their Black staff and were very exploitative," said former ZAPU member Reg Austin of Indians in Bulawayo. "But there was also a very strong part of the Indian community who were committed to the kind of values of freedom of the movement and were accepted on that basis. It was a mutual acceptance of each other."[62] These quotidian relationships were more difficult to create in spaces like Salisbury as more and more Indian families relocated to their own neighborhoods or white suburbs. In Bulawayo, however, the Indian presence in spaces like the African location of Makokoba was pervasive, from the goods that came from their stores to their monetary donations to the mission school of St. Columbia's and Jairos Jiri, a society which took care of the city's physically disabled residents.[63]

Indians in Rhodesia, even those born outside the subcontinent, came to symbolize a transnational form of Indian decolonization translated into local politics and ideologies. ZAPU more than ZANU was influenced by the ideas of the Indian National Congress from the years leading up to India's independence. Although this was not a key feature of the party's ideology, its Indian members served as symbol of a greater transnational resistance to colonialism, enabling ZAPU's policy of nonracialism.[64] "That was distinctive about ZAPU," according to Austin. "It was launched in a way which consistently emphasized its nonracial quality."[65] Its members included Suman Mehta and Dr. Hasu Patel from Salisbury, as well as the notable British academic Terence Ranger. Kantibhai Patel, who had migrated from Gujarat to Northern Rhodesia, and then to Southern Rhodesia in the 1950s, emerged as one of the leaders in ZANU, rather than ZAPU. He was responsible for the organization of a cell for the party in the Indian neighborhood of Ridgeview in the years leading up to elections in 1979, his involvement in the Indian nationalist movement in his home village of Dharmaj attracting him to the rural mobilization tactics of ZANU.[66] Rather than serving as an "essential reference point" as it did for Black South African politics, India as an idea became a localized strand of thought in Rhodesia that was subsumed under a larger ideology of Marxist nationalism and the idea that Indians could live separately but still be a part of an imagined postcolonial future.[67]

GONAKUDZINGWA

The *dukkan*'s boundaries which kept Indian families socially separate from Black Africans, and the men's involvement in the nationalist movement hidden, would soon be breached. In 1960, the Southern Rhodesian government passed the Law and Order (Maintenance) Act, which allowed it wider powers to arrest people associated with antigovernment politics.[68] The act, which was then maintained by the Rhodesian Front government, also allowed for greater powers of detention and was the "foundation of Rhodesian security legislation." Suspected persons could be searched and arrested without a warrant, public meetings could be banned, and provisions were made for the physical restriction of political detainees.⁶⁹ That year, the offices and homes of known members of the NDP were raided, including the party's main offices in Salisbury. Several arrests were made, leading to demonstrations in both Salisbury and Bulawayo.⁷⁰

The interior rooms and social intimacies of the *dukkan* became a target. Indian men had faced physical threats in the past, such as when Indian shops were raided in Umtali in 1899.⁷¹ This time, however, the safety of their families was also at stake when the interior spaces of the home were breached in a violent way. One night in 1963, Haribhai's home above M. V. Naik and Sons was raided by armed policemen. They overran all of the rooms in the house, turning the lights on, rushing into bedrooms "without any regard for children or women, no sense of decency." They opened all the closets, searching for secret financial documents, knowing that Haribhai was one of the main fundraisers for the party. Later, Haribhai told the family that he had been tipped off about the raid and had managed to hide all his paperwork.⁷² Suman Mehta's business was raided several times in the 1960s.⁷³ In 1962, secret police raided the home and business of L. Govan, an Indian member of the party living in the town of Sinoia, soon after ZAPU was banned. Security forces in Southern Rhodesia believed that the building had been used as the main headquarters for the party.⁷⁴

General Indian ambivalence to politics played out in complicated ways on Lobengula Street as the *dukkan* faced its first threats of physical danger. On 19 July 1960, police arrested three members of the NDP: Michael Mawema, Sketchley Samkange, and Leopold Takawira, prompting a march from the township of Highfields to the city center, which ended with tear gas and the invasion of townships. Narendhra Morar, who grew up in Bulawayo, recalled that Bulawayo was initially quiet. The NDP called for a meeting in Makokoba in response to the violence on 24 July. Police banned all meetings in the city. Despite this, more than a thousand people gathered. Singing "Nkosi Sikelel'i Afrika," the demonstrators proceeded toward Lobengula Street.⁷⁵ They looted Indian stores on Lobengula Street, leading to many families calling the police for help. Indian women came out to feed the security forces, who killed at least twelve Black Africans that day and injured many more.⁷⁶ The history of the Zhii riots, as they were later named, complicates narratives of Indian involvement in the nationalist movement as their homes and shops were caught in the crossfire.

It was not only their businesses that were now in danger. By 1963, raids by security forces had borne fruit in the form of physical arrests, resulting in the detention of hundreds of political prisoners. There were no trials after the arrests. Those who were famously detained included Josiah and Ruth Chinamano, Joshua Nkomo, and Leopold Takawira, among others. Less famously, other detainees included Amratlal Naik, Suman Mehta, Ramanbhai Naik, and Don Naik. Ranjit Naik still remembered his brother's arrest: One night in 1964 at about two in the morning, several police showed up at the family's home in Gwanda and served a restriction order to Amratlal. He was first taken to a jail in Gwanda, then transferred to another prison in Bulawayo, before being transported to Gonakudzingwa, where he was detained with Ramanbhai Naik and Suman Mehta.[77] When Ramanbhai was arrested, he was transferred immediately to the airstrip in the town of Gwelo, where there was a cargo plane waiting to transport him and eleven others who had been arrested—and were all chained together—to Gonakudzingwa.[78]

Located just 1.2 miles from the border with Mozambique in Tribal Trust Lands, Gonakudzingwa was surrounded by nothing but wilderness for miles. Fences put up around the camp were flimsy; anyone who tried to escape would die of thirst and hunger long before they were able to reach any sort of human settlement—or encounter lions and elephants in the surrounding game reserve. By 1965, there were 604 political detainees in Southern Rhodesia, in Gonakudzingwa and two other camps.[79] In May 1966, there were 320 Africans in detention at Gonakudzingwa alone.[80] By the time the war ended, there were still about 50 detainees at the prison.[81] Reports by humanitarian groups such as Amnesty International revealed that colonial attitudes about racial segregation pervaded the physical space of the camp. There was a "difference in the way the government treated political opponents, showing a preference to Asians, much to the disgust of the Asians concerned."[82] While all the detainees could meet during the day, under the supervision of guards, they were kept apart at night. White prisoners were considered "Scale 1," which gave them access to more resources. Indians and Coloureds were on "Scale 2," while Black Africans were classified as "Scale 3."[83]

Despite these divisions, both Black and Indian members of ZAPU continued to collaborate and work together. The *dukkan* was transferred to the bush, allowing continued interactions between Black and Indian men even while their living quarters were separated. The separate spaces Indians occupied in the camp became a focal point for collaboration rather than contention.

One notable example was through the diet plans offered for Scale 2, or Asian and Coloured prisoners. Indians advocated for a vegetarian diet based on the upper-caste restrictions of the Naiks and Mehta, who identified as part of the higher *anavil* caste who did not eat meat. Joshua Nkomo allegedly took on the task of supporting these dietary requirements, which meant that the Indian prisoners would get better-quality supplies. "Nkomo made it his duty to see what my living conditions were like," Ramanbhai Naik later recounted, "and told everyone that Naik is one of us, but he has his own way of life, and we must try and make it as comfortable as possible."[84] After some negotiation, the Asian prisoners were given supplies for a vegetarian diet. But the intimacies of the camp allowed more social integration than would have taken place outside. African prisoners frequently made appeals to improve their own rations. When these requests were denied, the Indian men would share their cooking with their Black compatriots. Some, such as Vote Moyo, expressed a liking for the "hot chillies" that they used—while others, like John Mabhena, could not handle the spice levels. To ensure discipline in the

Figure 14. Suman Mehta (*back row, third from right*) along with other ZAPU detainees at Gonakudzingwa. (*The Herald*, 18 April 2005, HSA POL0012-13)

camps, the Black prisoners even took on the teetotalling practices of their upper-caste Indian colleagues, refraining from drinking any alcohol.[85]

Women were once again left behind. Between May 1965 and March 1966, no wives were allowed to visit the detention camp at all, while the return fare from Bulawayo was too costly for some.[86] The exception was Suman Mehta's wife, Lilli, who was permitted to live with her husband in the camp because of his poor health.[87] Extended family networks allowed the brothers of those detained to take over as heads of households, carrying on the business and taking care of the children: "Apart from having an absent father and husband, life went on."[88] But even as they continued to maintain the family business, women were largely left out of the anecdotes and memories that men shared about their time in detention. Families suffered, even as those lives went on. The detention of political prisoners meant that the barrier between the domestic interior of the *dukkan* and the outside world had been shattered, and women in particular bore the brunt of maintaining the homes their husbands and fathers left behind.

While the prisoners were essentially cut off from their families and their lives outside the wire, Gonakudzingwa became a space for political organization. Lobengula Street was extended to the detention camp, as both Black and Indian detainees continued to collaborate as they had once done across the shop counters of Bulawayo. The camps became "spaces in which detainees actively negotiated their incarceration and challenged rules of detention" through "academic and political education, political debate" and the development of "powerful critiques of colonial rule through writings that were smuggled out of detention."[89] Despite the separation of their living quarters, Black African and Indian detainees shared these experiences together, creating lifelong bonds that extended beyond their imprisonment. But ZAPU and ZANU leaders were separated and imprisoned in different camps, with ZAPU leaders primarily at Gonakudzingwa in the south, and ZANU leaders at Sikombela (located near the town of Que Que) and Wha Wha (located near Gwelo). The goal of the Rhodesian authorities was to prevent political alliances between the two parties.[90] ZANU leaders who were incarcerated with Robert Mugabe at Wha Wha later emerged as the victors in general elections held in 1980.

The prison camps thus became reflective of what the postcolonial future would look like. In 1976, ZANU and ZAPU merged once more to form the Patriotic Front, but divisions remained. After independence, ZAPU's leaders would be marginalized from mainstream politics. Nkomo was appointed to Mugabe's cabinet, but in 1982 he was accused of plotting a coup, leading to the events of Gukurahundi, which saw the mass executions of Ndebele dissidents in Matabeleland the next year. The memory of that violence lived on.[91] Haribhai Naik felt a "total disillusionment" in the country after Gukurahundi, one from which he never recovered.[92] ZAPU's history was erased from postcolonial state narratives of resistance. Indians who participated in the nationalist movement were celebrated regularly by government-controlled media sources, but in the same breath investments from China and India were lauded, suggesting that Indian allies in the nationalist movement were "foreign" rather than part of an indigenous guerrilla struggle against imperialism.[93] Haribhai and the other men of Indian origin who were once part of the ZAPU leadership were never recognized by the national government for their role in the struggle, and after their deaths they were not buried in Heroes' Acre, whose sacred and political burial grounds are reserved for those who were designated heroes by the ZANU-PF regime according to a selective nationalist history and memorialization.[94] But unlike state narratives which villainized ZAPU, Indians were not perceived as enemies of the state in the same way, and so their erasure suggests an even deeper marginalization of their legacies.

Lobengula Street was a physical frontier between Black and white in Bulawayo but also within the resistance movement itself. Its customers became nationalist recruits; its funds were used to support underground activities. Even as a minority, the few Indian men who fought for freedom for all Rhodesians came to represent their entire communities in postcolonial Zimbabwe. In so doing, they grounded themselves and their legacies as part of a Zimbabwean future rather than a Rhodesian settler imperialist past. Others would later co-opt the histories of these select few to rewrite their colonial origins, drawing a straight line from the pioneers who arrived at the turn of the century to their revolutionary sons and grandsons. But the men at the center of the movement left in their wake complicated family legacies that romanticized accounts of "the struggle" rendered invisible. Haribhai was not arrested, but the sacrifices he and those who were detained made on the part of their families left behind remnants of trauma. Haribhai was dedicated "to a fault" to the nationalist movement. He neglected his family and the business. After the raids, the Vashee family, on whom M. V. Naik and Sons was still financially dependent, gave Haribhai an ultimatum. He had to either give up his involvement with politics or he would lose the business. Eventually, he chose the former. With a large extended family to take care of, he had no choice.[95] The daily struggles, as well as the quotidian acts of collaboration between Black and Indian, are often forgotten. Patriarchal hagiographic narratives of Indian involvement in the nationalist movement that erased general opposition to their participation point to stories forgotten rather than remembered. But the lives of the women and children who were literally left behind when their husbands and fathers were arrested in Bulawayo would be brought to the center of attention with an event that took place in 1978, one that would destroy the boundary between the private and public faces of the *dukkan* in a life-changing way.

EPILOGUE

Air Rhodesia Flight 825

On 3 September 1978, a scheduled passenger flight from Kariba took off for Salisbury just after five o'clock in the evening. Most of the passengers were residents of Salisbury who had been vacationing at the lake. About five minutes after departure, a group of Zimbabwe People's Revolutionary Army (ZIPRA) guerrillas fired a Soviet-made infrared homing missile at the plane. It critically damaged the Viscount aircraft, which was forced to make an emergency landing just outside the town of Karoi. Of the fifty-two passengers and crew, thirty-eight died on impact. ZIPRA insurgents later allegedly approached the plane and shot ten of the survivors. Three others were hiding in the bush and managed to escape; another five had left to look for water. The passenger list released the following day revealed that eight of those who died from the crash itself were members of the same family: Ramesh Gulabh, Shankatula Gulabh, Veena Gulabh (aged eight), Leena Gulabh (aged four), Prababen Natu Lalloo, Neela Lalloo (aged twenty), Ramola Lalloo (aged eleven), and Mrs. D. A. Dulabh.[1] The Lalloos lived in Salisbury; the Gulabhs in Bulawayo. Mrs. Gulabh and Mrs. Lalloo were sisters; Shankatula had decided to take her sister and her children on holiday with them after Prababen's husband had died a few months before.[2]

If not for an unlucky coincidence, the family would not have been in Kariba, and not on that particular flight back to Salisbury at all. Winter was just coming to an end, and Bulawayo, located farther south in the country, was "still chilly." Ramesh Gulabh had thought he would take the family to Kariba for a week. When he first inquired with the travel agent, he was told the flight was fully booked. The travel agent's office in Salisbury kept following up with the airline for him. A few days later, enough seats opened up, and Ramesh was able to book eight for the entire family. They were all excited to go to the lake, a frequent holiday spot for white and Asian Rhodesians after the artificial dam's construction in 1959. They spent a weekend there and, on Monday, arrived at the airport at four o'clock, in good time to catch the flight back to Salisbury at five.[3]

News of the crash reverberated around the country. Initially, its cause remained a mystery. The next day, however, Joshua Nkomo publicly took responsibility for the shooting in an interview with the BBC, claiming that the airplane was actually being used for military purposes. The Rhodesian state classified the shooting as an act of terrorism. While the initial crash shocked the country, the killing of the survivors caused even more reactions of horror. The story continued to dominate the headlines of newspapers well into the rest of the year as the mystery surrounding the shootings after the crash continued. According to eyewitness reports by the three survivors who hid in the bush when insurgents approached the scene of the crash, "ten 'shocked and numbed' survivors . . . were ordered to their feet by terrorists in the vicinity of the crash and shot dead at point blank range." According to these reports, the "terrorists . . . opened fire with communist-made Kalashnikov assault rifles and 10 of the passengers . . . died in a hail of fire."[4] Those in hiding stayed in the bushes for two hours; "then the terrorists came back. They raided the aircraft wreckage, looting suitcases that were strewn around." One survivor, a Mr. Hansen, was "sure he heard a terrorist's bayonet as he drove it several times into the body of a seriously injured survivor."[5]

The event shattered the illusions of domestic security that the *dukkan* throughout its existence in Rhodesia had aimed to maintain. The shop had grounded Indian families in Africa but was also constructed to keep them "safe" from the outside world. Women and children had now been killed because of the war, and the space behind the shop counter had been breached in a violent and public way. Hundreds of people gathered at Mrs. Prababen Lalloo's home in Milton Park in Salisbury for the joint funeral of the eight family members: "The house was a scene of overwhelming grief as the six coffins, two of them small and white, were laid on the lawn. Two wreaths lay on Mrs. Lalloo's coffin, representing her two daughters, Neela and Ramola, whose bodies were not identified."[6] A busload of about fifty people came from Bulawayo for the funeral, gathering at one of the family's homes in Salisbury. "The whole area was full of coffins, people were screaming and crying," said one family member. After the funeral, the coffins were taken to the Pioneer Cemetery for the final cremation rites.[7]

The plane crash took place as Black nationalists were struggling to negotiate a transition to full majority rule. They were denigrated as "terrorists," their legitimate political goals for freedom dismissed. The deaths of the white and Indian passengers received more coverage in the news than did any killings of Black civilians during the entire course of the war. "For days on end, White Rhodesia was overwhelmed by shock, grief, and anger," reactions that were exacerbated by another ZIPRA attack on Umtali's residential suburbs only days later.[8] White Rhodesians mourned the passengers at mass church services across the country. The minister of transport and power, Bill Irvine, voiced his "utter disgust at the vile action of the Patriotic Front in shooting down an unarmed aircraft carrying civilian passengers, many of them women and children. The subsequent slaughter by the Patriotic Front killers of the injured and dazed survivors, who included defenceless women and children, was an action more barbaric than anything that can be read in the annals of Ghengis Khan."[9] In government meetings, the "killers" were demonized as "vermin," "sub-humans," "Neanderthals," and "animals."[10] Rumors that one of the survivors had been raped before being bayoneted were later refuted by pathology reports, but stories like these were characterized by similar tinges of racialized and gendered immorality.[11] Ian Smith took advantage of the crash to delay negotiations toward majority rule, arguing that such an act of terrorism necessitated closing the door to the nationalist leaders in exile.[12]

The nationalist movement saw the shooting down of the plane as a necessary act of war. While Nkomo took credit for downing the plane, he denied responsibility for the shooting of the survivors: "We brought that plane down, but it is not true that we killed any survivors," he told the press. "The Rhodesians have been ferrying military personnel and equipment in Viscounts and we had no reason to believe that this was anything different." He argued that ZIPRA was "not interested in killing civilians, but when people start using civilian aircraft how do you know when the plane is up there?" He further added that "there had been a massive outcry in the West because white civilians had been killed," when thirty Black Africans were killed per day in Rhodesia. "So the life of a black person is different from a white person? Any European child is supposed to be worth a million blacks."[13] He pointed the blame for the subsequent shootings at the Selous Scouts security forces, and therefore at the Rhodesian government, who had been accused of killing and torturing civilians in the rural areas while pretending to be members of the guerrilla forces of the nationalist movement.[14] Several parts of the country were placed under martial law, and in response to the plane crash, ZIPRA's bases in Zambia were attacked by Rhodesian forces in October 1978 in an assault known as Operation Gatling. While the Rhodesian government claimed that it had killed more than 1,500 ZIPRA personnel, historians later uncovered that many of those killed were actually unarmed civilian refugees living at the ZIPRA camp.[15] In a move characteristic of the nervous and fragile white state, minor attacks which threatened the security of white citizens were met with retribution on a much larger scale. Black lives were expendable; white lives were mourned.

The Rhodesian government was fighting a losing battle as the rest of the world pressured it to give up power. In February 1979, ZIPRA forces shot down another passenger Viscount plane, and all fifty-nine passengers died in the crash. In one of his last speeches as prime minister, Smith condemned the British government for their traitorous abandonment of the Rhodesian cause by exerting pressure on the government to transition to majority rule.[16] In 1978, the country's Internal Settlement was negotiated, leading to the election of Bishop Abel Muzorewa, head of the United African National Council, to power. Muzorewa supported the Rhodesian plan for separate electoral seats by race, ensuring the continued influence of the Rhodesian Front. But the settlement did not include the heads of ZANU and ZAPU, both of whom commanded the guerrillas taking part in the war. After failing to gain international recognition, fresh elections were negotiated at the Lancaster House talks in the United Kingdom in 1979. By 1980, ZANU-PF, under the leadership of Robert Mugabe, had been elected to the government. Rhodesia was now known as Zimbabwe.

Black Zimbabwe and white Rhodesia remained divided, despite the fact that white farmers were allowed to keep their land for the time being. Postcolonial Zimbabwe memorialized the retributory Rhodesian strikes against the nationalist guerrilla camps, part of the new government's project of national construction that propagated the story of a united Black struggle against white rule. In 1998, a monument to those who died during Operation Gatling was erected in Zambia, dedicated by both the Zimbabwean and Zambian governments. Former self-proclaimed Rhodesians continued to mourn the Viscount crashes as part of their "imperial nostalgia" which valued white lives over Black.[17] In 2012, the Viscount Memorial was built on the same grounds as the Voortrekker Monument in Pretoria, part of a legacy that memorialized white power in the region. The names of the dead passengers and crew were engraved on two granite slabs that were topped by a symbol of an aircraft, while the Rhodesian flag was set on a pole in the ground beside the monument.[18] The memorial was dedicated not only to the lives lost in the crash but to the idea of Rhodesia as a whole, which for white Rhodesians had been lost with the election of Robert Mugabe. After independence, many white Rhodesians migrated to the United Kingdom, as well as to the United States and Canada, creating networks of diasporic nostalgia through communities of "Rhodies."

The Indian community's response demonstrated that the relative safety and security they had taken for granted in Rhodesia was destroyed. But many did not explicitly take sides in the war, one those in Salisbury in particular had claimed was not theirs to fight. By remaining neutral, they felt they would survive the political transition taking place. In Salisbury, the Indian men who had worked within the system to protect their rights of mobility, and whose sons had been recruited into the Rhodesian army, faced the direct effects of the violence of the war on their families for this first time. But they blamed the Indian men who were members of the nationalist movement, primarily based in Bulawayo, for the deaths of an entire family. Rather than publicly blaming either the white state or the Black nationalists, they chose to condemn those within the community. The two political spheres that had once remained separated between two cities had finally collided in a tragic and devastating way. The family's public statements were guarded, questioning the violence that had led to the crash but without making an explicit statement of support or condemnation for either side in the war. Chagan Lalloo, who spoke to the press on behalf of the family after the funeral, articulated fears about the security and safety of residents of the country but also called for peace, declaring that any retaliation would lead to more "needless deaths." "Security, peace and a smooth transition of power which can be enjoyed by all the inhabitants of this country, is what we now pray for," he told the press.[19] But when Suman Mehta, a known member of ZAPU and a neighbor, attempted to attend the funeral, the grieving family told him to leave. According to Mehta's son, the whole community "turned against him" in the aftermath of the plane crash, and despite being good friends with the Lalloo family, "he was lambasted and called a killer."[20] The next day, Mehta was arrested and detained briefly at Chikurubi Prison in Salisbury for "being an active member of Zapu following the shooting down of two Rhodesian civilian planes by Zipra forces."[21]

As Rhodesia became Zimbabwe, many Indians struggled to define their political identities as members of either collective—of those who mourned the end of Rhodesia, or of those who celebrated the birth of Zimbabwe. As Black majority rule became an increasing reality, there were many Indians in Rhodesia who feared their status in a postcolonial world, with the specter of 1972 in Uganda still looming from the recent past. They feared the loss of their shops and their assets, and of being exiled. Black majority rule was associated with another form of racialized rule for many Indians in Rhodesia, who had never lived in a country in which racial hierarchies did not predicate access to the rights of citizenship. In an interview in 1970, Mehta said he believed that there was still "quite a proportion of people who think they are safer under white rule, and that everything is fine as long as a white government is in power . . . they accept eventual majority rule as inevitable, but they are frightened."[22] It is probable that many Indians did not vote for Mugabe and ZANU-PF, or did not vote at all.[23]

Retroactively, in a postcolonial reality, the crash was remembered differently. Indians were not forced to leave. Their businesses remained safe, and they automatically became Zimbabwean citizens after independence. The family's condemnation of Mehta as a "killer" was forgotten. In 1978, just after the tragedy, Amrat Lalloo had described the event "as a holocaust to us as a family and as a community." He emphasized the history and the role that the family had played in Rhodesian society, saying that "as a family, we have been involved in national as well as community affairs in both business and social spheres. We are one of the oldest families in the community with our roots in Rhodesia going back to the early 1900s." In 1978, this was "the biggest tragedy the community has suffered," in his words.[24] But by 2018, two decades after Mehta's death, Lalloo, as well as the rest of the Indian community, revered him publicly as a hero of the nationalist movement and therefore of the country as well as the entire community. Lalloo's response to the crash exactly forty years later was that it was "accepted in times of war that these sorts of tragedies do occur," recalling Mehta as a dear friend.[25] At the same time, the family held a memorial that year for the eight members who had been lost in 1978, conducting a *havan*, or a ritual involving fire into which offerings are poured and burnt, at the Aumkar temple in Ridgeview on 16 September, described as a commemoration of the "Viscount air disaster."[26] The family, and the Hindu community in Salisbury at large, memorialized the deaths of the civilian passengers who had been lost. But they did so in isolation from the context of the war in which the family had lost their lives, in contrast to the nationalist memorialization of the deaths of the thousands of Africans that had occurred in retribution. To make an overt political statement about the Viscount crash four decades later would be to suggest that Indians still found affinity with Rhodesia and the principles it stood for. Instead, the ceremony was held privately within the community.

The events of 1978 and 1979, which took place as the Rhodesian government made its final, desperate attempts to violently defeat the guerrillas and maintain control, held different meanings for all involved. While it is clear who shot down the plane, and why, the mystery surrounding the shooting of the survivors remains. Was it ZIPRA guerrillas who came back to take care of those who had survived the crash? Or was it the Black Selous Scouts of the Rhodesian troops, notorious for their acts of barbarity done in the name of the state, posing as members of the nationalist movement? For the Rhodesian government and the white settler population who lost some of their own citizens, family members, and neighbors to yet another "terrorist attack," the shooting down of the plane was one in a series of events that demonstrated that they would not, and could not, hand the country over to the "barbarians" responsible for the deaths of innocent white Rhodesians. Today, the event is remembered as one that signaled disaster and impending doom for the glorious days of white Rhodesia, which is still nostalgically commemorated by those who refuse to call themselves Zimbabweans and instead reminisce about the "good old days" through diasporic digital newsletters and Facebook community groups. Black Zimbabweans instead remember the hundreds of civilians who were killed in retribution for the plane crash, and the thousands more who were killed during the war, lives lost in the anticolonial struggle.

Even with the attainment of majority rule based on the principle of "one man, one vote," race remained the most salient category for ideas of belonging on the eve of independence. But Indians, an in-between population in Rhodesia in many interpretations of the term, claimed belonging with white

Rhodesia *and* with Black Zimbabwe, by different groups at different times. For the Hindu community, the deaths of eight members of a single family were a blow to all who knew them. The vilification of Mehta for his involvement with the same movement that was responsible for the shooting down of the plane revealed the divisions that existed between those who chose the safety of participation in Rhodesian society in Salisbury in comparison to those families, mainly located in Bulawayo, who had sacrificed both their finances and their freedom for the cause of Black majority rule. While these men and their families, including Mehta, are now recalled as heroes by the Indian community as they emphasize their commitment to being Zimbabwean, the lives of the eight who lost their lives because of the war between Black and white in Rhodesia are still quietly remembered.

CONCLUSION

> I told myself how desperately I loved this country that somehow could not accept me. Was there really something prohibitively negative in me, and in those like me, with our alien forbidding skins off which the soul of Africa simply slipped away?
>
> —M. G. VASSANJI, The In-Between World of Vikram Lall, 302

Kamuben Rama was well known to many people in Zimbabwe. Her family had once been involved in the nationalist movement; she and Suman Mehta's wife, Lilli, were good friends before Lilli's death. The family into which she married ran a shop that sold textiles and materials for clothing. It essentially became her store. Later, she imported traditional clothing from India to sell to women in Harare. In postcolonial Zimbabwe, she hosted numerous fundraisers for charities. For national Independence Day celebrations on 18 April 1980, she trained a group of thirty Indian dancers, young women from the community, to perform for the entire country. She met Indira Gandhi when the prime minister visited Harare soon after independence, and called Sally Mugabe, Robert Mugabe's first wife, a dear friend who would often visit her shop to buy materials.[1] Zulekha Ebrahim was another woman who made connections through her work. She trained as a fashion designer under a white Rhodesian woman, later opening her own store. While she initially designed dresses for the wives of white farmers, her later customers included everyone from Abigail Vera to Graça Machel.[2] She became renowned for her wedding dress designs.[3]

Both women—one Hindu, one Muslim—were born in Rhodesia and were married into traditional Indian families and households but, through their shops, made names for themselves as notable Zimbabweans. The sari that Joshua Nkomo allegedly once donned to evade arrest is symbolic of these women's participation in Zimbabwean history through their careers in fashion, even as their social identities were tied to the domestic traditions of the *dukkan*. The idea that Indians were an insular diaspora erases the fact that their history is also African history. While communities used traditional notions of gender to erect boundaries around their homes, their shops became spaces for engagement with the worlds and modernities in between which they were located. Across generations, Indians became Zimbabwean, pointing to the complexities and multiplicities of that identity in the postcolonial era.

An African Indian identity in Zimbabwe is deeply and intimately tied to the shop. Through it, Indians have made historic claims to being Zimbabwean. The *dukkan* is a lens into the wider worlds which Indians occupied as both colonizing settlers and colonized subjects, located in between Black Africans and white Europeans. After Rhodesia became Zimbabwe, most Indian families retained their livelihoods as traders and business owners. Indians were not forced or pressured to leave Zimbabwe, or to give up their shops as part of postcolonial indigenization policies. Studies of diasporas often center oceanic narratives, the transient, migratory nature of those who left one land for another on boats across waters. In these stories, the historical moments in which diasporic subjects participate are fleeting, invisible, and washed away by broader waves of change over time. But Indians in Zimbabwe grounded themselves in firmer soil through their shops, which established their presence and their visibility on urban land. This book has told the stories of many families and individuals who lived in Rhodesia. What they all have in common is that their stories begin and end in the space of the *dukkan*, a physical site as well as a metaphorical space for the remaking of identities that enabled Indian families to set down roots in colonial modernity. Ideas about gender and the protection of women were central to the spaces that men constructed. Over generations, these ideals shifted, allowing both men and women to participate in the wider worlds that surrounded them. At the end of the day, however, they all returned to the safe space of the *dukkan* that tied their identities as Indians living in Africa to a real home.

The history of Indians in Rhodesia is the history of the country's transition to becoming Zimbabwe. The "pioneers" who migrated across the Indian Ocean to territory controlled by the British South Africa Company were part of the settler colonial process that established the foundations of the colony called Southern Rhodesia. The hostility they faced, both at the gates of constructed borders as well as within them, was part of the white settler state's attempt to define the boundaries of belonging. In the stories they told about this early history, Indian patriarchs established themselves as colonized subjects looking for new opportunities, even as they participated in the displacement of Black Africans. But kept away from rural land and African reserves through seminal land legislation, Indians found themselves sharing intimate urban spaces with Coloured and Black Africans. They engaged with them across the shop counter, the first iterations of the *dukkan* enabling their permanent settlement. Their lives were shaped by segregation controls, but they also transgressed these boundaries daily in their intimate lives. Their experiences shaped Indian elite conceptions about gender and purity and became the foundation for the expansion of families across generations.

Indian patriarchs brought their families over from India, and children were now being born in Africa rather than on the subcontinent. Because they had chosen to make their lives in colonial urbanity, they created community purity schools funded by the colonial state to uphold their ideologies of race, caste, and gender gleaned from the subcontinent in an African context. They informed racialized colonial education policies to protect the extension of their lives beyond the *dukkan*. But they did not remain unchallenged, and debates over who belonged to the community went beyond a simple definition of racial identity, reflecting how the localized experiences of ordinary people in towns and cities deeply shaped colonial policy. During the Federation period, groups across racial lines collaborated and interacted, challenging divisive policies that were masked by performative liberalism and the limited integration of Black Africans into systems of governance. Those who confronted the strictures of segregation made their voices heard in the courts, allowing for contestations over law and justice and challenging how nonwhite populations could live their lives in the privacy of their homes, and where they could find space for themselves beyond them.

A new generation of Rhodesian Indians created identities for themselves that were still tied to the *dukkan,* but which grounded them as active participants in civic society too. In a tale of two cities, Indians in Salisbury used their historical experience with the immigration and legal system to fight for their rights to physical and social mobility as Southern Rhodesia became the renegade Rhodesia, resisting calls for a transition to Black majority rule. In Bulawayo, however, Indians used their shops, which became part of a political underground network of resistance to the white state, to participate in the nationalist movement. Indians fought on both sides of the war determining Rhodesia's future, both as recruits to the army and members of Black nationalist political parties. When Rhodesia eventually met its end, Indian shops survived the transition into a postcolonial future, even those whose owners were ambivalent about Black majority rule. Their lives were determined by the history of the place they had migrated to, and which they chose to make home. In turn, their influence on the country's economic, political, and social landscape was reflected in the vibrant trading streets that could be found deep in the center of cities like Harare and Bulawayo, historical sites that marked how long they had been there and the inheritance they would pass down to their children and grandchildren.

Although Rhodesia died, its legacies lived on. In the 1980s, the Zimbabwean government attempted to redress some of the basic social inequalities nonwhite populations had faced. Free education and health care were offered, and Zimbabwe's literacy rates soared. But it had yet to deal with the issue of rural land reform, and most agricultural farms remained in the hands of white farmers and cooperatives. Taking back the land was key to dominant narratives of resistance, and by 2000, the Zimbabwean state began a process known as fast-track land reform, which aimed to redistribute land from white settler farmers, who dominated the agricultural sector, to Black smallholders. That process has been detailed in depth by other scholars.[4] Beyond the political and economic ramifications of the process, land reform revealed the inherent racialism that existed in Zimbabwean society at all levels, where race, because of the nature of the colonial project in Rhodesia, became inherent to the anticolonial politics and public rhetoric of Zimbabwe and definitions of indigeneity and nativism. Indians, who neither owned land nor worked on it, were left out of the land reform process and therefore were marginalized from the political construction of the new nation. In mainstream state-dominated narratives of Zimbabwe and its history, Zimbabweans of Indian origin neither belong nor are they unwelcome. They simply exist.

As a result, race was a defining factor of citizenship legislation during this period. In 2001, the registrar-general, Tobaiwa Mudede, announced that all Zimbabwean citizens with "foreign" origins had to renounce their claims to alien citizenship in order to retain or acquire their Zimbabwean nationality, per his interpretation of the amended Citizenship of Zimbabwe Act. According to the new rules, Zimbabwean citizens born before 26 January 1950 of Indian parents, or of an Indian father, had to produce a letter from the Indian government stating that they had no claims to Indian citizenship.[5] Indian citizenship laws were clear in that any Indian who voluntarily acquired the citizenship of another country would automatically cease to be a citizen of India. The Citizenship of India Act of 1955 covered citizenship by descent if a person's father was a citizen of India, but required formal registration and did not allow for dual citizenship—making Indian citizenship a moot point if another citizenship was acquired voluntarily or at birth.[6] Descendants of grandparents born in India did not have an automatic claim to an Indian nationality, either. After several months of back-and-forth between the registrar's office and the Indian embassy, the Indian authorities eventually agreed to issue statements declaring that Zimbabwean residents of Indian origin were not automatically Indian citizens.[7] Eventually, all persons of Indian origin were required to obtain this paperwork from the Indian High Commission when they turned eighteen years of age.[8]

But Indians' "foreign origins" were not a defining factor when it came to economic claims to belonging beyond land reform. Instead, race became a way for Indians to claim inclusion as a formerly colonized group rather than as migrant settlers. In September 2007, in the aftermath of a contentious implementation of land reform that pitted Black against white, the Zimbabwean Parliament passed the Indigenisation and Economic Empowerment Act. According to the terms of the new legislation, 51 percent of all businesses had to be owned by "indigenous Zimbabweans." The act defined an indigenous Zimbabwean as "any person who, before the 18th April, 1980, was disadvantaged by unfair discrimination on the grounds of his or her race, and any descendant of such person."[9] Indians and their descendants born after 1980 were included in that definition, based on the grounds that they had suffered economic discrimination. They did not have to give up a majority share in their businesses, and the act was eventually repealed in 2019.[10]

State narratives of the country's history erased Indians. Citizenship laws suggested that Indians were still a "foreign" presence. Indigenization laws, however, suggested that because of their historic experiences of disenfranchisement, they were African. What is clear is that race on its own has its limitations as a category of identity based on actual lived experience. Indian history in Zimbabwe, which they lived through and beyond the shop, demonstrates how caste, class, religion, and gender were all modes of identity that people negotiated on the ground in their everyday lives. Across the shop counter, Indians both engaged with other communities and contested the terms of their belonging. Through these experiences that were both defined by and transcended race, Indians made historical and geographic claims to belonging. Indians have since become Zimbabwean, and their history, along with that of the many other peoples with whom they shared urban spaces, is as much the history of the country as was the struggle for land and for majority rule.

Many of my generation, whose great-grandparents and grandparents were the first to migrate, have become part of the "brain drain" from the continent to Western countries. But when asked where home lies, we all say Zimbabwe. India, on the other hand, has become a distant ancestral land, a culturally defining point but not a real home to which we return. I was born at the Ambuya Nehanda hospital in Harare to parents who had been born in Salisbury and Bulawayo. My maternal grandfather was also born in Bulawayo. But I am still asked on a regular basis, both in Zimbabwe and outside, which part of India I come from. A racialized "Indian" identity continues to be associated with the nation long after the Indian nation itself fractured and then disassociated itself politically from its diaspora.[11]

Engseng Ho would argue that where you are buried is more important than where you were born. The first generations of Indian migrants were born in India but buried in Rhodesia. As migrants, they made what Ho calls a "shift in allegiance—from origins to destinations."[12] Rather than asking where we come from, then, a better question to ask might be how we got here, and how we were part of Rhodesia becoming Zimbabwe. Indians in Zimbabwe occupied different spaces and different modernities that intersected, and that defy exclusive definition. The stories of individuals are the ones that tell us what Zimbabwe means to the people who lived in it, and those who were buried there. Ultimately, this book has been the story of the worlds Indians occupied forming part of their larger transition to becoming Zimbabwean, both willingly and reluctantly, both consciously and subconsciously.

Many people's origin stories began with Bhimjee Naik, the "original" pioneer. Even the *Rhodesia Herald* marked his death in 1942, noting him as the "first Indian trader in the colony."[13] Bhimjee's trading stores not only provided jobs to new immigrants but were symbolic of the hard work and sacrifice it took to establish the first iterations of the *dukkan*. Ironically, however, he eventually left Southern Rhodesia for good to retire in India, while his sons continued to manage his African businesses from a distance. Stories told about him emphasize how he arrived in Africa, not when he left. The first Indian pioneer was not buried in Zimbabwe, but those who later claimed him as a communal ancestor were. This retelling of his history reflected a psychological desire on the part of those who did stay to belong somewhere by literally making their symbolic ancestors belong to the new colony as well.

On the other hand, Ismail Bhika's father, the first Muslim "pioneer," set down firm roots in Rhodesia. Ismail was born in Salisbury in 1930 and never went to India himself. He learned how to read Arabic at the community mosque but also went to a school attended by Indian, Coloured, and Chinese children, where he learned to read and write in English. He left school at the age of fifteen to work in the family businesses, which until his recent death, were still located in downtown Harare, including Bhika Bros. on Rezende Street. He played soccer and tennis at the Universals Sports Club in Ridgeview and was eventually conscripted into the Rhodesian army. While he believed the family still had relatives living in Bharuch in Gujarat, their family was "completely engrossed in business and trying to develop all the time" in Zimbabwe.[14] His life was firmly grounded in the family shops, even as he found a life outside of it.

Taraben Naik's grandchildren have all left Zimbabwe, creating "double diasporas" of Indian-Zimbabweans scattered across the globe.[15] As a wife and mother, she witnessed the debates over the education of Indian children, and what their lives should look like both inside the shop and outside of it. In turn, the next generation attended Gujarati schools and *madrasas* run by local community institutions but also enrolled in multiracial private schools and became more socially integrated with the rest of their generation. But as a result of a series of postcolonial economic crises, Zimbabwe is experiencing a "brain drain" across different class groups.[16] Taraben's grandchildren are a part of this pattern. At the same time, they still conform to patriarchal ideas about caste and religion when it comes to endogamy and marriage, expectations which determine the expansion of their families. Even beyond Zimbabwe's borders, the *dukkan* continues to influence their lives across time and space.

Family names live on through the legacies passed down to their children that went beyond the physical inheritance of the shop. Although Suman Mehta was not a lawyer, the court case he initiated became seminal in future legal challenges to segregation. His son, Deepak, did become a lawyer and an advocate in postcolonial Zimbabwe. But Suman's history has mostly been forgotten, or rewritten. He was appointed high commissioner representing Zimbabwe to Canada in the 1980s, but he was not accorded the honor of being buried in National Heroes' Acre when he died in 1989.[17] He is instead brought up in narratives of "Asian" participation in the resistance struggle rather than in general histories of Zimbabwean nationalism. But his story is critical for understanding the generational shift that took place for those born in Rhodesia, who saw it as their only homeland in which they were determined to stay and find a place for themselves, both within the structures of white minority rule as well as Black politics.

All of these narrative threads come together in the story of one family. Two of the men at the center of the final chapters of this book shared the first name and were born in the early 1920s. They led extraordinarily different lives, however, and left behind diverging legacies. Haribhai Patel's shop in Harare, Smartwear Outfitters, has since been dissolved. The wealth generated from the business allowed the family to purchase properties across the city. Haribhai's son, Bharat, benefited from his father's financial success and was able to avoid conscription into the Rhodesian army by leaving to study law in London. He returned to Zimbabwe in 1982 to work in the Ministry of Justice. As the country's deputy attorney general in the early 2000s, he served as one of the architects of the land reform program. Today, he is a judge of the Constitutional Court in Zimbabwe.[18] He fulfilled his father's dream for his son to become a judge, a form of upward class mobility in colonial society—but also a position he would use to attempt to correct the imperial legacies which had led to his success but oppressed the majority of the country's people.

Not all Indian families prospered economically. Haribhai Naik's daughter, Hansa, became a teacher, one of the two professional career options available to Indian women in Rhodesia.[19] Her family struggled financially because of their involvement in the nationalist movement, but she was able to make a

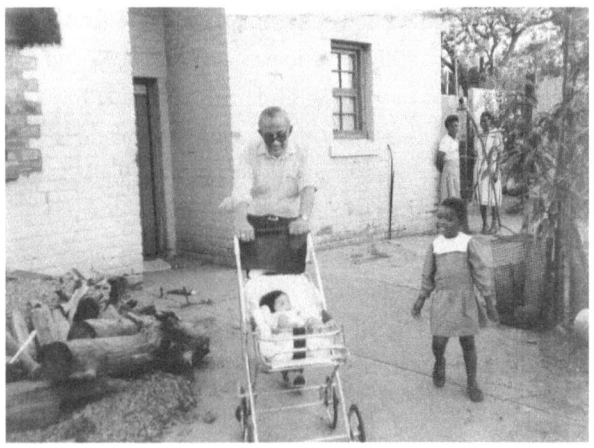

Figure 15. Author as a baby with her grandfather, Haribhai Naik, November 1989, Bulawayo. (Author's family collection)

career for herself as an educator in postcolonial Zimbabwe. The Naik family is now fractured and scattered across the globe as one by one they all left their home on Lobengula Street. M. V. Naik and Sons, once a center of a vibrant social and political scene, was dissolved. The building is now rented out to Black businessmen in Bulawayo. But Haribhai Patel and Haribhai Naik's lives collided when Bharat and Hansa married in 1976, and thirteen years later, the product of both their legacies was born. That child was me.

Before I was born, Haribhai Patel died in 1981 in Harare of cancer. His death precipitated Bharat and Hansa's return from London, where they had spent the first few years of their marriage. Dahiben, the matriarch of the family, died in 1987. Lilavatiben Naik died giving birth to Hansa in 1954. Her sister, Kusumben, helped raise both Hansa and me in her stead. The only grandparent I have known in life is my maternal grandfather, whom I called Bapa. I knew him as a quiet man whose presence gave my childhood a sense of peace and stability I did not realize was there until it was gone. I grew up in Harare, but also in M. V. Naik and Sons on Lobengula Street in Bulawayo, causing chaos with my cousins behind the shop counter. But the times I recall best were the quiet ones, the daily walks to the post office with my grandfather where we only exchanged occasional words, comfortable in our mutual silence. Beneath this placid exterior, however, Haribhai Naik felt deeply disillusioned with the country he had fought for, unacknowledged by those he had once counted as comrades. He had chosen his family over the cause, and for that, he would not be welcomed back into the fold. That choice led to a downward spiral for him.[20] One day in August 1997, when I was eight years old, he ordered a taxi that took him to the Hillside Dam.[21] His second wife, Urmilaben, thought this was a strange trip to make. He had said nothing to her about where he was going and had left his wallet and house keys behind, almost deliberately, in the living room. Later that day, his body was found in the lake. He was seventy-two years old when he died. His name is not one of those mentioned in occasional newspaper reports commemorating the Indian contribution to the nationalist movement. It cannot be found in any scholarly histories. He was not buried in Heroes' Acre. His story has been left to his granddaughter to tell instead.

NOTES

INTRODUCTION

1. "Rhodesia Banishes Nkomo and 3 Aides; Racial Fights Erupt," *New York Times*, 17 April 1964.
2. Dr. Vivek Solanki, interview by the author, 14 November 2018. Solanki's maternal relatives were part of the Rana family.
3. Indians in Zimbabwe mostly claimed peasant origins in their oral histories, which was not the case for free migrants to East Africa and South Africa, many of whom came from trading communities in Gujarat and expanded into Indian Ocean trade networks to make their way to the African coast. While some of them came from wealthier families, most Indians in Zimbabwe came from villages in Gujarat that were made up of predominantly farming communities.
4. Musoni, "Contested Foreignness," 318.
5. Southern Rhodesia Government Census 1911, National Archives of Zimbabwe, Harare (hereafter cited as NAZ), C5 11/1–2.
6. Rhodesia 1969 Census, Interim Report, Volume I: The European, Asian and Coloured Population, NAZ RG3/STA520.
7. Brownell, *The Collapse of Rhodesia*, 8.
8. D. M. Desai, *The Indian Community in Southern Rhodesia* (Herald Press, 1948), 9, Hindu Society Archive (hereafter cited as HSA), Harare, HIS0001.

9. Indigenisation and Economic Empowerment Act, in *The Statue Law of Zimbabwe* (2007), 83–86, Library of the High Court of Zimbabwe (hereafter cited as LHCZ), Harare. In 2017, Indians were officially classified as Kenya's forty-fourth tribe.
10. Ruramisai Charumbira unpacks the gendered construction of both the white colonial and Black postcolonial states in *Imagining a Nation*. The myth that Nkomo routinely dressed up as a woman to escape evasion would return to haunt him in 1983, when rumors surfaced that he had disguised himself as a woman to cross the border to Botswana to self-exile in London after the Gukurahundi massacres of ZAPU dissidents (Nkomo, *The Story of My Life*, 1–4).
11. Sana Aiyar makes this argument about Indians in East African history in *Indians in Kenya*, 262.
12. These two strands of historiography are articulated succinctly by Ranger in "Nationalist Historiography, Patriotic History and the History of the Nation," as well as by Raftopoulos and Mlambo in *Becoming Zimbabwe*. The inherited and interconnected legacies of nationalist myths between the white colonial and the Black postcolonial states are best argued by Charumbira in *Imagining a Nation*.
13. Mbembe and Balakrishnan, "Pan-African Legacies, Afropolitan Futures."
14. Hofmeyr argues for a "desegregated" approach to Indian Ocean history, which allows for a deracialization of terms such as "slave, indentured laborer, and settler" in "The Complicating Sea," 588. I take that argument a step further to consider what this means for racialized identities themselves.
15. Ranger, "The Invention of Tradition in Colonial Africa"; Ranger, "The Invention of Tradition Revisited."
16. Musoni, "Contested Foreignness."
17. Oonk, *Global Indian Diasporas*.
18. Bruce Hall argues that instead of race being understood exclusively as a "Euro-American ideology," there are instead "African histories of race that do not obey colonial logics" (Hall, *A History of Race in Muslim West Africa*, 1–2).
19. Biko, "The Definition of Black Consciousness," in *I Write What I Like*, 48–49.
20. Biko, "The Definition of Black Consciousness," 52–53.
21. Kwarteng, *Ghosts of Empire*, 5; Elkins, *Legacy of Violence*.
22. Examples of anthropological and ethnographic studies of Indians in Rhodesia that treat Indians as unchanging migrant middlemen populations include Dotson and Dotson, *The Indian Minority of Zambia, Rhodesia, and Malawi*; Kosmin, "Ethnic and Commercial Relations in Southern Rhodesia"; and Connelly, "Temporary Middlemen."
23. South African Indian scholars treated Indian history, and particularly narratives of indentured labor communities, as distinctly South African history,

demonstrating how apartheid shaped their experiences as well as how their history influenced the country's political trajectory. Examples include, but are not limited to, Desai, *Arise Ye Coolies*; Desai and Vahed, *Inside Indian Indenture*; and Vahed and Bhana, *Crossing Space and Time in the Indian Ocean*.
24. Hofmeyr, "The Complicating Sea"; Koshy and Radhakrishnan, *Transnational South Asians*; Bahadur, *Coolie Woman*; Bald, *Bengali Harlem*.
25. Newer works on Indians in Zimbabwe include Mpofu, "'Undesirable' Indians"; and Musoni, "Contested Foreignness."
26. Aiyar, *Indians in Kenya*.
27. Bertz, *Diaspora and Nation in the Indian Ocean*.
28. Brennan, *Taifa*.
29. Shankar, *An Uneasy Embrace*.
30. Soske, *Internal Frontiers*.
31. Safran, "Diasporas in Modern Societies."
32. Fatima Meer, South African nationalist, argued that Indians in South Africans were "not a diaspora of India in South Africa because we claimed South Africa for our own and in order to entrench that claim, we have had to struggle hard and long alongside our South African brothers and sisters" (Shubha Singh, "Discovering the Diaspora," *The Hindu*, 11 April 2003, https://frontline.thehindu.com/the-nation/article30216344.ece).
33. Tallie, *Queering Colonial Natal*, 3–8.
34. Smith, *Settlers at the End of Empire*, 8.
35. Vahed and Bhana, *Crossing Space and Time in the Indian Ocean*, 7.
36. For example, the entire collection of *Lotus* magazine, created by Indians in Bulawayo, is held at the home of a widow of a former Indian member of the nationalist movement in London. The National Archives in Zimbabwe holds some issues of *Lotus* in its collection, but not all.
37. Mbembe, "The Power of the Archive and Its Limits," 23.
38. Stoler, *Along the Archival Grain*, 46–47.

1. UNDESIRABLES AND PIONEERS

1. Crossing the *kala pani*, or dark waters of the Indian Ocean, would cause a loss of caste, "according to the strictures of Hinduism" (Bahadur, *Coolie Woman*, 19).
2. "Rao Bahadur Bhimjee R. Naik Family," in *The South African Indian Who's Who* (1939), 281, HSA PION0005-06.
3. N. J. Patel (one of Naik's former employees), interview by Dr. Hasu H. Patel, 11 September 1968.

4. See, for example, Robertson, *Rhodesian Rancher*; Clements, *This Is Our Land*; and Tanser, *A Scantling of Time*; among others. These writings detailing the white settler process have been coined "Rhodesiana."
5. Vansina, *Oral Tradition as History*, 30.
6. Charumbira, *Imagining a Nation*, 9–11.
7. *The South African Indian Who's Who*, 281.
8. Charumbira "uses gender as a concept that helps us understand the historical processes that shaped the remaking and reinforcement of sociopolitical relationships between women and men, but especially men and men—the colonizer and the colonized" (Charumbira, *Imagining a Nation*, 12).
9. O'Sullivan, *No Birds of Passage*, 8–9. The literature on Indians in Africa has inherited this legacy of treating their history as that of strangers and diasporic migrants.
10. Sekuru Kaguvi was a spiritual leader associated with the man called Gumboreshumba, who claimed to speak for the spirit Kaguvi. *Kaguvi* was also a term given to spirit mediums in the past who claimed to speak for the Shona deity Mwari. Nehanda, also known as Mbuya Nehanda, was a spirit medium of Nehanda, a female *mhondoro*, or ancestral spirit. Because of their connection to the ancestors, they were leaders in the First Chimurenga, or revolt, against the British South Africa Company in 1896–97. Their legacies were later recalled during the guerrilla war against the white minority state, or the Second Chimurenga.
11. Oonk, *Global Indian Diasporas*, 11.
12. Pearson, *Port Cities and Intruders*; Metcalf, *Imperial Connections*; Machado, *Ocean of Trade*; among others.
13. Metcalf and Metcalf, *A Concise History of Modern India*, 126–27.
14. Rajyagor, *History of Gujarat*, 446.
15. Suzuki, *The Nature of Whiteness*, 33.
16. D. M. Desai, *The Indian Community in Southern Rhodesia*, 9.
17. N. J. Patel, interview.
18. Dr. Hasu Patel, interview by the author, 25 October 2018.
19. D. M. Desai Jr., interview by Dr. Hasu Patel, date unknown.
20. Yusuf Adam, interview by the author, 17 May 2018.
21. Ismail Bhika, interview by the author, 31 October 2018. Written information about the colonies in Africa was rare in the villages. The first Gujarati vernacular newspaper was published in Bombay in 1822, but it was only after Gandhi's return from South Africa in 1915 that Gujarati media increased and spread to rural outposts, initiated with his creation of the newspaper *Navjivan* in 1919.
22. See chapter 2.
23. N. J. Patel, interview.

24. Dr. Hasu Patel, interview.
25. D. M. Desai, interview. The Indian Passport Act of 1920 necessitated the use of passports for travel within the confines of the British Empire.
26. N. J. Patel, interview. *Puris* are small rounds of deep-fried bread.
27. Kalshekar, "1908 Asiatics Ordinance in Perspective," 5.
28. Tanser, *A Scantling of Time*.
29. Yusuf Adam, interview.
30. M. P. Patel, interview by Dilip Chouhan, date unknown, HSA HIS0006.
31. By 1910, the new Union of South Africa had tightened regulations on the immigration and activities of Indian migrants.
32. Charumbira, *Imagining a Nation*, 116–17.
33. Charumbira, *Imagining a Nation*, 76.
34. Nandy, *The Intimate Enemy*.
35. Immigration Ordinance Amendment Ordinance, in *The Statute Law of Southern Rhodesia* (1903), 10–11, LHCZ.
36. Registers of Immigrants entering Territory via Umtali, NAZ S1826.
37. Southern Rhodesia's immigration laws stemmed from a longer history of transnational legislation against Asian and "undesirable" European immigration dating back to the Naturalization Act of 1790 of the United States, which only allowed naturalization of white citizens, to the Chinese Exclusion and Immigration Acts of the late nineteenth century. In 1885, Canada imposed a Chinese Immigration Act, and in 1901, the Immigration Restriction Act in Australia was part of a "White Australia" policy.
38. Minutes of proceedings and papers laid before the Conference presented to Parliament by Command of His Majesty regarding Reciprocity of Treatment between India and the Dominions, Lloyd George Papers, Parliamentary Archives of the United Kingdom (hereafter cited as PAUK), London, LG/F/117/2 Cd 9177.
39. Sergeant's report at Umtali Station on 27 March 1905, Registers of Immigrants entering Territory via Umtali, NAZ S1826.
40. See correspondence in Immigration: Alien General Policy, NAZ F119/IMM/3.
41. "Total deportations under Section 2, Ordinance 7 of 1914," NAZ A3/14/1–5.
42. J. B. Patel, interview by Dilip Chouhan, date unknown, HSA HIS0008.
43. J. B. Patel (Babulal's son), interview.
44. A. Long, Agent of the Union of South Africa, Governor General's Office, Pretoria, to M. Chamney, Esq., Pretoria, 21 June 1915, No. 15/777, National Archives of the United Kingdom (hereafter cited as NAUK), Richmond, DO119/911.
45. Ismail Bhika (Mohammed's son), interview.
46. A. Long, Agent of the Union of South Africa, Governor General's Office, Pretoria, to M. Chamney, Esq., Pretoria, 26 March 1915, A. 2624, NAUK DO119/911.

47. Chief Immigration Officer, Bulawayo, Southern Rhodesia, to the Staff Officer, Immigration Department, Salisbury, 11 July 1916, NAZ A3/14/1–5.
48. Correspondence between Bhimjee R. Naik and the Administrator of the BSAC, November 1909, NAZ A3/14/4.
49. Ranchod Naron, Prag Kesav, Valabh Fakir, and Nursi Premji to the Resident Commissioner, Salisbury, 29 January 1912, NAZ A3/14/4.
50. Palley, *The Constitutional History and Law of Southern Rhodesia*, xvii.
51. Southern Rhodesia Government Census 1911, NAZ C5 11/1–2.
52. Musoni, "Contested Foreignness," 323.
53. Chief Immigration Officer to the Secretary of Home Affairs, Salisbury, "Alien immigrants consorting with native women," 30 January 1956, NAZ F119/IMM/3.
54. Bishi, "Immigration and Settlement of 'Undesirable' Whites in Southern Rhodesia."
55. Owen Thomas, "Scheme for Land Settlement of Rhodesia," 15–16, NAZ A11/2/9/9.
56. Thomas, "Scheme for Land Settlement of Rhodesia," 15–16, NAZ A11/2/9/9.
57. Secretary, Department of the Administrator, to M. Ebrahim, Chairman of the British Indian Association, Salisbury, 2 November 1918, NAZ A3/12/30/1. African mobility was similarly associated with the spread of disease through the migrant labor system (van Onselen, *Chibaro*).
58. *The South African Indian Who's Who*, 281.
59. "Report on Chamber of Commerce Meeting," *Bulawayo Chronicle*, 8 February 1895, cited in Kalshekar, "1908 Asiatics Ordinance in Perspective," 4–5. The term "banyan," a type of tree in India, was a corruption of the term *baniya*, or the caste name for traders in India.
60. G. O. Robertson, Acting Resident Magistrate, to the Resident Commissioner, Salisbury, 17 January 1899, NAZ S1428/23.
61. Details of initial incident reported in G. O. Robertson, Acting Resident Magistrate, to the Resident Commissioner, Salisbury, 17 January 1899, NAZ S1428/23.
62. Herbert H. Castens, Acting Public Prosecutor, "Proceedings of the Foreign Department, December 1899: Anti-Indian Riot in Umtali (Southern Rhodesia)," National Archives of India (hereafter cited as NAI), New Delhi, Abhilek Patal Digitized Collections PR_0000000092433, file no. 2.
63. JNO. W. Corderoy (former justice of the peace for Umtali district), to the Civil Commissioner, Umtali, 6 January 1899, NAZ S1428/23.
64. A. W. Suter to the Administrator, Salisbury, 5 January 1899, NAZ S1428/23.
65. Petition from Nathoo Vadey & Co. and Allarakia Hassim, Indian Merchants, to His Excellency the Viceroy and Governor-General of India, 23 January 1899, NAI PR_000001429436.
66. N. J. Patel, interview.

67. J. B. Patel, interview. Lobengula similarly sent two envoys to the queen when the Rudd Concession tricked the Ndebele state out of the rights to its land, as well as a letter repudiating the Concession.
68. Asiatics Ordinance 1908, in *Minutes of the Proceedings of the Legislative Council and Ordinances*, First Session, Fourth Council, NAZ.
69. Kalshekar, "1908 Asiatics Ordinance in Perspective," 20.
70. Desai, *The Indian Community in Southern Rhodesia*, 9.
71. Interview of British Indians with the Administrator, 23 April 1915, NAZ A/3/14/4.
72. Petitions, 1916, NAZ A3/14/5/5; Musoni, "Contested Foreignness," 330–31.
73. British South Africa Company in London to William Henry Milton, Administrator of Mashonaland, Salisbury, 12 June 1908, Gell Family Papers, Derbyshire Records Office (hereafter cited as DRO), Manchester, United Kingdom.
74. Palley, *The Constitutional History and Law of Southern Rhodesia 1888–1965*, xviii.
75. See correspondence in "Importation of Indian Labour into Rhodesia," 1903, NAI PR_000000092710, file no. 13–15.
76. Prashad, "The *Desi* Diaspora," 320.
77. Aiyar, "Anticolonial Homelands Across the Indian Ocean," 994–95. See also T. Patel, "From the Subcontinent with Love," 458. Indian publications specifically condemned anti-Indian immigration restrictions in Southern Rhodesia (see "Notes of the Day: Indians in Rhodesia," *Bombay Chronicle*, 26 April 1924, NAI PR_000000250844, file no. 23–26).
78. Petition of the British Indian population of Southern Rhodesia to the Secretary of State for the Colonies, 10 July 1908, 3–4, NAUK DO 119/523.
79. In the Transvaal, the Asiatics Registration Act was passed in 1906, canceled by London, and then repassed in 1908.
80. White, *Unpopular Sovereignty*, 5.
81. C. T. Davis to Colonial Office, London, 19 June 1924, NAI PR_000000250844, file no. 23–26.
82. White, *Unpopular Sovereignty*, 4.

2. BETWEEN WHITE PICKET FENCES AND BLACK RESERVES

1. Ismail Bhika (Mohammed's son), interview by the author, 31 October 2018.
2. See chapter 1.
3. Ismail Bhika, interview.
4. Superintendent, Criminal Investigation Department, British South Africa Police to the Mining Commissioner, Bulawayo, 10 November 1921, NAZ M/3/11/22.

5. Ernest W. S. Montagu, Secretary for Mines and Works, to the Secretary, Department of the Administrator, "Issue of Prospecting License to Maken Lalla," 27 September 1922, NAZ M/3/11/22.
6. C. Holderness, Solicitor, Gatooma to the Secretary, Department of Administrator, Salisbury, 7 March 1923, NAZ M3/11/22.
7. Kosmin, "Ethnic and Commercial Relations in Southern Rhodesia," 230.
8. Montagu to Secretary, Department of the Administrator, "Issue of Prospecting License to Maken Lalla."
9. "The Labour Problem in Rhodesia and Proposed Importation of Chinese," *Bulawayo Chronicle*, 1901, cited in Kosmin, "Ethnic and Commercial Relations in Southern Rhodesia," 96.
10. Kosmin, "Ethnic and Commercial Relations in Southern Rhodesia," 96; "Statistical Yearbook of Southern Rhodesia," Department of Statistics, 1947, NAZ SRG3/STA591.
11. Kosmin, "Ethnic and Commercial Relations in Southern Rhodesia," 110.
12. *Report of the Cost of Living Committee*, 1913, 44, NAZ.
13. Dr. Vivek Solanki, interview by the author, 14 November 2018.
14. Tulsidas K. Doolabh, "The Bulawayo of Yesterday," *Bulawayo Kshatriya Mandal 75th Anniversary Commemorative Magazine* (1994), 16, HSA CURE011.
15. Mlambo, *A History of Zimbabwe*, 60–61.
16. Yusuf Adam, interview by the author, 17 May 2018.
17. Gerald Chikozho Mazarire, "Reflections on Pre-Colonial Zimbabwe c. 850–1880s," in *Becoming Zimbabwe*, ed. Raftopoulos and Mlambo.
18. Response by Southern Rhodesian government to questions posed by Apa Pant, Indian commissioner to East and Central Africa, regarding the treatment of Indians in the Federation of Rhodesia and Nyasaland, March 1951, personal collection of Dr. Hasu Patel.
19. Kosmin, "Ethnic and Commercial Relations in Southern Rhodesia," 3.
20. H. Moyana, "Land and Race in Rhodesia," *African Review* 5, no. 1 (1974), 24.
21. W. J. Atherstone, Surveyor General, to the Civil Commissioner, Department of Lands, Victoria, 1904–1905, personal collection of Dr. Hasu Patel. See also correspondence in NAZ S1542/S9.
22. Correspondence in NAZ L2/2/81/2.
23. Percy Inskipp, Commercial Representative, Bulawayo, to the Director of Land Settlement, Salisbury, 16 March 1914, NAZ S246/433.
24. Chief Native Commissioner, Salisbury, to the Chief Clerk, Department of Lands, 9 November 1933, NAZ S235/438.
25. Southern Rhodesia, *Second and Final Report of the Census Taken on 3rd May, 1921* (Sessional Papers, A1, 1923), table XXXIX, NAZ C6/1.

26. Mushonga, "White Power, White Desire," 1–2.
27. R. Robertson, Secretary, Department of the Administrator, to Mrs. Longden, President of the Rhodesian Women's League, Bulawayo, 22 November 1921, NAZ A3/18/35.
28. Southern Rhodesia Government Census 1921, NAZ C6/1.
29. D. H. Moodie, Native Commissioner in Rusape, to Superintendent of Natives in Umtali, 10 June 1921, NAZ A3/18/35.
30. "The Problem of Unattached Women in Settled Areas," undated memorandum, NAZ S482/179/3/49.
31. Discussions of prostitution tend to generalize women as victims rather than as active agents in their economic and social lives (see White, *The Comforts of Home*, 3).
32. Scholars of gender have argued that reproduction and sexuality became the subject of colonial intervention "because so many people viewed its regulation as fundamental to the construction of political and moral order" (Thomas, *Politics of the Womb*, 4).
33. "Undesirable Traders," Resident Commissioner, Salisbury, 1904, NAZ RC 3/7/10.
34. D. H. Moodie, Native Commissioner in Rusape, to Superintendent of Natives in Umtali, 10 June 1921, NAZ A 3/18/35.
35. Speech of Chief Maranke, report of meeting of chiefs and Governor at Umtali, 28 June 1929, NAZ S138/22. Jon Soske argues that this was part of a larger struggle of the African patriarchal elite to deal with loss of control over women (Soske, "'Wash Me Black Again,'" chapter 4).
36. A. C. Jennings for the Chief Native Commissioner to the Under Secretary, Department of Lands, Salisbury, 13 April 1934, NAZ S1542/S9.
37. Chief Native Commissioner to the Chief Clerk, Department of Lands, Salisbury, 3 July 1933, NAZ S1542/S9.
38. Chief Native Commissioner to the Honourable Minister of Native Affairs, 24 December 1934, NAZ S1542/S9.
39. Testimony of Nyatsanza to the Chairman of the Native Production and Trade Commission, 1944, 1170, NAZ ZBJ/1/1/2/1.
40. Testimony of Natives Mwamuka, Rev. Marakanke, and Sgt. Chineta, 1201–7, NAZ ZBJ/1/1/2/1. The "European" stores in question, rather than being owned by migrants of British stock, were instead run by Jewish and Greek traders, "middlemen" in the colonial economy who were less likely than Indian traders to allow haggling (see Kosmin, "Ethnic and Commercial Relations in Southern Rhodesia").
41. West, *The Rise of an African Middle Class in Colonial Zimbabwe*, 3.

42. Testimony of Natives Mwamuka, Rev. Marakanke, and Sgt. Chineta.
43. Dr. George Kahari, interview by the author, 7 November 2018.
44. Aiyar, *Indians in Kenya*, 76.
45. Mlambo, *A History of Zimbabwe*, 137.
46. Mlambo, *A History of Zimbabwe*, 85.
47. Assistant Native Commissioner to the Chief Native Commissioner, Salisbury, 11 January 1926, NAZ S138/41.
48. Report of a commission appointed to enquire into the running of the Bulawayo location, 1930, NAZ S235/440.
49. Report of a commission appointed to enquire into the running of the Bulawayo location, 1930, NAZ S235/440.
50. See correspondence in NAZ S1542/S9.
51. Map and list of private property on Indians in Location, Bulawayo City Council, 1930, NAZ-Bulawayo BLG 3/373.
52. K. R. Vashee, President, and M. Narsing, Secretary of the British Indian Association, to the Chairman, Native Affairs Commission, Bulawayo, 14 March 1930, NAZ S235/440.
53. Report of Location Superintendent to the Town Clerk, Bulawayo, 1930, NAZ-Bulawayo BLG 3/373.
54. Report of a commission appointed to enquire into the running of the Bulawayo location, 1930, NAZ S235/440.
55. Report by the 1930 Native Affairs Commission, Section on the Report of Trading Stores in the Location, Bulawayo Sanitary Board, NAZ S235/440.
56. R. J. Hudson, Ex Parte Municipal Council of Bulawayo, 25 February 1931, NAZ-Bulawayo BLG 3/373.
57. Report by the 1930 Native Affairs Commission, Section on the Report of Trading Stores in the Location, Bulawayo Sanitary Board, NAZ S235/440.
58. A similar process took place for Africans in urban spaces who attempted to transgress the boundaries imposed on them by the Native Affairs Department—health regulations in towns and cities effectively blocked Africans from trading aspirations (West, *The Rise of an African Middle Class in Colonial Zimbabwe*).
59. Dr. Hasu Patel, interview by the author, 25 October 2018.
60. Ranger, *Bulawayo Burning*, 16.
61. M. V. Naik is the author's great-grandfather.
62. Case against C. N. Pandya, NAZ MS 841/35.
63. "Statistical Yearbook of Southern Rhodesia."
64. Gunvantrai Naik (their son and author's great-uncle), interview by the author, 27 November 2018.
65. Dr. Hasu Patel, interview.

66. Aiyar, *Indians in Kenya*, 76.
67. *African Weekly*, 28 June 1944, Library of Congress (hereafter cited as LOC), Washington, DC, Newspaper 3198, control no. sn97059031.
68. *African Weekly*, 26 July 1944, LOC, Newspaper 3198.
69. *Bantu Mirror*, 12 July 1941, LOC, control no. sn97059030.
70. Burke, *Lifebuoy Men, Lux Women*.
71. Ranjit Naik, interview by the author, 23 August 2018. Antoinette Burton has argued that "even when they function as the foundation for new developmental hierarchies, Africa and Africans repeatedly demonstrate how structurally dependent Indians were on them for their own political and economic fates" (see Burton, *Africa in the Indian Imagination*, 5).
72. Dr. Busani Mpofu, interview by the author, 12 June 2020.
73. Dr. Francis Musoni, interview by the author, 5 June 2020.
74. Unlike the case in other colonial cities like Durban, Black resentment toward Indians never erupted into large-scale violence, as it did during the 1949 anti-Indian pogrom. For an account of the 1949 "Durban riots," see Soske, "'Wash Me Black Again,'" chap. 3.
75. T. Patel, "Played Out on the Edges of the Cricket Boundary," 469.
76. Sale of Liquor to Natives and Indians Act 1898/1899, in *Statute Law of Southern Rhodesia Volume II* (1899); Possession of Arms and Ammunition (Natives and Asiatics) Act 1897, in *Statute Law of Southern Rhodesia* (1897), LHCZ.
77. Colonial Secretary to the Honourable the Premier, "Possession of liquor and firearms by Indians and Coloured People," 3 November 1924, NAZ S246/728; J. A. C. Brundell, Criminal Investigation Department, Bulawayo, to the Office of the Colonial Secretary, Salisbury, 18 January 1924, NAZ S1180/1/6.
78. H. Patel, "Asian Political Activity in Rhodesia," 81–82.
79. Cohn, *Colonialism and Its Forms of Knowledge*, 3–6.
80. Asiatic Census Return Schedules 1926, Central Statistical Office, NAZ C7/1/1-30. Gujarat was part of the Bombay Province in colonial India. His son, Ismail, said his father had remarried in 1925; the information here suggests that he only married Ismail's mother after the census was taken in 1926.
81. Asiatic Census Return Schedules 1936, Central Statistical Office, NAZ S899/1-45. Ismail Bhika noted having two sisters; one listed on this census schedule likely passed away. This was likely the same family found in 1926, but some of the details in this schedule contradict information from Ismail.
82. Asiatic Census Return Schedules 1926, NAZ C7/1/1-30; Asiatic Census Return Schedules 1936 and 1941, NAZ S899/1-45.
83. Just as there was no "Indian" nationality, a "Rhodesian" or "Southern Rhodesian" nationality did not exist until 1949 with the introduction of the Southern Rhodesia Citizenship and British Nationality Act.

84. Until 1948, no concept of a separate nationality of citizenship existed for the United Kingdom and Ireland, with British nationality being defined under the nexus of British subjecthood. The creation of a composite nationalist distinction between citizens of the United Kingdom and citizens of the British colonies did not happen until after Indian and Pakistani independence.
85. Director of Census to the Secretary, Department of the Administrator, Salisbury, 14 January 1921, NAZ C 6/1.
86. Muzondidya, *Walking a Tightrope*, 1.
87. Muzondidya, *Walking a Tightrope*, 12.
88. Their lives reflected what Muzondidya calls the "multiple identities" of the "colonial experience" that defined Coloured communities (Muzondidya, *Walking a Tightrope*, xii).
89. Mandaza, *Race, Colour and Class in Southern Africa*, 143.
90. Barrier, *The Census in British India*, 74–75.
91. Southern Rhodesia Government Census 1921, NAZ C6/1.

3. PURITY SCHOOLS AND HINDU DAUGHTERS

1. Bulawayo Ramakrishna Youth League magazine (1972), 15, NAZ.
2. Tara Naik, interview by the author, 12 September 2018.
3. Yengde, *Caste Matters*.
4. Mitra, *Indian Sex Life*, 6.
5. Soske, "Navigating Difference."
6. Scholars of childhood in Africa use generation as "a useful lens for understanding change within African societies under colonial rule" (Duff, *Childhood and Youth in African History*, 8).
7. Chatterjee, *Unfamiliar Relations*, 21.
8. Ranger, "The Invention of Tradition in Colonial Africa"; Chanock, *Law, Custom and Social Order*; Mann and Roberts, *Law in Colonial Africa*; Ranger, "The Invention of Tradition Revisited"; Spear, "Neo-Traditionalism and the Limits of Invention in British Colonial Africa"; among others.
9. Sinha, *Specters of Mother India*, 5. Histories of the British Empire written in recent decades highlight the central ideological and political role of the Raj in constructions of colonial policy in later African colonies (see, for example, Metcalf, *Imperial Connections*; and Blyth, *The Empire of the Raj*). The role of ordinary Indians who were not civil servants or colonial administrators in informing colonial policy has drawn less attention, particularly in the Central

African territories where Indians were a smaller and less visible population than they were in East and South Africa.
10. Bulawayo Ramakrishna Youth League magazine, 12–13.
11. Tara Naik, interview.
12. Jasu Bhagat, interview by the author, 26 September 2018.
13. "Central Africa's Only Hindu Temple," *Rhodesia Herald*, 17 December 1951, NAZ.
14. Sumant Patel, interview by the author, 29 November 2018.
15. Yusuf Adam, interview by the author, 17 May 2018.
16. "Mohammedan's Place of Worship in Salisbury," *Rhodesia Herald*, 19 December 1951, NAZ.
17. Moosa Hassan and Basheer Mahomed, interview by the author, 28 January 2019.
18. "How Islam Came to Zimbabwe," *Sunday News*, 8 December 2019, https://www.sundaynews.co.zw/how-islam-came-to-zimbabwe/.
19. Shree South Africa Rhodesia Rajput Mandal silver jubilee brochure (1970), 11, HSA CURE0007.
20. Hemant Naik, interview by the author, 17 September 2018.
21. Dirks, *Castes of Mind*, 5; Cohn, *Colonialism and Its Forms of Knowledge*.
22. Shobana Shankar has further argued that "caste in India differed from caste in Africa, which is often overlooked" (Shankar, *An Uneasy Embrace*, 6).
23. Bulawayo Ramakrishna Youth League magazine, 29.
24. In Gujarat, land tenure systems followed the *ryot* rather than the *zamindar* pattern, meaning that agriculturists were small landowners rather than tenants (Dotson and Dotson, *The Indian Minority of Zambia, Rhodesia, and Malawi*, 131).
25. Dotson and Dotson, *The Indian Minority of Zambia, Rhodesia, and Malawi*, 134–35.
26. Mpofu, "'Undesirable' Indians," 559.
27. Pragbhai R. Vaghmaria and Lalloobhai Rama, "Bulawayo Kshatriya Mandal: A Survey," *Bulawayo Kshatriya Mandal 75th Anniversary Commemorative Magazine* (1994), 3, HSA CURE011.
28. Caste was recognized within cultures, communities, and families, but one's caste status did not determine eligibility for marriage.
29. Extract from conclusions of a meeting of cabinet held in the Prime Minister's Room on 24 May 1949, ref. S.R.C. (49) twenty-ninth meeting, NAZ S482/179/3/49. In South Africa, children of mixed race with Asian parentage were considered "Coloured." Rhodesian Coloured elites, however, emphasized "European" origins in public debates over education, even as the descendants of Indian and African or Coloured parents would eventually be included as part of the Coloured community over generations.
30. Muhamod Ebrahim-Patel, interview by the author, 23 January 2019.
31. See chapter 2.

32. Mlambo, *A History of Zimbabwe*, 52.
33. Compulsory Education Act, *Statute Law of Southern Rhodesia 1930*, LHCZ.
34. "Education of Asiatic Children," memorandum, 10 December 1947, NAZ S824/62.
35. Mlambo, *A History of Zimbabwe*, 102.
36. R. Challiss, "Coloured and Asian Education in Southern Rhodesia, 1890–1930," undated, document no. 33728, NAZ.
37. H. M. Patel, President, and Members of the Committee of the Hindoo Society, to V. A. Lewis, Minister for Internal Affairs, Salisbury, 17 May 1935, NAZ S245/832.
38. Vijay Mehta, interview by the author, 28 November 2018.
39. "Indian Vernacular Teaching," memorandum, 1945–1960, NAZ F209/547.
40. This setup followed in the tradition of colonial personal law in India, whereby Hindu families' legal affairs were regulated by the state, but Muslim families were governed by Islamic laws.
41. Minister of Education's response to petition presented by the Indian Community requesting support for an Indian school in Bulawayo, 23 March 1937, NAZ S245/832. Indian and Jewish relationships dated back to their solidarity over their exclusion from Rhodesian society in the early years of their settlement (see Kosmin, "Ethnic and Commercial Relations in Southern Rhodesia").
42. Duff, *Childhood and Youth in African History*, 98.
43. Inspector of Schools, Bulawayo, to the Director of Education, Salisbury, 18 May 1934, ref. 1802/34, NAZ S824/580.
44. H. M. Patel, President, and Members of the Committee of the Hindoo Society to V. A. Lewis, Minister for Internal Affairs, Salisbury, 17 May 1935, NAZ S245/832.
45. G. Tanser for Chief Education Officer to the Secretary, Department of Internal Affairs, Salisbury, 16 April 1946, NAZ S245/831.
46. A. R. Mackenzie, Director of Education to the Secretary, Department of Internal Affairs, Salisbury, 9 June 1937, NAZ S245/831.
47. Stan O'Donnell, Senior Social Welfare Officer, to the Director of Social Welfare, Bulawayo, 22 April 1959, NAZ F209/G/5/04.
48. Duff, *Childhood and Youth in African History*, 95.
49. Memorandum written by Bulawayo Indian School Advisory Committee, Bulawayo, 1935, NAZ S824/580.
50. Agent of the Government of India in South Africa, Durban, to Mr. O'Keefe, Minister of the Interior, Salisbury, 13 October 1934, NAZ S245/1053.
51. Heuberger, "Transnational Belonging," 87. Muslim Indians in Southern Rhodesia did not automatically affiliate with Pakistan, as other diasporic populations

did, because they located their origins in Gujarat, which remained a part of India after 1947.
52. Memorandum written by a committee of the Rhodesian Born Indian Association, presented to the Ministry of Internal Affairs, 17 July 1935, NAZ S245/1053.
53. Minutes of meeting of the Bulawayo Muslim Society, 26 January 1936, NAZ S245/1053.
54. Guardians of Mohamedan children to the Minister of Internal Affairs, Salisbury, 20 January 1936, NAZ S245/1053.
55. Guardians of Mohamedan children to the Minister of Internal Affairs, Salisbury, 20 January 1936, NAZ S245/1053.
56. British Indian Association and Islamic Society of Umtali to the Minister of Internal Affairs, Salisbury, 29 June 1935, NAZ S245/1053.
57. These complex contestations over generational mobility and the ability of sons to overthrow the leadership of their fathers have been articulated in Africanist histories as centered around ideas of security and its antithesis, insecurity (McKittrick, *To Dwell Secure*, chapter 2).
58. Education Department applications for employment as teacher, 140, NAZ S824/802/1. In the 1950s and 1960s, training colleges were created to prepare Indian and Coloured teachers for these schools; colonial officials often complained that local Indians were not interested in taking on the teaching profession and instead requested teachers from abroad (see correspondence in NAZ F119/IMM4/3/1/1).
59. Report by Mr. Cowie, inspector for the Department of Education, at the Hindoo School in Salisbury, 20 February 1939, NAZ S824/802/1.
60. H. D. Sutherns, Acting Assistant Director of Education, to the Chief Inspector, Salisbury, 16 February 1939, NAZ S824/802/1.
61. Memorandum re: Hindoo School Salisbury, undated, NAZ S824/802/2.
62. Memorandum re: Hindoo School Salisbury, undated, NAZ S824/802/2. Parents reported having been insulted by Bitshoo in the past.
63. Confidential report by Inspectors of Schools to the Minister of Education, undated, NAZ S824/802/2.
64. H. D. Sutherns, Acting Assistant Director of Education, to the Chief Inspector, Salisbury, 16 February 1939, NAZ S824/802/1.
65. Secretary of the Hindoo Society to the Chief Education Officer, Salisbury, 5 March 1943, no. 2208/202/118, NAZ S824/802/2.
66. A. G. Cowling, Chief Education Officer, to the Secretary, Department of Internal Affairs, Salisbury, 18 August 1942, NAZ S824/802/2.
67. H. D. Sutherns, Chief Education Officer, to the Secretary, Department of Internal Affairs, Salisbury, 16 November 1945, NAZ S245/1053.

68. A. G. Cowling, Chief Education Officer, to the Secretary of the Education Committee, Education Department, Salisbury, 14 November 1940, NAZ S824/802/1.
69. Education Department to the Primary School Council, Moffat Primary School, Salisbury, 8 September 1945, NAZ S824/580.
70. Chairman of the Moffat School Advisory Board to the Secretary for Education, Salisbury, 5 March 1949, NAZ S824/580; meeting of the Coloured community at Moffat School on 26 September 1945, NAZ S824/580.
71. A. R. Mackenzie, Director of Education, to the Secretary, Department of Internal Affairs, Salisbury, 9 June 1937, NAZ S245/831.
72. Tara Naik, interview.
73. Ministry of Internal Affairs, "Exemption of Indian Girls from Compulsory Education," 26 August 1942, NAZ S245/882.
74. Naik v. The King, in *Official Reports of the High Court of Southern Rhodesia 1944*, 66, LHCZ.
75. A. G. Cowling, Secretary, Department of Internal Affairs for the Minister, 6 October 1945, NAZ S245/882.
76. P. C. Bowles of Allen Bowles to the Minister of Internal Affairs, Salisbury, 11 September 1945, NAZ S245/882.
77. Request for exemption from school, sent from Chief Education Officer to the Secretary for Internal Affairs, 30 December 1947, NAZ S245/882.
78. Thomas, *Politics of the Womb*, 4.
79. "Exemption of Indian Girls from Compulsory Education."
80. A. G. Cowling, Secretary, Department of Internal Affairs for the Minister, 6 October 1945, NAZ S245/882.
81. "Exemption of Indian Girls from Compulsory Education."
82. Historians of generation and childhood in Africa have articulated these conflicts as a clash between modern and traditional categories of childhood (Duff, *Childhood and Youth in African History*, 9).

4. THE *DUKKAN* AND THE COURTROOM

1. Deepak Mehta, interview by the author, 27 March 2018.
2. Natu Patel and Suman Mehta, interview by Dr. Hasu Patel, 29 March 1970.
3. Deepak Mehta, interview.
4. Personal law in the British Raj regulated marriage, divorce, inheritance, and guardianship. This was known as "customary law" in British African colonies, and "civil law" as applied to white settler citizens.
5. Sharafi, *Law and Identity in Colonial South Asia*, 11.

6. Karekwaivanane, *The Struggle over State Power in Zimbabwe*, 2.
7. Scholars of legal systems in African colonies argue that "law was a site in which competing conceptions of political authority were given expression, and in which people's understandings of themselves as citizens were formed and performed" (Verheul, *Performing Power in Zimbabwe*, 3).
8. This chapter is part of the shift in historiography of legal history in colonial Africa from the anthropological domain of legal scholarship to that of social and cultural history and the relationship between law and culture, and the use of legal records as a lens into domestic affairs (see Waller, "Legal History and Historiography in Colonial Sub-Saharan Africa").
9. Acting Master, High Court v. Estate Mehta (1957); Mehta, N. D., the estate of, v. Acting Master of the High Court (1958), in *Rhodesia and Nyasaland Law Reports*, LHCZ.
10. Deepak Mehta, interview.
11. Sharafi, *Law and Identity in Colonial South Asia*, 6; Karekwaivanane, *The Struggle over State Power in Zimbabwe*, 3, 11.
12. Mamdani, *Citizen and Subject*.
13. Mann and Roberts, *Law in Colonial Africa*, 8.
14. Metcalf, *Imperial Connections*; Blyth, *The Empire of the Raj*.
15. "Multiracialism," as opposed to "nonracialism," aimed to give Africans limited representation in governance rather than allowing color-blind representation of elected officials.
16. "Immigration Policy: Asiatics," 25 November 1959, NAZ F119/IMM/4/5.
17. Wood, "The Reaction to Asian Migration on the Eve of Federation in British Central Africa," 332.
18. Immigration Act 1954, in *The Statute Law of the Federation of Rhodesia and Nyasaland* (1954), LHCZ.
19. Inter-Territorial Movement of Persons (Control) Act, no. 51, in *The Statute Law of Southern Rhodesia* (1954), 140, LHCZ.
20. See chapter 3.
21. Natu Patel and Suman Mehta, interview.
22. The Indian population in Nyasaland had historically demanded constitutional reforms under the Federation government, outnumbering the European population (9,000 to 7,000 in 1958), Nyasaland Asian Convention, NAUK CO1015/1751.
23. "Asians and Federation," Southern Rhodesian Indian Conference Central Committee, 18 March 1953, personal collection of Dr. Hasu Patel.
24. Acting Secretary, Immigration Department, "Policy: Asian Immigration," Salisbury, 25 September 1959, NAZ F119/IMM/4/5.
25. Secretary for Home Affairs to the Secretary of the Asian Association, Salisbury, 28 August 1954, NAZ F119/IMM/4/5.

26. "Immigration Policy: Asiatics," 25 November 1959, NAZ F119/IMM/4/5.
27. "Immigration Policy: Asiatics," 25 September 1959, NAZ F119/IMM/4/5.
28. "H. N. Patel: Son of N. K. Patel," 8 October 1959, NAZ F119/IMM/4/5.
29. "Representations to the Prime Minister by the Lusaka Indian Association," Salisbury, 5 May 1956, NAZ F119/IMM/4/5; note to the Minister of Immigration, Salisbury, 29 May 1956, NAZ F119/IMM/4/5.
30. "Representations to the Prime Minister by the Lusaka Indian Association," Salisbury, 5 May 1956, NAZ F119/IMM/4/5.
31. "Immigration Policy: Asiatics," 25 September 1959, NAZ F119/IMM/4/5. The policy assumed women had no claims to rights of residency if they married foreign men.
32. Secretary for Home Affairs to the Federal Chief Immigration Officer, 28 December 1961, NAZ F119/IMM/4/2.
33. The act was the subject of much debate when implemented in India: It adopted policies regarding the regulation of the family according to upper-caste preferences when it came to monogamy but was opposed by Hindu nationalists over the allowance of divorce, which was anathema to elite Hindu conceptions of marriage. The eventual compromise gave women more freedom over conjugal autonomy but gave the nuclear family greater authority over the control of ancestral property (see Subramaniam, "Making Family and Nation").
34. The Hindu Marriage Act, Act 25 of 1955, 18 May 1955, High Court of India, https://highcourtchd.gov.in/hclscc/subpages/pdf_files/4.pdf. The postcolonial state took on the task of regulating Hindu domesticity but left Islamic law to be enforced by the upholders of religious institutes, a continuation of colonial personal law systems for Muslims but not Hindus.
35. "Procedure Governing the Introduction of Indian Wives and Minor Children into the Federation," 8 November 1958, NAZ F119/IMM/4/5.
36. "Procedure Governing the Introduction of Indian Wives and Minor Children into the Federation," 8 November 1958, NAZ F119/IMM/4/5.
37. The High Court dealt with serious civil law issues, whereas lower magistrate courts were the courts of first instance for most criminal cases.
38. Acting Federal Attorney-General to the Secretary for Home Affairs, 24 December 1956, NAZ F119/IMM/4/5.
39. Ferera (Pvt.) Ltd. v. Estate Karimshah and others, in *Official Reports of the High Court of Southern Rhodesia 1953*, 35–43, LHCZ.
40. Patel v. Master of the High Court and others, in *Official Reports of the High Court of Southern Rhodesia 1953*, 160–64, LHCZ.
41. "Discrimination Disallowed: Court Ruling on Indian's Request," *Rhodesia Herald*, 7 June 1952, NAZ.
42. "Rent Policy on Asiatics: No Ejectments If Values Would Drop," *Bulawayo Chronicle*, 29 April 1948, NAUK DO 35/3088.

43. Desai & Co. v. Bindura Town Management Board, Salisbury, 6 June 1952, in *Official Reports of the High Court of Southern Rhodesia*, 136–39, LHCZ.
44. "Gatooma Ordered to Grant Indian a License," *Rhodesia Herald*, 12 July 1952, NAZ.
45. "Gwanda Adamant in Refusing T.M.B.," *Rhodesia Herald*, 29 August 1952, NAZ.
46. "Amendments to License and Stamp Act," *Rhodesia Herald*, 26 September 1952, NAZ.
47. "A Warning to Shopkeepers in Southern Rhodesia," Reuters, 3 April 1958, NAUK DO 35/4739.
48. See notes section of "Africans, Asians and Coloureds in the Federal Public Service" file, 1952–1953, NAUK CO 1015/229.
49. Circular minute from H. N. Parry, Secretary, Office of the Prime Minister and External Affairs, to all Ministers and Heads of Ministries, Salisbury, 22 April 1959, NAZ F148/AGF/72/1.
50. Section 142 of Government Notice 704 of 1933, referenced in S. G. Hinde, Secretary for Local Government, to the Secretary of the Municipal Association of S. Rhodesia, Salisbury, 11 September 1959, NAUK DO 35/7635.
51. Notes of meeting held in Chief Superintendent's Office (Rhodesia Railways Limited) with representatives of the British Indian Office, 23 January 1953, personal collection of Dr. Hasu Patel.
52. Hindus, Muslims, and Jews were allocated the space of the Pioneer Cemetery in Salisbury in the 1920s to cremate and bury their dead, with Europeans and Christian Africans allocated burial spaces by their churches. When the cemetery was opened is unclear, but it was originally designated as a Commonwealth burial site for those who fought in World War I and was initially built to bury the white pioneers and soldiers of the colony.
53. See chapter 1.
54. Wiltse, *Contested Waters*, 3–6.
55. S. N. Mehta v. City of Salisbury, in *Rhodesia and Nyasaland Law Reports 1961*, 915–17, LHCZ.
56. Dr. Hasu Patel, interview by author, 25 October 2018.
57. S. N. Mehta v. City of Salisbury, in *Rhodesia and Nyasaland Law Reports 1961*, 911–12, LHCZ.
58. Natu Patel and Suman Mehta, interview.
59. Summary of judgment regarding S. N. Mehta v. City of Salisbury (1961), personal collection of Dr. Hasu Patel.
60. Deepak Mehta, interview. See also chapter 6.
61. Deepak Mehta, interview.
62. Mehta's case had the advantage of exploiting in Southern Rhodesia what John Cell termed the "constitutional ambiguity" of segregationist legislation in the

United States, an "internal contradiction" which South Africa's political system did not contain (Cell, *The Highest Stage of White Supremacy*, 250).

63. *Dawson v. Mayor City of Baltimore City*, 220 F.2d 386 (4th Circ. 1955), Casetext, https://casetext.com/case/dawson-v-mayor-city-of-baltimore-city.
64. *Holmes v. City of Atlanta*, 124 F. Supp. 290 (N.D. Ga. 1954), US District Court for the Northern District of Georgia, https://law.justia.com/cases/federal/district-courts/FSupp/124/290/1882491/.
65. Earl Warren and Supreme Court of the United States, *U.S. Reports: Brown v. Board of Education*, 347 U.S. 483 (1953), https://www.loc.gov/item/usrep347483/.
66. S. N. Mehta v. City of Salisbury, in *Rhodesia and Nyasaland Law Reports 1961*, 919–20, LHCZ.
67. S. N. Mehta v. City of Salisbury, in *Rhodesia and Nyasaland Law Reports 1961*, 921, LHCZ.
68. S. N. Mehta v. City of Salisbury, in *Rhodesia and Nyasaland Law Reports 1961*, 922–23, LHCZ.
69. S. N. Mehta v. City of Salisbury, in *Rhodesia and Nyasaland Law Reports 1961*, 925–28, LHCZ.
70. With the implementation of Federation, a Federal Supreme Court was created to oversee appeals from the High Courts of the three separate territories of Southern Rhodesia, Northern Rhodesia, and Nyasaland.
71. City of Salisbury v. S. N. Mehta, in *Rhodesia and Nyasaland Law Reports 1961*, 1000–1020, LHCZ.
72. Chamboko v. Mabelreign Town Management Board, in *Rhodesia and Nyasaland Law Reports 1962*, 450–55; Mabelreign Town Management Board v. Chamboko, in *Rhodesia and Nyasaland Law Reports 1962*, 493–501, LHCZ.
73. Mabelreign Town Management Board v. Chamboko, in *Rhodesia and Nyasaland Law Reports 1962*, 496.
74. Karekwaivanane, *The Struggle over State Power in Zimbabwe*, 142. This was a stark contrast to the legal profession in West Africa.
75. Karekwaivanane, *The Struggle over State Power in Zimbabwe*, 98.
76. Karekwaivanane, *The Struggle over State Power in Zimbabwe*, 98.
77. See letters to the editor in September 1961 and April 1962 in the *Rhodesia Herald*, microfilm no. 646, LOC.

5. "RHODESIANS FIRST, ASIANS SECOND"

1. Bhanabhai Dahyabhai Patel is the author's paternal great-grandfather.
2. Patel family tree, which is inscribed on the wall of one of the family homes in Mandir, Gujarat. Translated from Gujarati into English by the author. Women

were not included in the family tree; the author is the first woman to have her name added.
3. Asiatic Census Returns 1941, Central Statistical Office, NAZ S899/1-45.
4. Bharat Patel (author's father), interview by the author, 7 September 2018.
5. Dr. Vivek Solanki, interview by the author, 14 November 2018.
6. Bharat Patel, interview.
7. See chapter 4.
8. Monica Perales has similarly explored how Mexican American immigrants in the border town of Smeltertown in Texas navigated their geographic, racial, ethnic, political, and cultural identities over generations as both Mexican and American, identities that were not mutually exclusive and existed simultaneously, if sometimes awkwardly and with difficulty, for different groups of people at different times (Perales, *Smeltertown*).
9. Godwin and Hancock, "*Rhodesians Never Die*"; Hughes, *Whiteness in Zimbabwe*; White, *Unpopular Sovereignty*.
10. Tanser, *A Scantling of Time*.
11. Tanser, *A Scantling of Time*.
12. White, *Unpopular Sovereignty*, 10.
13. Unlike the case in Zambia, Kenya, Uganda, and Malawi, Indians in Rhodesia did not have British passports and therefore did not qualify for British residency upon "independence." Southern Rhodesia had instead created its own localized citizenship in 1949 with the Southern Rhodesia Citizenship and British Nationality Act.
14. Constitution of the Asian Association, Salisbury, 1965, personal collection of Dr. Hasu Patel.
15. Asian Association, Salisbury, to the Constitutional Commission, memorandum, August 1967, personal collection of Dr. Hasu Patel.
16. "The Younger Generation," Bulawayo Ramakrishna Youth League magazine, 32.
17. Omnia Saed, "Listen to Wells Fargo, the Revolutionary 1970s Heavy Rock Band from Zimbabwe," 3 June 2016, *OkayAfrica*, https://www.okayafrica.com/wells-fargo-heavy-rock-band-zimbabwe/.
18. Dhansuk Jamnadas Nagar, Jayanti Gosni Kanjee, Ratnaprabha Bardolia, Premlata B. Patel, and Kantilal Nathoo Lalla (Hindu Youth Movement Committee), interview by Dr. Hasu Patel, 1967–68.
19. Hindu Youth Movement Committee, interview.
20. "Family Unit," Bulawayo Ramakrishna Youth League magazine, 15.
21. Hindu Youth Movement Committee, interview.
22. The Bombay Nurses, Midwives & Health Visitors Registration Act, 1935, certificate of examining board granted to Dahiben D. Patel, 24 August 1948, author's personal collection.

23. Hansa Patel (author's mother), interview by the author, 9 April 2024.
24. Hansa Patel, interview.
25. Educated Black Africans and elite leaders of African political parties similarly dismissed "tribe" and "ethnicity" as backward precolonial conceptions.
26. "The Younger Generation," Bulawayo Ramakrishna Youth League magazine, 32.
27. "Survey," Bulawayo Ramakrishna Youth League magazine, 33–43.
28. Bharat Patel, interview.
29. Beverly Whyte, "Twilight Citizens," *Illustrated Life Rhodesia*, 18 October 1972, HSA HIS0010.
30. "Housing," Bulawayo Ramakrishna Youth League magazine, 12.
31. Whyte, "Twilight Citizens."
32. Ivaska, *Cultured States*, 2.
33. Peter Godwin and Ian Hancock justify their omission of Black Africans from their history of Rhodesia by arguing that Rhodesians themselves ignored them: "White Rhodesia is examined as a separate entity because, in the minds of nearly all its inhabitants, it existed as one" (Godwin and Hancock, "*Rhodesians Never Die*," 11).
34. Immigration Act, No. 43, 1966, *The Statute Law of Rhodesia 1966*, 424, LHCZ.
35. Land Tenure Act, No. 55, 1969, *The Statute Law of Rhodesia 1969*, 469, LHCZ.
36. Land Tenure Act, No. 55, 1969, *The Statute Law of Rhodesia 1969*, 492, LHCZ.
37. Moosa Hassan and Basheer Mahomed, interview by the author, 28 January 2019.
38. T. Patel, "Played out on the Edges of the Cricket Boundary," 475–77.
39. Rhodesia 1969 Census, Interim Report, Volume I: The European, Asian and Coloured Population (Central Statistical Office: Salisbury, 1971), NAZ RG3/STA520.
40. Despite international sanctions, Rhodesian exports of tobacco and chrome were booming, enabled by legislation in countries such as the United States, which in 1971 passed an amendment validating an exception to the embargo of Rhodesia with regard to imports of chrome ore, sponsored by Senator Harry F. Byrd Jr. of Virginia. India and Pakistan also accused the United Kingdom of consistently violating sanctions by continuing trade with Rhodesia.
41. Peter Niesewand, "Smith Move to Evict Asian 'Infiltrators,'" *The Guardian*, 13 November 1970, NAZ MS 308/54.
42. "Belvedere Residents May Back Property Bill," *Rhodesia Herald*, 1 June 1967; "Newington Hits at Indian Immigrants," *The Citizen*, 1 September 1972; LOC.
43. "Property Bill Is on the Way," *Rhodesia Herald*, 14 February 1970, LOC microfilm collection no. 646.
44. H. Patel, "Asian Political Activity in Rhodesia," 81–82.

45. Heads of Denominations Statement on Residential Property Owners (Protection) Bill 1971, sent to the editor of the *Rhodesia Herald* and the minister of Local Government and Housing, 8 February 1971, NAUK FCO36/921.
46. R. Elliott Kendall, "Rhodesia's New Housing Legislation," *Methodist Recorder*, 18 February 1971, NAUK FCO36/921.
47. Statement by the Bulawayo Asian Association, 25 August 1972, personal collection of Dr. Hasu Patel. This particular statement was a reference to Idi Amin's infamous expulsion of Asians from Uganda that year.
48. "'Dead Duck' is Now an Alderman," *Sunday Mail*, 26 August 1973, NAZ MS 308/54.
49. "Vote for Adam," published by M. A. Adam, Advocates' Chambers, Salisbury, 1963, personal collection of Dr. Hasu Patel.
50. "Vote for Ismail" postcard, Salisbury, 1971, personal collection of Dr. Hasu Patel.
51. See chapter 4.
52. Secretary, Department of Internal Affairs, to the Secretary to the Prime Minister, 5 January 1938, NAZ S262/39.
53. Notes of Mussa Essof Hassan, an Indian politician, personal collection of Dr. Hasu Patel.
54. See chapter 3.
55. Brian Raftopoulos, interview by the author, 2 October 2018.
56. Ibbo Mandaza, interview by the author, 15 October 2018.
57. Notes of Mussa Essof Hassan regarding the meeting, which took place in 1967 in Arcadia, 24 June 1970, personal collection of Dr. Hasu Patel.
58. In 1969, only one person in forty was allowed to vote, and the electorate consisted of approximately 91,000 registered voters, 81,500 of whom were white, and 6,600 African. Figures taken from P. B. Harris, "The Rhodesian Referendum: June 20th, 1969," *Parliamentary Affairs* 23 (1969): 72–80. Because the European voter roll did not disaggregate according to race between European, Asian, and Coloured, it is difficult to estimate what percentage of each of those three groups paid qualifying amounts of income tax.
59. "Cash Available to Fight Bill," *Rhodesia Herald*, 23 April 1971, NAUK FCO36/921.
60. Notes of Mussa Essof Hassan.
61. "RF Rank and File Uneasy on P.O.P. Bill," *Sunday Mail*, 23 May 1971, NAUK FCO36/921.
62. Kendall, "Rhodesia's New Housing Legislation."
63. D. J. E. Ratford, Rhodesia Political Department, to W. A. Ward Esq., Salisbury, telegram, 16 December 1971, NAUK FCO36/921.

64. Anthony Rider, "Secret Meetings Spark off Row," *"Mail" Africa Bureau*, 21 August 1974, NAZ MS308/54.
65. Dr. Hasu Patel, interview by the author, 15 November 2018.
66. ANC Press Statement by Bishop A. T. Muzorewa, President, 19 September 1974, personal collection of Dr. Hasu Patel.
67. Natu Patel and Suman Mehta, interview by Dr. Hasu Patel, 29 March 1970.
68. Notes of Mussa Essof Hassan. The Gujarati quote in this statement loosely translates as, "you grow up in your father's house, you work in your father's house," pointing toward the security that most Indians of his generation felt because their homes and incomes were guaranteed.
69. White Rhodesians referred to the conflict as the "Bush War," dismissing the legitimate political goals of the nationalists, who instead called the war the "Second Chimurenga," connecting it to the first notable rebellion, or the First Chimurenga, against British rule in 1896–97. *Chimurenga* is a Shona word which means "revolutionary struggle."
70. Secretary of Defence, Salisbury, to the Joint Asian and Coloured Community, 30 October 1973, personal collection of Dr. Hasu Patel.
71. Bharat Patel, interview.
72. Narendhra Morar, "Colour, Class and Caste in Rhodesia/Zimbabwe: My Family and Other Indians," unpublished memoir, 89.
73. Hemant Naik, interview by the author, 17 September 2018.
74. Hemant Naik, interview.
75. Norma Kriger has examined the current ruling party's efforts to mobilize political support in the countryside during the war, arguing that peasants suffered from "guerrilla coercion" rather than being willing participants in what had been portrayed as a popular rebellion. Using direct peasant voices, which she accuses older scholarship of neglecting, she suggested that peasants took part in the guerrilla war only partly to remove the policies of the white settler government. A more pressing motive for participation, she states, was the opportunity to "transform oppressive village structures" in the face of the "breakdown of law and order" (Kriger, *Zimbabwe's Guerrilla War*, 8).
76. Bharat Patel, interview.
77. ZANLA stood for the Zimbabwe African National Liberation Army. Dr. Hasu Patel, interview, 1 November 2018.
78. National Democratic Party Resolutions, 1961, NAUK DO 158/34.
79. Kriger, *Zimbabwe's Guerrilla War*, 5–7.
80. White, *Fighting and Writing*.
81. Sumant Patel, who served in the Rhodesian army, interview by the author, 29 November 2018.
82. Dr. Vivek Solanki, interview.

6. THE *KUMALOS* OF LOBENGULA STREET

1. Asiatic Schedules, Colony of Southern Rhodesia, census taken on 4 May 1926, NAZ C7/1/1-30.
2. Roberts, Letts & Gill, applicants' attorneys to the Bulawayo Municipal Council, c/o the Town Clerk, Municipal Offices, Bulawayo, 20 January 1925, NAZ-Bulawayo BLG 4/1.
3. Gunvantrai Naik (author's great-uncle), interview by the author, 27 November 2018.
4. *Kumalo*, or *Khumalo*, was the Ndebele term given to a royal. In the colonial period, the *khumalos* were given colonial authority to act as traditional leaders on behalf of the Southern Rhodesian state (see "Obituary: Mr. M. V. Naik," *Lotus* 4, no. 2 [June 1958]: 36, collection held by Hansa Naik).
5. See chapter 2.
6. Representations of female guerrilla soldiers at Heroes' Acre in Harare have been subordinated to those of their male counterparts. On one panel, a woman carries a gun, while a male soldier wields another gun at an unseen enemy while seeking blessings from the ancestors. "She carries while he wields; that is how the nation's memory was imagined" (Charumbira, *Imagining a Nation*, 221).
7. See chapter 1.
8. Scholars have recently begun to criticize narratives of this alliance for its romanticization of collaboration at the expense of the realities of friction between Black African and Indian communities. Antoinette Burton frames this tension through the hierarchical positioning of "brown over black," with Indian nationalism conscripting Africa as the lowest tier in a "hierarchy of civilizations" in the creation of a racialized and superior identity in the postcolonial world (Burton, *Africa in the Indian Imagination*, xi, 5).
9. In Kenya and South Africa, Indian political parties allied themselves with African national congresses, but they were a separate and much more visible element of anticolonialism.
10. Lobengula's father, Mzilikazi, was Shaka Zulu's lieutenant, but he left Zululand during the period of northward migrations known as the *mfecane*.
11. Ranger, *Bulawayo Burning*, 14-16.
12. Ranger, *Bulawayo Burning*, 24.
13. Ranger, *Bulawayo Burning*, 31.
14. A. S. Mlambo, "From the Second World War to UDI, 1940-1965," in *Becoming Zimbabwe*, location 2883, Kindle.
15. Mlambo, *A History of Zimbabwe*, chapter 6.
16. Meredith, *The Past Is Another Country*, 40.

17. Lan, *Guns and Rain*.
18. Raftopoulos and Mlambo, *Becoming Zimbabwe*.
19. Scarnecchia, *The Urban Roots of Democracy and Political Violence in Zimbabwe*.
20. See chapter 2.
21. Mpofu, "'Undesirable' Indians," 563.
22. H. Patel, "Changing Asian Politics." In Salisbury, Suman Mehta's seminal swimming pool challenge in the courts was part of these larger protests against discrimination (see chapter 4).
23. *Lotus* was also the name given to a later publication by the Afro-Asian Writers' Association, a tri-quarterly journal based in Cairo, whose contributors included notable African, Asian, and Middle Eastern poets from Chinua Achebe to Ghassan Kanafani. Like the editorial board of the Rhodesian version of *Lotus*, the Cairo publication condemned colonial aggression across the globe, including US involvement in Vietnam and the Israel-Palestine conflict, suggesting that the lotus was not only an Indian and Hindu symbol but one that was co-opted by those who were committed to the principles of Afro-Asian anticolonialism (see Lewis and Stolte, "Other Bandungs," 17).
24. Biography of Ramanbhai Naik, researched and edited by Marieke Faber Clarke (Oxford, 2022).
25. "Lotus Group Secretary's Report," *Lotus* 3, no. 1 (March 1957): 54.
26. Hansa Patel (née Naik, author's mother), interview by the author, 18 September 2018.
27. Biography of Ramanbhai Naik, 14.
28. Hofmeyr, *Gandhi's Printing Press*.
29. Dombo, "African Newspapers Limited," 202.
30. "Editorial," *Lotus* 1, no. 1 (March 1955): 4.
31. This rhetoric was present in many African countries as antagonism against Indians rose after independence. One example in postcolonial Zimbabwe came from a ZANU-PF politician who called for the expulsion of Indians, as had been done en masse in Uganda in previous decades (Farayi Machamire, "Zanu PF Provincial Commissar Wants Indians Expelled," *Daily News*, 20 February 2017).
32. Soske, "Navigating Difference." See also chapter 2.
33. Soske, *Internal Frontiers*, 162.
34. C. C. Ngcebetsha, "Afro-Indian Understanding," *Lotus* 1, no. 2 (June 1955): 78.
35. Ngcebetsha, "Afro-Indian Understanding," 24, 78.
36. H. Patel, "Changing Asian Politics," 14.
37. "Editorial," *Lotus* 8, no. 9 (September 1962): 1.
38. Mlambo, *A History of Zimbabwe*, 147.
39. "A Palliative," *Lotus* 8, no. 9 (September 1962): 3.

40. "Editorial," *Lotus* 8, no. 12 (December 1962): 1–2.
41. "Editorial," *Lotus* 8, no. 12.
42. Reg Austin (former member of ZAPU and lawyer), interview by the author, 2 June 2020.
43. Sumant Patel, interview by the author, 28 November 2018.
44. Ranger, *Bulawayo Burning*, 241. Today, it is rented as a Praise and Worship Centre by a church in Bulawayo, which retained the name "K. R. Vashee Hindoo Hall" as well as the building's *aumkar* symbol mounted above the front door, a monument to the interwoven histories of the city's Indian families and nationalist past.
45. Most Indian women gave birth at home because of a lack of hospital facilities for Indians and Coloureds, even in urban centers.
46. Hansa Patel, interview, 18 September 2018.
47. Sibanda, *The Zimbabwe African People's Union, 1961–87*, 121.
48. Hansa Patel, interview, 18 September 2018.
49. Colonial officials in Kenya heard similar rumors of Indian financing of Mau Mau; Sana Aiyar identified Indian families who served as middlemen supplying food to forest fighters and keeping their money safe for them in their own bank accounts (Aiyar, *Indians in Kenya*, 193–96).
50. Hansa Patel, interview, 18 September 2018.
51. Biography of Ramanbhai Naik, 19. There were about 20,000 ZIPRA insurgents based in Zambia and Malawi.
52. Biography of Ramanbhai Naik, 25. She was not Haribhai's second wife, Urmila, who migrated from India after her marriage.
53. Biography of Ramanbhai Naik, 31–34.
54. Hansa Patel, interview by the author, 9 April 2024.
55. Hansa Patel, interview, 18 September 2018. Don Naik was the only Indian member of ZAPU to marry a Black woman. The community and his family ostracized him for this decision, and he eventually ended up divorcing his wife before relocating to the United Kingdom after being released from political detention.
56. "Indian Traders in Rural Areas Criticised," *African Daily News*, 18 December 1956, LOC Newspaper 3197, Madison LM133.
57. "Byo. Asians Said to Be Practising Colour Bar," *African Daily News*, 18 December 1958, LOC Newspaper 3197.
58. Dr. Busani Mpofu, interview by the author, 12 June 2020.
59. Dr. Francis Musoni, interview by the author, 5 June 2020.
60. Shamuyarira, *Crisis in Rhodesia*, 239.
61. "Byo. Asians Said to Be Practising Colour Bar."

62. Reg Austin, interview.
63. The former headmaster of the school, Canon Dhlula, said, "I could always rely on the Asian community" (quoted in biography of Ramanbhai Naik, 12). "Bulawayo Asians Give Assistance to Jairosi Jiri," *African Daily News*, 23 December 1958, LOC, Newspaper 3197.
64. The ANC in South Africa practiced multiracialism, allowing only Black African members from 1912 until 1969 but participating in a wider alliance with other racial political parties. ZAPU, on the other hand, was nonracial in that it allowed the membership and direct participation of non-Africans (see "A Lesson in the ANC's History of Multiracialism and Non-racialism," *Daily Vox*, 3 March 2016, https://www.thedailyvox.co.za/anc-multiracialism-nonracialism-history/).
65. Reg Austin, interview. According to Austin, there were a "few white" members of ZAPU—"unfortunately very few." But ZAPU stood in stark contrast to ZANU, allowing nonracial membership including Guy Clutton-Brock and Reg Austin. Austin's wife was also a member of the party. As Austin put it many years later, "I was a member of ZAPU, not just a white supporter."
66. Vijay Patel (Kantibhai Patel's son), interview by the author, 10 October 2018.
67. Soske, *Internal Frontiers*, 2.
68. Law and Order (Maintenance) Act, in *The Statute Law of Southern Rhodesia 1960*.
69. "Amnesty International Briefing: Rhodesia/Zimbabwe," *Issue: A Journal of Opinion* 6, no. 4 (1976): 34–37; Palley, *The Constitutional History and Law of Southern Rhodesia*, 590.
70. Central Africa Department, London, to Salisbury, 29 July 1960, NAUK DO35/7600.
71. See chapter 1.
72. Hansa Patel, interview, 18 September 2018; Gunvantrai Naik, interview.
73. Deepak Mehta, interview by the author, 27 March 2018.
74. Report by John Desmond Lennett, Detective Inspector in the Criminal Investigation Department, Sinoia, 22 October 1962, NAZ S3330/1/35/19/2/2/9.
75. Ranger, *Bulawayo Burning*, 222. Translated as "God Bless Africa," the song had become a nationalist anthem throughout Southern Africa.
76. Narendhra Morar, "Colour, Class and Caste in Rhodesia/Zimbabwe: My Family and Other Indians," unpublished memoir, 91–93.
77. Ranjit Naik, interview by the author, 23 August 2018.
78. Biography of Ramanbhai Naik, 43.
79. Palley, *The Constitutional History and Law of Southern Rhodesia*, 591.
80. Biography of Ramanbhai Naik, 43.
81. Jan Marsh, "Detainees in Rhodesia," 15 February 1980, NAZ MS 734/1/1.
82. Deepak Mehta, interview.

83. Marsh, "Detainees in Rhodesia," NAZ MS 734/1/1.
84. Report of statement made by Joshua Nkomo regarding his fellow prisoner in Gonakudzingwa, Ramanbhai Naik, in the early 1960s, quoted in biography of Ramanbhai Naik, 46.
85. Margaret Mabhena, widow of John Mabhena, quoted in biography of Ramanbhai Naik, 49; biography of Ramanbhai Naik, 47.
86. Biography of Ramanbhai Naik, 51.
87. Deepak Mehta, interview.
88. Hansa Patel, interview, 9 April 2024.
89. Munochiveyi, "The Political Lives of Rhodesian Detainees," 284.
90. Munochiveyi, "The Political Lives of Rhodesian Detainees," 296.
91. Msindo, *Ethnicity in Zimbabwe*, 231.
92. Hansa Patel, interview, 18 September 2018.
93. Sifelani Tsiko, "Look East Policy Rooted in Liberation Struggle," *The Herald*, 18 April 2005, HSA POL0012-1.
94. Charumbira, *Imagining a Nation*, conclusion. There were two exceptions. The first was the burial of Amratlal Naik, who remained involved in local politics in Gwanda and later became the town's mayor. Upon his death in 2014, he was buried in the regional heroes' burial ground after his family petitioned the state to recognize his achievements. The second was Kantibhai Patel, a member of ZANU, who was buried along with white nationalist Guy Clutton-Brock in the National Heroes' Acre. But the rhetoric surrounding the declaration of their status as national heroes emphasized their exception, lauded as rare examples.
95. Hansa Patel, interview, 18 September 2018.

EPILOGUE

1. "Passengers Aboard Flight 825," *The Herald*, 4 September 1978, LOC microfilm collection no. 646.
2. "Family of Eight Wiped Out," *The Herald*, 5 September 1978, LOC microfilm collection no. 646.
3. Amrat Lalloo (relative of the deceased family), interview by the author, 11 October 2018.
4. "Terrorists Kill 10 Survivors," *The Herald*, 5 September 1978, LOC microfilm collection no. 646.
5. "Three Describe a Night of Terror," *The Herald*, 5 September 1978, LOC microfilm collection no. 646.

6. "Asian Family in Peace Plea at Funeral," *The Herald*, 11 September 1978, LOC microfilm collection no. 646.
7. Amrat Lalloo, interview.
8. Godwin and Hancock, *"Rhodesians Never Die,"* 228.
9. "Missile Was the Cause of Crash," *The Herald*, 8 September 1978, The Hunyani Disaster, Compilation of Newspaper Reports, http://www.rhodesia.nl/viscount.htm.
10. Godwin and Hancock, *"Rhodesians Never Die,"* 229.
11. "Viscount Survivors 'Were Not Raped,'" *The Herald*, 20 September 1978, LOC microfilm collection no. 646.
12. Ronald Golden, "Only One Road to Take After Air Disaster—Smith," *The Herald*, 16 September 1978, LOC microfilm collection no. 646.
13. "Plane 'Yes': Massacre 'No'—Nkomo," *The Herald*, 6 September 1978, LOC microfilm collection no. 646.
14. Sibanda, *The Zimbabwe African People's Union*, 173.
15. See Sibanda, *The Zimbabwe African People's Union*, 202; and Moorcraft and McLaughlin, *The Rhodesian War*.
16. Moorcraft and McLaughlin, *The Rhodesian War*, 243.
17. Charumbira, *Imagining a Nation*, 6–7.
18. *Contact! Contact!*, monthly publication of the Rhodesian Services Association Incorporated, http://www.rhodesianservices.org/user/image/publication10-2012.pdf.
19. "Asian Family in Peace Plea at Funeral."
20. Deepak Mehta, interview by the author, 27 March 2018.
21. Sifelani Tsiko, "Look East Policy Rooted in Liberation Struggle," *The Herald*, 18 April 2005, HSA POL0012-1.
22. Natu Patel and Suman Mehta, interview by Dr. Hasu Patel, 29 March 1970.
23. In South Africa, where Indian political participation was divided between those who collaborated with the white ruling class and those who allied with the broader politics of the African National Congress, significant numbers of Indians voted for the National Party, rather than the ANC, in the elections that took place in April 1994 (Desai and Maharaj, "Minorities in the Rainbow Nation"). While it was "impossible to isolate" the exact numbers of Indian voters from South African election data, Desai and Maharaj made use of polls conducted by national newspapers before the election and data from predominantly Indian neighborhoods to conclude that the National Party gained significant support from working-class Indians (ibid., 120). While these class divides did not exist in Rhodesia as distinctly as they did within the Indian populations of South Africa, similar voting patterns could be expected from

many Indians in Rhodesia, especially in Salisbury, where support for the Patriotic Front was limited.
24. "Great Blow to Indian Community," *The Herald*, 8 September 1978, LOC microfilm collection no. 646. Amrat Lalloo also kept every copy of *The Herald* that had articles relating to the crash and shared them with the author.
25. Amrat Lalloo, interview.
26. Notice of *havan* from Hindoo Society of Harare to author, who is a member, email, 14 September 2018.

CONCLUSION

1. Kamuben Rama, interview by the author, 5 April 2018.
2. Abigail Vera was a relative of the Bulawayo-based nationalist Jerry Vera. Graça Machel is the widow of former Mozambican president Samora Machel and former South African president Nelson Mandela.
3. Zulekha Ebrahim, interview by the author, 20 March 2018.
4. Some scholars who have contributed to the discussion and debate over the results of land reform are Chambati, "Restructuring of Agrarian Labour Relations After Fast Track Land Reform in Zimbabwe"; Magaramombe, "'Displaced in Place'"; Marongwe, "Farm Occupations and Occupiers in the New Politics of Land in Zimbabwe"; Matondi, *Zimbabwe's Fast Track Land Reform*; Rutherford, "Commercial Farm Workers and the Politics of (Dis)placement in Zimbabwe"; among others. Many of these scholars have focused on the A2 farms, which reserved the most productive and fertile sections of land for members of the political elite, rather than the land being distributed through the A1 scheme to the war veterans and small-scale farmworkers to whom it had been promised.
5. This was the date that India formally became a republic, and the date on which Indian citizenship first came into official existence.
6. The Citizenship Act, 30 December 1955, https://www.indiacode.nic.in/bitstream/123456789/15380/1/the_citizenship_act%2C_1955.pdf.
7. Secretaries of Hindoo and Islamic Societies to Cde T. Mudede, Registrar General, Harare, 31 October 2001, personal collection of Dr. Hasu Patel.
8. T. Patel, "Three Times a State, Never a Nation," 249–50.
9. Indigenisation and Economic Empowerment Act, 2007, in *The Statue Law of Zimbabwe*, 83–86, LHCZ. Bharat Patel was the architect of that particular legal definition of "indigenous" during his tenure as acting attorney general.
10. T. Patel, "Three Times a State, Never a Nation," 248–49.

11. T. Patel, "From the Subcontinent with Love."
12. Ho, *The Graves of Tarim*, 3.
13. "Death of Rao Bahadur Bhimjee R. Naik," *Rhodesia Herald*, 4 June 1942, LOC microfilm no. 646.
14. Ismail Bhika, interview by the author, 31 October 2018.
15. Pirbhai, *Mythologies of Migration, Vocabularies of Indenture*, 12.
16. Dr. Masimba Mavaza, "Hunt for Greener Pastures Creates Severe Brain Drain," *The Herald*, 25 February 2023, https://www.herald.co.zw/hunt-for-greener-pastures-creates-severe-brain-drain/.
17. Deepak Mehta, interview by the author, 27 March 2018.
18. Bharat Patel, interview by the author, 7 September 2018.
19. Their second career choice was to train as nurses.
20. Hansa Patel, interview by the author, 18 September 2018.
21. The lake has been the site of many mysterious deaths since, including the deaths of a couple, the murder of a tourist, and a suicide.

BIBLIOGRAPHY

ARCHIVES AND PRIVATE COLLECTIONS

INDIA

National Archives of India, New Delhi
Abhilek Patal, Digitized Public Records

UNITED KINGDOM

British Library, London
India Office Records

Derbyshire Records Office, Manchester
Gell Family Papers

National Archives, Kew, Richmond

Parliamentary Archives, London
Lloyd George Papers

UNITED STATES

Library of Congress, Washington, DC
James Madison Memorial Building, Newspaper and Current Periodical Research Center

ZIMBABWE

Bulawayo National Archives, Bulawayo
Hindu Society Archive, Harare
National Archives of Zimbabwe, Harare
Private collection of Dr. Hasu Patel, Harare
Pioneer Cemetery

ORAL HISTORIES

BULAWAYO
Vijay Mehta
Gunvantrai Naik
Sumant Patel

HARARE
Yusuf Adam
Mahomed Basheer
Jasu Bhagat
Ismail Bhika
Ahamed Ebrahim
Zulekha Ebrahim
Muhamod Ebrahim-Patel
Moosa Hassan
George Kahari
Amrat Lalloo
Ibbo Mandaza

Deepak Mehta
Hemant Naik
Tara Naik
Bharat Patel
Hansa Patel
Hasu Patel
Vijay Patel
Kamla Rama
Vivek Solanki

UK

Ranjit Naik

VIRTUAL

Reg Austin
Busani Mpofu
Francis Musoni
Brian Raftopoulos

OTHER SOURCES

Aiyar, Sana. "Anticolonial Homelands Across the Indian Ocean: The Politics of the Indian Diaspora in Kenya, ca. 1930–1950." *American Historical Review* 116, no. 4 (2011): 987–1013.

Aiyar, Sana. *Indians in Kenya: The Politics of Diaspora*. Harvard University Press, 2015.

Bahadur, Gaiutra. *Coolie Woman: The Odyssey of Indenture*. University of Chicago Press, 2013.

Bald, Vivek. *Bengali Harlem and the Lost Histories of South Asian America*. Harvard University Press, 2013.

Barrier, N. G. *The Census in British India: New Perspectives*. Manohar, 1981.

Bertz, Ned. *Diaspora and Nation in the Indian Ocean: Transnational Histories of Race and Urban Space in Tanzania*. University of Hawai'i Press, 2015.

Biko, Steve. *I Write What I Like: Selected Writings*. University of Chicago Press, 1978.

Bishi, George. "Immigration and Settlement of 'Undesirable' Whites in Southern Rhodesia, c. 1940s–1960s." In *Rethinking White Societies in Southern Africa, 1930s-1990s*, edited by Duncan Money and Danelle van-Zyl Hermann, 59–77. Routledge, 2020.

Blyth, Robert J. *The Empire of the Raj: India, Eastern Africa and the Middle East, 1858–1947*. Palgrave Macmillan, 2003.

Brennan, James. *Taifa: Making Nation and Race in Urban Tanzania*. Ohio University Press, 2012.

Brownell, Josiah. *The Collapse of Rhodesia: Population Demographics and the Politics of Race*. I. B. Tauris, 2011.

Burke, Timothy. *Lifebuoy Men, Lux Women: Commodification, Consumption, and Cleanliness in Modern Zimbabwe*. Duke University Press, 1996.

Burton, Antoinette. *Africa in the Indian Imagination: Race and the Politics of Postcolonial Citation*. Duke University Press, 2016.

Cell, John W. *The Highest Stage of White Supremacy: The Origins of Segregation in South Africa and the American South*. Cambridge University Press, 1982.

Chambati, W. "Restructuring of Agrarian Labour Relations After Fast Track Land Reform in Zimbabwe." *Journal of Peasant Studies* 38l, no. 5 (2011): 1047–68.

Chanock, Martin. *Law, Custom and Social Order: The Colonial Experience in Malawi and Zambia*. Cambridge University Press, 1985.

Charumbira, Ruramisai. *Imagining a Nation: History and Memory in Making Zimbabwe*. University of Virginia Press, 2015.

Chatterjee, Indrani, ed. *Unfamiliar Relations: Family and History in South Asia*. Rutgers University Press, 2004.

Clements, Frank. *This Is Our Land*. Baobab Books, 1963.

Cohn, Bernard. *Colonialism and Its Forms of Knowledge: The British in India*. Princeton University Press, 1996.

Connelly, Nancy. "Temporary Middlemen: Hindu and Moslem Asians in Bulawayo." PhD diss., Dedman College, 1983.

Desai, Ashwin. *Arise Ye Coolies: Apartheid and the Indian, 1960–1995*. Impact Africa, 1996.

Desai, Ashwin, and Brij Maharaj. "Minorities in the Rainbow Nation: The Indian Vote in 1994." *South African Journal of Sociology* 24, no. 4 (1996): 118–25.

Desai, Ashwin, and Goolam Vahed. *Inside Indian Indenture: A South African Story, 1860–1914*. HSRC, 2010.

Dirks, Nicholas B. *Castes of Mind: Colonialism and the Making of Modern India*. Princeton University Press, 2001.

Dombo, Sylvester. "African Newspapers Limited and the Growth of Newspapers for Africans in Southern Rhodesia." *Media History* 25, no. 2 (2019): 183–207.

Dotson, Floyd, and Lillian O. Dotson. *The Indian Minority of Zambia, Rhodesia, and Malawi.* Yale University Press, 1968.

Duff, S. E. *Childhood and Youth in African History.* Palgrave Macmillan, 2022.

Elkins, Caroline. *Legacy of Violence: A History of the British Empire.* Alfred A. Knopf, 2022.

Godwin, Peter, and Ian Hancock. *"Rhodesians Never Die": The Impact of War and Political Change on White Rhodesia, c. 1970–1980.* Oxford University Press, 1993.

Hall, Bruce. *A History of Race in Muslim West Africa, 1600–1960.* Cambridge University Press, 2011.

Heuberger, Gretchen. "Transnational Belonging: The Effects of the Independence and Partition of India on the Indo-African Diaspora." *Columbia Undergraduate Journal of South Asian Studies* 1, no. 2 (2010): 75–90.

Ho, Engseng. *The Graves of Tarim: Genealogy and Mobility Across the Indian Ocean.* University of California Press, 2006.

Hofmeyr, Isabel. "The Complicating Sea: Indian Ocean as Method." *Comparative Studies of South Asia, Africa and the Middle East* 32, no. 3 (2012): 584–90.

Hofmeyr, Isabel. *Gandhi's Printing Press: Experiments in Slow Reading.* Harvard University Press, 2013.

Hughes, David M. *Whiteness in Zimbabwe: Race, Landscape, and the Problem of Belonging.* Palgrave Macmillan, 2010.

Ivaska, Andrew. *Cultured States: Youth, Gender and Modern Style in 1960s Dar es Salaam.* Duke University Press, 2011.

Kalshekar, Ali. "1908 Asiatics Ordinance in Perspective." Lecture, Henderson Seminar, University of Rhodesia, 1974.

Karekwaivanane, George Hamandishe. *The Struggle Over State Power in Zimbabwe: Law and Politics Since 1950.* Cambridge University Press, 2017.

Koshy, Susan, and R. Radhakrishnan, eds. *Transnational South Asians: The Making of a Neo-Diaspora.* Oxford University Press, 2008.

Kosmin, Barry Alexander. "Ethnic and Commercial Relations in Southern Rhodesia: A Socio-Historical Study of the Asian, Hellene, and Jewish Populations, 1898–1943." PhD diss., University of Rhodesia, 1974.

Kriger, Norma J. *Zimbabwe's Guerrilla War: Peasant Voices.* Cambridge University Press, 1991.

Kwarteng, Kwasi. *Ghosts of Empire: Britain's Legacies in the Modern World.* Public Affairs, 2011.

Lan, David. *Guns and Rain: Guerrillas and Spirit Mediums in Zimbabwe.* James Currey, 1985.

Lewis, Su Lin, and Carolien Stolte. "Other Bandungs: Afro-Asian Internationalism in the Early Cold War." *Journal of World History* 30, nos. 1–2 (2019): 1–20.

Machado, Pedro. *Ocean of Trade: South Asian Merchants, Africa and the Indian Ocean, c. 1750–1850.* Cambridge University Press, 2014.

Magaramombe, G. "'Displaced in Place': Agrarian Displacements, Replacements and Resettlement Among Farm Workers in Mazowe District." *Journal of Southern African Studies* 36, no. 2 (2010): 361–75.

Mamdani, Mahmood. *Citizen and Subject: Contemporary Africa and the Legacy of Late Colonialism.* Princeton University Press, 1996.

Mandaza, Ibbo. *Race, Colour and Class in Southern Africa.* Sapes Books, 1997.

Mann, Kristin, and Richard L. Roberts, eds. *Law in Colonial Africa.* Heinemann, 1991.

Marongwe, N. "Farm Occupations and Occupiers in the New Politics of Land in Zimbabwe." In *Zimbabwe's Unfinished Business: Rethinking Land, State and Nation in the Context of Crisis,* edited by A. Hammar, B. Raftopoulos, and S. Jensen, 155–90. Weaver, 2003.

Matondi, P. *Zimbabwe's Fast Track Land Reform.* Zed Books, 2012.

Mbembe, Achille. "The Power of the Archive and Its Limits." In *Refiguring the Archive,* edited by C. Hamilton, V. Harris, J. Taylor, M. Pickover, G. Reid, and R. Saleh, 19–27. Springer, 2002.

Mbembe, Achille, and Sarah Balakrishnan. "Pan-African Legacies, Afropolitan Futures." *Transition* 120 (2016): 28–37.

McKittrick, Meredith. *To Dwell Secure: Generation, Christianity, and Colonialism in Ovamboland, Northern Namibia.* Heinemann, 2002.

Meredith, Martin. *The Past Is Another Country: Rhodesia, UDI to Zimbabwe.* Pan Books, 1979.

Metcalf, Barbara, and Thomas R. Metcalf. *A Concise History of Modern India.* Cambridge University Press, 2001.

Metcalf, Thomas R. *Imperial Connections: India in the Indian Ocean Arena, 1860–1920.* University of California Press, 2007.

Mitra, Durba. *Indian Sex Life: Sexuality and the Colonial Origins of Modern Social Thought.* Princeton University Press, 2020.

Mlambo, Alois. *A History of Zimbabwe.* Cambridge University Press, 2014.

Moorcraft, Paul, and Peter McLaughlin. *The Rhodesian War: A Military History.* Pen and Sword Books, 2008.

Mpofu, Busani. "'Undesirable' Indians, Residential Segregation and the Ill-Fated Rise of the White 'Housing Covenanters' in Bulawayo, Colonial Zimbabwe, 1930–1973." *South African Historical Journal* 63, no. 4 (2011): 553–80.

Msindo, Enocent. *Ethnicity in Zimbabwe: Transformations in Kalanga and Ndebele Societies, 1860–1990.* University of Rochester Press, 2012.

Munochiveyi, Munyaradzi Bryn. "The Political Lives of Rhodesian Detainees During Zimbabwe's Liberation Struggle," *International Journal of African Historical Studies* 46, no. 2 (2013): 283–304.

Mushonga, Munyaradzi. "White Power, White Desire: Miscegenation in Southern Rhodesia, Zimbabwe." *African Journal of History and Culture* 5, no. 1 (2013): 1–12.

Musoni, Francis. "Contested Foreignness: Indian Migrants and the Politics of Exclusion in Early Colonial Zimbabwe, 1890 to 1923." *African and Asian Studies* (2017): 312–35.

Muzondidya, James. *Walking a Tightrope: Towards a Social History of the Coloured Community of Zimbabwe*. Africa World Press, 2005.

Nandy, Ashis. *The Intimate Enemy: Loss and Recovery of Self Under Colonialism*. Oxford University Press, 1983.

Nkomo, Joshua. *The Story of My Life*. Methuen, 1984.

Oonk, Gijsbert. *Global Indian Diasporas*. Amsterdam University Press, 2007.

O'Sullivan, Michael. *No Birds of Passage: A History of Gujarati Muslim Business Communities, 1800–1975*. Harvard University Press, 2023.

Palley, Claire. *The Constitutional History and Law of Southern Rhodesia 1888–1965*. Clarendon Press, 1966.

Patel, Hasu. "Asian Political Activity in Rhodesia from the Second World War to 1972." *Rhodesian History*, no. 9 (1978): 63–82.

Patel, Hasu. "Changing Asian Politics." *Central African Examiner* 4, no. 7 (1960).

Patel, Trishula. "From the Subcontinent with Love: India and Activist Diplomacy in 20th Century Central Africa." *Comparative Studies of South Asia, Africa, and the Middle East* 41, no. 3 (2021): 455–68.

Patel, Trishula. "Played out on the Edges of the Cricket Boundary: The History of an Indian Cricket Team in Rhodesia/Zimbabwe, 1934–1995." *Journal of Southern African Studies* 45, no. 3 (2019): 465–83.

Patel, Trishula. "Three Times a State, Never a Nation: Indians in Rhodesia/Zimbabwe." In *Xenophobia, Nativism, and Pan-Africanism in 21st Century Africa*, edited by Sabella Abidde and Emmanuel Matambo, 233–53. Springer, 2021.

Pearson, Michael. *Port Cities and Intruders: The Swahili Coast, India, and Portugal in the Early Modern Era*. Johns Hopkins University Press, 1998.

Perales, Monica. *Smeltertown: Making and Remembering a Southwest Border Community*. University of North Carolina Press, 2010.

Pirbhai, Miriam. *Mythologies of Migration, Vocabularies of Indenture: Novels of the South Asian Diaspora in Africa, the Caribbean, and Asia-Pacific*. University of Toronto Press, 2009.

Prashad, Vijay. "The *Desi* Diaspora: Politics, Protest, and Nationalism." In *India and the British Empire*, edited by Douglas M. Peers and Nandini Gooptu, 313–33. Oxford University Press, 2012.

Raftopoulos, Brian, and Alois Mlambo, eds. *Becoming Zimbabwe: A History from the Pre-Colonial Period to 2008*. Weaver, 2009.

Rajyagor, S. B. *History of Gujarat*. S. Chand, 1982.

Ranger, Terence. *Bulawayo Burning: A Social History of a Southern African City, 1893–1960.* Weaver, 2010.

Ranger, Terence. "The Invention of Tradition in Colonial Africa." In *The Invention of Tradition,* edited by Eric Hobsbawm and Terence Ranger, 211–62. Cambridge University Press, 1983.

Ranger, Terence. "The Invention of Tradition Revisited: The Case of Colonial Africa." In *Legitimacy and the State in Twentieth Century Africa,* edited by Terence Ranger and Olufemi Vaughan, 62–111. Palgrave Macmillan, 1993.

Ranger, Terence. "Nationalist Historiography, Patriotic History and the History of the Nation: The Struggle over the Past in Zimbabwe." *Journal of Southern African Studies* 30, no. 2 (2004): 215–34.

Robertson, Wilfrid. *Rhodesian Rancher.* Blackie and Son, 1935.

Rutherford, B. A. "Commercial Farm Workers and the Politics of (Dis)placement in Zimbabwe: Colonialism, Liberation and Democracy." *Journal of Agrarian Change* 1, no. 4 (2001): 626–51.

Safran, William. "Diasporas in Modern Societies: Myths of Homeland and Return." *Diaspora* 1, no. 1 (1991): 83–99.

Scarnecchia, Timothy. *The Urban Roots of Democracy and Political Violence in Zimbabwe: Harare and Highfield, 1940–1960.* University of Rochester Press, 2008.

Shamuyarira, Nathan. *Crisis in Rhodesia.* A. Deutsch, 1965.

Shankar, Shobana. *An Uneasy Embrace: Africa, India and the Spectre of Race.* Oxford University Press, 2021.

Sharafi, Mitra. *Law and Identity in Colonial South Asia: Parsi Legal Culture, 1722–1947.* Cambridge University Press, 2014.

Sibanda, Eliakim. *The Zimbabwe African People's Union, 1961–87: A Political History of Insurgency in Southern Rhodesia.* Africa World Press, 2005.

Sinha, Mrinalini. *Specters of Mother India.* Duke University Press, 2006.

Smith, Jean P. *Settlers at the End of Empire: Race and the Politics of Migration in South Africa, Rhodesia and the United Kingdom.* Manchester University Press, 2022.

Soske, Jon. *Internal Frontiers: African Nationalism and the Indian Diaspora in Twentieth-Century South Africa.* Ohio University Press, 2017.

Soske, Jon. "Navigating Difference: Gender, Miscegenation and Indian Domestic Space in Twentieth-Century Durban." In *Eyes Across the Water: Navigating the Indian Ocean,* edited by Pamila Gupta, Isabel Hofmeyr, and Michael Pearson, 197–219. University of South Africa Press, 2010.

Soske, Jon. "'Wash Me Black Again': African Nationalism, the Indian Diaspora, and Kwa-Zulu Natal, 1944–1960." PhD diss., University of Toronto, 2009.

Spear, Thomas. "Neo-Traditionalism and the Limits of Invention in British Colonial Africa." *Journal of African History* 44, no. 1 (2003): 3–27.

Stoler, Ann Laura. *Along the Archival Grain: Epistemic Anxieties and Colonial Common Sense.* Princeton University Press, 2010.

Subramaniam, Narendra. "Making Family and Nation: Hindu Marriage Law in Early Postcolonial India." *Journal of Asian Studies* 69, no. 3 (2010): 771–98.

Suzuki, Yuka. *The Nature of Whiteness: Race, Animals, and Nation in Zimbabwe.* University of Washington Press, 2017.

Tallie, T. J. *Queering Colonial Natal: Indigeneity and the Violence of Belonging in Southern Africa.* University of Minnesota Press, 2019.

Tanser, G. H. *A Scantling of Time: The Story of Salisbury, Rhodesia 1890–1900.* Stuart Manning, 1965.

Thomas, Lynn. *Politics of the Womb: Women, Reproduction, and the State in Kenya.* University of California Press, 2003.

Vahed, Goolam, and Surendra Bhana. *Crossing Space and Time in the Indian Ocean: Early Indian Traders in Natal, A Biographical Study.* Unisa, 2015.

van Onselen, Charles. *Chibaro: African Mine Labour in Southern Rhodesia, 1900–1933.* Pluto, 1976.

Vansina, Jan. *Oral Tradition as History.* University of Wisconsin Press, 1985.

Vassanji, M. G. *The In-Between World of Vikram Lall.* Alfred A. Knopf, 2004.

Verheul, Susanne. *Performing Power in Zimbabwe: Politics, Law, and the Courts Since 2000.* Cambridge University Press, 2021.

Waller, Richard. "Legal History and Historiography in Colonial Sub-Saharan Africa." *Oxford Research Encyclopedias, African History* (2018).

West, Michael O. *The Rise of an African Middle Class: Colonial Zimbabwe, 1898–1965.* Indiana University Press, 2002.

White, Luise. *The Comforts of Home: Prostitution in Colonial Nairobi.* University of Chicago Press, 1990.

White, Luise. *Fighting and Writing: The Rhodesian Army at War and Postwar.* Duke University Press, 2021.

White, Luise. *Unpopular Sovereignty: Rhodesian Independence and African Decolonization.* University of Chicago Press, 2015.

Wiltse, Jeff. *Contested Waters: A Social History of Swimming Pools in America.* University of North Carolina Press, 2007.

Wood, J. R. T. "The Reaction to Asian Migration on the Eve of Federation in British Central Africa: Gleanings from the Welensky Papers." *Journal of Contemporary African Studies* 1, no. 2 (1982): 329–38.

Yengde, Suraj. *Caste Matters.* Penguin Random House, 2019.

INDEX

Italicized page numbers refer to illustrations.

Adam, Mahomed Ali, 109, 127
Africa and Africans: Africanization, 6 (*see also* indigeneity: indigenization); Black, 3, 5, 7, 9–15, 17–18, 22, 25, 29–30, 35, 40–43, 44–56, 61–63, 65–67, 69, 72–73, 79, 82, 88–89, 93–96, 100–101, 103–9, 115–16, 119, 124, 126–29, 134, 139–41, 144–61, 165–67, 169–70, 172–75, 191n74, 202n25, 202n33, 205n8, 208n64 (*see also* indigeneity; native); history, 6, 9, 11–13, 30, 117, 172, 176; identity, 3, 6, 8–13, 47, 86, 89, 172, 176; institutions, 3, 5–6, 8, 14, 177; non-Africans, 54, 63, 76, 86, 99, 126, 208n64
African National Congress (ANC) in South Africa, 208n64, 210n23
African National Council (ANC) in Rhodesia, 130, 166
Afrikaners, 31, 34–35
Afrikaans, 61
Afro-Asian collaboration and solidarity, 12, 17, 141, 146, 148, 152
Afropolitanism, 9
alcohol, 55–56, 63, 122, 159
"alien" groups, 5, 10, 62, 64, 124–26, 142, 171, 175
amenities, public, 92, 101, 103–4, 106, 108, 126–27
Amin, Idi, 127, 203n47
ancestors, 2, 5, 8, 17, 18, 22–25, 32, 117, 133, 141, 143, 176–77, 184n10, 198n33, 205n6
Anglo-Boer War, 40
anticolonialism. *See* colonialism

apartheid, 10, 14, 92, 124, 126, 129, 183n23. *See also* South Africa
Arabic, 77, 177
Arcadia, 76, 85, 105, 107
army, Rhodesian, 2, 17, 115, 132–34, 167, 174, 177, 178
arrests, 1, 7, 37, 155–57, 160–61, 168, 172. *See also* detention
Asians: as colonial racial category, 4, 11, 17, 21, 23, 31, 33, 38, 46, 48, 50–52, 56–57, 63, 65–66, 75, 77, 79–81, 85, 90, 95, 98–99, 104–5, 107–8, 115, 117–18, 126–32, 134, 144, 147–48, 152–54, 157–58, 164, 178; education of, 76–78, 80; labor of, 40; neighborhoods, 125
Asian Association, 91, 95, 117–18, 127
Asiatics. *See* Asians
Asiatics Ordinance of 1908, 38–39, 41
Atlantic Ocean, 92, 104, 106

Banda, Hastings, 152
banyans, 21, 36–37, 186n59
Beadle, Hugh, 106–9
Bechuanaland. *See* Botswana
Beira, 21, 28–31, 36
belonging, 2–3, 5–11, 15–17, 22–24, 29–32, 35–36, 38–39, 41–43, 47, 66–67, 75, 81–82, 89, 92–93, 101, 110–11, 114–15, 118, 122, 124, 139–41, 143, 146, 169, 173, 175–77
Belvedere, 125
Bengal, 25, 66
Biko, Steve, 10
Bindura, 102–3
Bombay, 21, 25–26, 27, 28, 64, 66, 93, 137, 184n21, 191n80
Botswana, 24, 132, 182n10

brahmin: Brahminic ideology, 16, 70; priestly caste, 70, 73, 75
Britain and the British, 34, 40, 115, 133; colonialism, 29, 204n69; identity, 42, 64; indirect rule, 94; music, 118; nationality, 192n84, 201n13; government, 25, 40–41, 166; settlers, 4, 24, 35, 189n40; subjects, 39, 64. *See also* British Empire; England; United Kingdom
British Empire, 12, 19, 23–24, 29–31, 38–39, 49, 82, 117, 145, 185n25
British Indian Association, 39, 56
British Indians, 28, 35, 38–39, 41, 63–66
British Protected Persons, 65
British Raj, 27, 39–40, 196n4. *See also* India
British South Africa Company (BSAC), 3, 21, 23, 48, 173, 184n10
Bulawayo, 3, 7, 17, 20, 31, 39, 44, 47, 48, 51, 54, 55–57, 59, 60, 68, 71, 72, 74–75, 76, 81, 85, 88, 97, 103, 111, 113, 116, 121, 125, 132, 135–36, 137–39, 141–46, 148, 148–54, 156, 159, 161, 163–65, 167, 170, 174, 176, 179, 183n36
Bulawayo Indian School, 78, 80
businesses, 1, 2, 7–8, 17, 18, 22, 29, 32–38, 42, 45–48, 52, 55, 58, 60–62, 64, 67, 68, 70–72, 77, 83, 86, 91, 93–103, 113, 115, 117, 120, 131, 137–38, 142, 150–51, 153–54, 156–57, 159, 161, 168, 172, 175, 177, 178, 179. *See also dukkan*; shops; stores; trading

Cameron Street, 57, 72
Cape Colony, 40
caste, 5, 7, 12–16, 33, 46, 66–67, 69–71, 73–76, 78–82, 88–89, 112, 121–22,

125, 153, 173, 176, 178, 183n1, 186n59, 193n22; *jati*, 73, 79; lower, 69, 73, 76, 143; *mandal*, 71, 73–76, 79, 82; upper, 45, 69, 73, 75, 76, 77, 79–80, 87, 89, 143, 153, 158–59, 198n33; *varna*, 73
census, 15, 20, 39, 46, 54, 62–67, 75
Central Africa, 3, 5, 96, 151
Central African Asian Conference, 96
Central Baths, 90, 101, 105, 107
Charter Road, 47, 56–57, 73
chilapalapa, 61, 72
childhood, 80, 179, 192n6, 196n82
Chimurenga: First, 184n10; Second, 131–32, 184n10, 204n69
China, 160
Chinamano, Josiah, 157
Chinamano, Ruth, 157
Chinhoyi, 156
Chipinge, 1
Chitepo, Herbert, 109
Christians, 98, 100. *See also* Roman Catholics
citizens, 8, 30, 53, 92–95, 98, 101, 105–8, 110, 112, 117, 126–27, 166, 168–69, 175, 185n37, 196n4, 197n7; citizenship, 6, 10–11, 41, 115, 133, 168, 175–76, 191n83, 192n84, 201n13, 211n5. *See also* subjects
Citizenship Act of India of 1955, 175
Citizenship of Zimbabwe Act of 2001, 175
civilization, 6, 8, 10, 24, 42–43, 61, 69, 79, 81, 117
Civil Rights League, 144
class, 6, 13, 46, 51, 56–57, 61, 77, 80, 87, 89, 93, 104, 121, 125, 127–29, 133; hierarchy, 75–76, 126, 153, 176–77; lower, 35, 61, 66–67, 70, 74, 143, 145; middle, 5, 52, 104, 116, 120, 131;

mobility, 17, 115, 178; second-, 53, 95, 106–7; working, 143, 210n23
colonialism: administration, bureaucracy, government, state, and system, 2, 7, 10, 15–16, 19, 25, 29, 39, 46–46, 53, 55, 60, 62, 65, 67, 69, 71, 76–77, 81–82, 85–86, 88–89, 94, 110, 142, 159, 182n10, 182n12, 192n6, 205n4, 207n49; anticolonialism, 5, 9, 11, 139–41, 155, 169, 174; commonwealth, 40; constitution, 106; diaspora, 110; economy, 29, 189n40; education, 70, 76, 78, 82, 85, 88, 173, 195n58; experience, 8, 10, 12, 61, 65; gender ideology, 56, 63, 97, 189n32; identity, 39, 66, 89; knowledge, 71, 92, 94; law, legislation, policy, and regulation, 37, 41, 70, 80, 89, 91–92, 95, 99–100, 109, 173, 192n9, 194n40, 197n8, 198n34; modernity, 5, 49, 61; narrative, 20, 116, 142–43; origin, 42, 141; period, 73–74, 154; postcolonial, 4, 6, 9, 11, 98, 116, 130, 131, 134–35, 140, 145, 149, 155, 159–60, 168, 171, 172, 174, 177, 178–79, 182n10, 182n12, 198n34, 208n8; precolonial, 4, 18, 24, 49, 61, 75, 146, 202n25; project, 8–9, 11–12, 20, 22, 62, 148, 174; racial category, ideology, and hierarchy, 4, 7–8, 10, 13, 35, 46, 66, 74–76, 79, 84, 139, 146, 153, 157, 182n18; settler colonialism, 12–15, 18, 23, 29–30, 40–41, 45, 52, 62, 173; society, 45, 77, 118, 146; space, 34, 38, 69, 70, 89, 143, 149; subject, 64; urbanity, 5, 173, 191n74; village network, 28; violence, 29, 206n23. *See also* imperialism
Colonial Office, 41

colonization, 10, 12, 15, 18, 20, 24, 43, 95, 172, 175, 184n8; decolonization, 6, 8, 10, 18, 135, 155

colonized, the, 12, 13, 15, 18, 20, 23–24, 30, 40, 43, 62, 71, 88, 92, 95, 124, 172, 175, 184n8

colonies, 3, 5, 12, 21, 26, 32–33, 36, 38, 40–42, 46–47, 54, 56, 63–64, 67, 73, 76, 78, 80, 82, 88, 96–99, 128, 177, 184n21, 192n84, 196n4, 197n7, 199n52; Crown, 41; self-governing, 3, 30, 41–42, 54, 72, 95; settler, 4, 23, 124

Coloured people, 10, 13, 35, 46–47, 48, 50, 53, 54–55, 63, 65–67, 69, 73, 75–77, 79–82, 84–85, 89, 96, 104–5, 107, 115, 124, 126, 128–30, 131–34, 154, 157, 158, 173, 177, 192n88, 193n29, 195n58, 203n58, 207n45

Commonwealth, the, 31, 40, 199n52

communalism, 13, 67, 69–70, 75–76, 81, 87–88, 91, 144

consumers. *See* customers

"coolies," 37, 38

councils, 55; city, 94; Gatooma Town Council, 103; Indian Women's Council, 146; Legislative Council, 30, 35; local, 92, 104, 110, 127; municipal, 91, 115; Order in Council, 40; Salisbury City Council, 129; school, 84; urban, 20

courts, 16, 20, 88–89, 91, 92, 99, 103, 105, 110–11, 115, 127, 132, 173, 178, 224n22; Constitutional Court of Zimbabwe, 178; Federal Supreme Court, 108–9; High Court, 87, 91, 93, 99, 100, 101–2, 105–9, 198n37; Master of the High Court, 93, 100; Supreme Court of the United States, 92, 106

customers, 5–6, 8, 15, 33, 35, 44–45, 49, 51, 53–55, 58, 60–62, 69, 72, 113, 133, 137–39, 144, 149–50, 152–54, 160, 172

Dabengwa, Dumiso, 152

Dalit, 69, 75

decolonization. *See* colonization

Delhi, 20

descendants, 1, 4, 6, 11–12, 17–18, 22, 32, 48, 73, 75, 112, 135, 141, 175, 193n29

detention, 1, 137, 140, 152, 155–60, 168, 207n55. *See also* arrests

Dharmaj, 26, 31, 47, 155

dhobi, 33, 74

diaspora, 3, 6, 9–10, 13–14, 23, 40, 42, 70, 74, 101, 110, 135, 145, 167, 169, 172, 176, 177, 184n9, 194n51; South Asian diaspora in Africa, 6, 9, 13–14, 23

discrimination, 6, 39–41, 42, 82, 90, 95–96, 102–10, 123, 130, 154, 175, 206n22

domesticity, 2, 5–6, 12–17, 46–47, 53, 60–61, 67, 69–72, 75, 82–84, 86, 88–89, 91–92, 94–97, 99, 109–10, 114, 122, 125, 135, 140–41, 145, 146–47, 152–54, 164, 172, 197n8, 198n34

domestic workers. *See* servants

Dominions Office, 38

dukkan, 2–3, 5–8, 14, 15, 17, 22, 29, 33–34, 39, 43, 46, 60, 64, 67, 69, 73, 76–77, 79–80, 82, 86–87, 89, 91–93, 94, 96, 98, 100, 106, 110, 114–15, 118–20, 122, 125, 128, 131–32, 135, 139–41, 147–48, 149, 152, 155–57, 159, 161, 164, 172–74, 177, 178. *See also* businesses; shops; stores

Durban, 145, 191n74

East Africa, 4, 5, 25, 28, 71, 146, 181n3, 182n11, 193n9
education, 16, 20, 26, 35, 47, 56, 61, 63, 69, 70, 72, 74–75, 77–78, 80, 82, 86, 88–89, 96, 114, 118, 119–23, 127, 128, 135, 144–45, 152, 159, 173, 174, 177, 179, 202n25; Department of Education, 68, 75, 77–78, 83–85; institutions, 15, 56, 77; policy, 70–71, 76, 79; Quranic, 78. *See also* schools
Education Act of 1930, 76, 87
Education Ordinance of 1899, 76
elections, 41, 103, 111, 126–30, 147–48, 155, 159, 166–67, 197n15, 203n58, 210n23. *See also* voting
elite, 10, 41, 43, 45–46, 50, 55, 61, 67, 69–70, 76, 78–80, 84, 86, 89, 95, 104, 111, 138–39, 144–46, 152, 173, 189n35, 193n29, 198n33, 202n25, 211n4
endogamy, 5–6, 12, 23, 69, 72—74, 76, 80, 121, 141, 153, 178. *See also* kinship; marriage
England, 25, 38, 112, 117, 127, 135, 149. *See also* Britain and the British; United Kingdom
English: language, 26, 31, 32–33, 35, 42, 61, 72, 77, 150, 152, 177, 200n2; law, 94; origin, 35, 118, 120; people, 42. *See also* Britain and the British
ethnicity, 9–10, 34, 73, 140, 142–43, 201n8, 202n25
Europe and Europeans: countries, 34; culture, 113; imperialism, 25; language, 31, 33; origin, 193n29; population, 4–5, 16, 21–22, 25, 34, 37, 42, 48, 50, 62–65, 72, 76–79, 94–98, 100, 101, 103–9, 112, 123, 125, 148, 153, 166, 172, 185n37, 197n22, 199n52, 203n58; schools, 84; space, 57, 115, 123, 124, 126, 129–32, 142; traders, 52–53, 189n40. *See also* whites

farming: community, 25, 181; farms, 4, 43, 51, 54, 113, 134; farmers, 5, 26, 33, 44–45, 48, 112, 166, 172, 174; industry, 49, 75; markets, 5, 33, 45, 48–49; pastoral, 73. *See also* gardens, market
fast-track land reform, 5, 174, 211n4
Federation of Rhodesia and Nyasaland, 3, 92–93, 95–99, 103, 108, 111, 117–18, 126, 147
females, 119–20; ancestral spirits, 184n10; Black, 51; children, 70, 83, 122–23; family members, 140; guerrillas, 205n6; labor and workers, 34, 46; migrants, 76; sexual purity, 119, 153. *See also* women
Founders High School, 85

Gandhi, Indira, 171
Gandhi, Mohandas, 40, 184n21
gardeners, 48, 50, 64, 72
gardens, market, 5, 33, 45, 47, 54–55, 64. *See also* farming
Gatooma. *See* Kadoma
gender, 6, 8, 13–14, 22, 29, 51, 70–71, 73, 75, 81–82, 85, 89, 91, 99, 108, 165, 173, 176, 189n32; anxieties about, 50, 172; colonial ideas of, 34, 56, 80, 98, 182n10, 184n8; equality, 120; labor, 46, 152; roles, 7, 15, 16, 87, 114
general dealers, 45, 47, 102–3, 112–13, 125, 137. *See also* hawkers; traders

generations, 2–3, 7–8, 11, 13–14, 16, 18, 22, 24, 34, 38, 42, 45–46, 63–67, 69–71, 73, 76, 80–83, 85–86, 89, 91, 93–94, 96, 110, 112–15, 118–19, 121–22, 127, 131, 135, 139, 172–74, 176–78, 192n6, 193n29, 195n57, 196n82, 201n8; transgenerational, 18
Global South, 17, 19, 141
Goa, 4; Goan, 77, 83
gold, 4, 23, 24, 26, 29, 44, 47–48, 112, 142
Gonakudzingwa, 140, 155, 157–59
Greeks, 34–35, 189n40
Grey Street, 57
guerrillas, 17, 115, 131–34, 138, 141, 142–43, 160, 163, 166, 169, 184n10, 204n75, 205n6
Gujarat: Gujarati culture, 51, 72, 122; Gujarati identity and origin, 14, 21; Gujarati language, 2, 18, 31, 58, 61, 77, 122, 150–51, 200n2, 204n68; Gujarati people, 1, 4, 22–26; Gujarati schools, 77, 78, 149, 177; region of, 4, 25, 27, 28, 33, 38, 42, 48, 58, 60, 66, 73, 75, 82, 112, 149, 155, 177, 181n3, 191n80, 193n24, 195n51
Gukurahundi, 143, 160
Gwanda, 103, 157, 209n94
Gwelo. *See* Gweru
Gweru, 39, 54, 65, 142, 157, 159

Harare, 1, 17, 19–20, 22, 26, 29, 32, 36–37, 39, 45, 47, 54, 57, 58, 60, 64, 68, 72–73, 75–76, 77, 78, 79, 82–85, 88, 90–91, 93–94, 101, 104–5, 107–9, 111, 112–16, 120, 122, 125, 127, 129–30, 135, 138, 142, 144, 145, 152, 154–56, 163–65, 167–70, 171, 174, 176, 177, 178–79, 205n6, 206n22

Hassan, Mussa Essof, 129, 131
hawkers, 5, 45, 55, 60. *See also* general dealers; traders
Heroes' Acre, 160, 178, 180, 205n6, 209n94
hierarchy: caste, 15, 74, 76–77, 81, 125; class, 75–76, 126, 153; racial, 8, 10, 13–14, 43, 46, 52, 61–62, 66–67, 75, 126, 147, 153, 168, 191n71, 205n8; social, 71, 75–76
Hindi, 31, 122
Hindoo/Hindu: Hinduism, 66, 72, 77, 79, 87, 95, 144, 149, 206n23; marriage, 39, 82, 97–100, 198nn33–34; people, 4, 13–16, 19, 33, 45, 47, 66, 68–76, 77–87, 89, 96, 118–20, 123, 143, 169–70, 172, 199n52; personal law, 101, 194n40; schools, 77, 78, 80–85, 87–88, 93, 149
Hindoo/Hindu Society, 77, 78, 79, 81, 84, 88, 84, 207n44, 211n36
Hindu Marriage Act of 1955, 98–99, 198nn33–34
Hindu Youth Movement, 119, 123
homeland, 4, 5, 11, 13, 14, 22, 114, 118, 178
Hughes, Sir Edgar, 147
Hwange, 48

immigration. *See* migrants; migration
Immigration Act of 1954, 95–96
Immigration Act of 1966, 126
immorality, 45, 51, 53, 67, 165. *See also* morality
Imperial Conference of 1918, 30
imperialism, 25; administration and government, 10, 41, 66, 134; citizen and subject, 8, 29–30, 95, 110, 133;

collective, 15, 22; ideology, 24, 62, 160, 167, 178; immigration, 20; metropole, 4, 135; network, 2; power of disallowance, 40–41; space and territory, 9, 11, 23, 38, 43, 71. *See also* colonialism
indenture, 4, 25, 40, 182n14. *See also* labor and laborers: indentured
independence: fight for, 2; Indian, 98, 155, 192n84; period of, 5, 17, 117, 143, 154, 159, 167–69, 171, 201n13, 206n31. *See also* liberation movement
Independence Day, 1980, 171
India: colony of, 31, 40, 42, 65, 71, 74, 77, 191n80; as a concept, 14, 37, 127, 140, 155, 176; culture and traditions from, 13, 45, 69, 73–75, 88, 118, 120, 186n59, 193n22; imports from, 72, 171; marriage in, 93–95, 97–99, 194n40; migration from, 4–5, 8, 16, 22, 25–26, 29, 34, 36, 27, 39, 46, 61, 63–64, 66, 69, 71, 82, 86, 89, 91, 97–99, 112–14, 117, 119–20, 131, 135–36, 137, 150, 152, 173, 176, 177, 183n32, 207n52; Partition of, 13; Republic of, 119, 160, 175, 202n40, 211n5. *See also* British Raj; Partition; South Asia; subcontinent
India High Commission, 145
Indian National Congress, 40, 155
Indian Ocean, 1, 3–5, 9–10, 13–14, 18, 21, 23–25, 32, 34, 41, 44, 46, 60, 67, 69, 74, 86, 88, 92, 104, 112, 114, 145, 173, 181n3, 182n14
India Office, 40
indigeneity, 9–10, 174; indigenization, 6, 172, 176; indigenous, 6, 9, 22, 43, 61, 63, 79, 84, 140, 142, 160, 175,

211n9. *See also* Africa and Africans: Black
Indigenisation and Economic Empowerment Act of 2007, 175
insularity, 2, 6, 8–9, 12–13, 15–16, 61, 67, 75, 110, 140, 154, 172. *See also* isolation
intangible factors of discrimination, 92, 101, 107, 109
Internal Settlement, 166
Inter-Territorial Movement of Persons (Control) Act of 1954, 95–96
invention of tradition, 10
Islam. *See* Muslims and Islam
Islamic Society, 73, 82
Ismail, G., 127
isolation, 7, 9, 12–13, 47, 61, 119, 169. *See also* insularity
Italians, 34

Jewish people, 98, 199n52; relationships with Indians, 78, 194n41; traders, 189n40

Kadoma, 1, 48, 103, 142
Kaguvi, 24, 184n10
Kariba, 163–64
Karoi, 163
Kenya, 4, 6, 13, 25, 182n9, 201n13, 205n9, 207n49
kinship, 6, 15, 22–24, 28, 32–34, 42, 46, 58, 69–71, 89, 91, 114, 132. *See also* endogamy; marriage
Kopje, 54, 57, 85, 104, 115, 116
Koran, 77–78
kumalo, 138, 149–50, 205n4
Kwekwe, 54, 152, 159

labor and laborers, 4, 7, 15, 23, 25, 39, 52, 91, 95, 114; activism, 135, 142–43; Black laborers, 4, 15, 54, 61, 124, 127, 136, 182n14 (*see also* workers); caste, 74–75; domestic or female, 46, 69, 86, 100, 122, 140, 152; indentured, 25, 40, 182n23 (*see also* indenture); male, 34, 71; migrants, 49, 73, 144, 186n57; network, 39

Lancaster House, 166

Land Apportionment Act of 1930, 49, 56, 108, 124

Land Tenure Act of 1969, 115, 124, 126

language: African, 61; barriers, 61; *chilapalapa*, 61; civilizational, 69; colonial, 79, 84; English, 118; European, 31, 33; Gujarati, 77, 122, 151; Indian, 35, 114; of infiltration, 125; legal, 108, 124, 126; linguistic region, 27; patriarchal, 61; political, 127, 133; of purity, 15, 81; of sacrifice, 28; tests, 31, 39 (*see also under* literacy); vernacular, 70, 77, 84, 118, 149, 184n21; of white Rhodesians, 14, 23, 29, 134

laundry, 1, 33–34, 48

laws and legal systems: African colonial system, 91–93, 95, 100–101, 106, 108–10, 174, 197n7; bylaws, 104, 107–9, 126; citizenship, 117, 175–76; civil, 94–95, 97, 99–100, 101, 196n4; colonial, 40, 89, 91, 93, 99, 197nn7–8; court cases and challenges, 16, 20, 33, 51, 86–89, 90–93, 97–98, 99–103, 105–11, 129, 178, 198n37, 199n62; customary, 70, 94, 196n4; customary legal systems, 95; discriminatory and segregationist, 34, 38–39, 41, 50, 62–64, 89, 91–93, 95–96, 102–3, 108–10, 125–26, 128, 130, 173, 199n62; disputes, 97, 105; education, 88; family and personal, 16, 91, 93–95, 98–101, 194n40, 196n4, 198n34; history, 197n8; immigration, 34, 40–41, 95–96, 99–100, 185n37; justification, 103, 124; land, 5, 45, 49–50, 124, 173, 185n37; legal affairs, 194n40; legal ambiguity, 92, 99; legal definitions, 79, 211n9; legal divides, 94; legal pluralism, 94; legal profession, 200n74; legal status, 39, 101, 128; legal tradition, 94; martial, 166; municipal, 103, 108; ordinance, 30, 38–39, 41, 76; patriarchal code, 101; postcolonial, 6; restrictions, 108; rights, 104, 107; Roman-Dutch, 91; security, 155; South African system, 94; Western standards, 97

Law and Order (Maintenance) Act of 1960, 155

legislation. *See* laws and legal systems

Legislative Council, 30, 35

liberation movement, 1, 8, 24, 134, 151. *See also* independence

licenses: general dealer's and trading, 5, 36–37, 39, 45, 47, 50, 52–53, 55–56, 92, 101–3; prospecting, 5, 26, 47–48

License and Stamp Act of 1952, 103

literacy, 86, 128, 174; illiteracy, 24, 35; tests, 30–31, 41 (*see also* language: tests)

Lobengula, 3, 24, 141–42, 187n67, 205n10

Lobengula Street, 7, 17, 18, 44, 54, 56–57, 59, 137–38, 141–42, 144–45, 149–50, 154, 156, 159–60, 179

locations, 15, 44–45, 49, 54–57, 76, 142, 154. *See also* townships
London, 3, 20, 37–41, 122, 132, 178–79, 182n10, 186n36
Lotus Group, 144–48, 150, 152
Lotus magazine, 139, 145, 147–48, 183n36, 206n23
Louis Mountbatten School, 85

Machel, Graça, 172, 211n2
Madras, 66
majority rule, 4–5, 18, 116, 130, 131, 135, 142, 147, 165–66, 168–70, 174–76
Makokoba, 59, 154, 156
Malawi, 4, 73, 95–96, 117–18, 146, 152, 197n22, 200n70, 201n13, 207n51
males: adult, 41–42, 46, 48, 50, 56, 58, 91, 97, 137; elite, 45, 70; head of family, 15, 71–72; kinship, 34; labor, 34, 49, 71; peers, 120; pioneer narratives, 29–30; politics, 110; soldiers, 205n6; teachers, 83, 87. *See also* patriarchy
marriage, 7, 16, 22–23, 35, 38, 60, 64, 69–71, 73, 76, 82, 86–88, 91, 93, 95, 97–101, 105, 110, 113–14, 120–22, 128, 152, 171–72, 178, 179, 191n80, 193n28; arranged, 119, 122; certificates, 39; laws, 91, 93–94, 97–100, 128, 196n4, 198n33; mixed, 66, 69–70, 75–76, 79–82, 146, 153, 207n55 (*see also* miscegenation). *See also* endogamy; kinship; monogamy; polygamy
Marxism, 119, 143, 155. *See also* socialism
Mashonaland, 21, 24, 26
Matabeleland, 24, 51, 141, 143, 144, 160

Mehta, Suman, 90–94, 96, 101, 105–11, 114–15, 127, 131, 135, 152, 154–59, 167–68, 170, 171, 178, 199n62, 206n22
memory, 19, 22, 27, 29, 159–60, 205n6
middlemen, 5–6, 46, 62, 66, 75, 138, 182n22, 189n40, 207n49
migrants: "immigrant race," 34; Indian, 6, 10, 12, 14, 22–23, 25–26, 30–33, 35–36, 38–39, 42, 45–46, 63–64, 71, 74, 76, 91, 92, 96, 99, 106, 113, 118, 135, 141, 176–77, 181n3, 182n22, 184n9, 185n31; labor of, 49, 73, 144, 186n57; "prohibited" or "undesirable" immigrants, 23, 31, 33–35, 51, 96, 185n37; white, 15, 35, 175, 189n40. *See also* settlers
migration: immigration, 16, 20, 23, 30–33, 35, 36, 38–42, 58, 64, 66, 68, 71, 89, 91, 95–101, 104, 110, 137, 174, 185n37, 187n77; Indian Ocean, 24–25; of Indians, 4, 8, 10, 13, 23–25, 30, 36, 47, 58, 60, 69, 73–74, 91, 95–98, 112–13, 155, 173–74, 176, 185n31, 207n52; of labor networks, 39, 42, 96, 149; *mfecane*, 205; narratives, 14, 22, 26, 29, 172; policy, 31, 34; process, 7, 38, 74; rights, 23; of white Europeans, 4, 54, 63, 124, 167. *See also* migrants; mobility: transnational
Milton Park, 90–91, 106, 164
mining, 26, 48–49, 102, 112, 125
miscegenation, 13, 16, 34, 50, 61, 65, 69, 76, 80–81, 104, 128. *See also* marriage: mixed; race: mixed
mobility: social, 52, 74, 104, 115, 167, 174, 178, 195n56; transnational, 23, 25, 29, 36, 38–40, 95–96, 186n57 (*see also* migration)

modernity, 5–6, 11–12, 20, 49, 61–62, 74, 104, 114–15, 116, 118–22, 124–25, 135, 172, 176, 196n82
Moffat School, 85
Moffat Street, 47, 56–57
Mohammedan. See Muslims and Islam
monogamy, 94, 100, 198n33. See also marriage
morality, 13, 16, 35, 45, 51, 55–56, 69–70, 79–82, 83, 88–89, 114, 119, 189n32. See also immorality
Morgan High School, 85
mosques, 73, 125, 177
Moyo, Jason, 152, 153
Mozambique, 1, 4, 21, 28, 33, 132, 157
Mugabe, Robert, 142, 149, 159–60, 166–68, 171
Mugabe, Sally, 171
municipalities, 20, 45, 54–56, 62, 73, 91–92, 101–5, 108, 113, 115, 117, 124, 126–29, 142–43
Municipal Act of 1952, 104, 108
music, 16, 114, 118–19, 122
Muslims and Islam, 4, 13–14, 19, 33, 38, 45, 69, 73–74, 75, 77, 81, 87, 89, 90, 96–99, 125, 128–29, 143, 172, 177, 194n51; children, 78, 82; community, 72–73, 75, 77; customs and rites, 39, 97, 99; family, 16, 65, 70, 72, 75, 82–84, 194n40, 199n52; Islamic law, 198n34; marriage, 97–100, 198n34; religion, 87; schools, 77–78, 177; state, 81; Sunni, 73
Mutare, 1, 21–22, 28, 30–31, 33, 36–37, 39, 51–53, 54, 134, 142, 156, 165
Muzorewa, Bishop Abel, 130, 166
Mzilikazi, 24, 142, 205n10

Naik, Amratlal, 152, 157–58, 209n94
Naik, Bhimjee, 21–22, 24–25, 31–33, 36–39, 41, 177
Naik, Don/Dhirubhai, 144, 152, 157, 207n55
Naik, Haribhai, 137–38, 140, 149, 150, 151–53, 156, 160–61, 178, 179, 180
Natal, 40, 83
National Democratic Party (NDP), 91, 111, 134, 142, 147, 149, 152, 156
nationalism: activities and agendas, 11, 144; anthems, 208n75; aspirations and ideology, 134, 140, 155; elite and leaders, 138, 145, 165; guerrillas, 132, 138, 166; Hindu, 198n33; historiography, 13, 140, 182n12; Indian, 40–41, 70, 145, 155, 205n8; members and recruits, 40, 111, 115, 141, 152, 160, 167, 204n69, 209n94, 211n2; movements, 2, 7, 17, 109–10, 130–31, 135, 138, 140–43, 144–50, 152, 154–56, 160–61, 165–69, 171, 174, 178, 180, 183n36; myths, 2, 9, 143, 160, 169, 182n12; past, 207n44; political parties, 1, 132, 174; South African, 183n32; white settler, 93
native: eating houses, 33, 45, 47, 54–56, 65, 143; land and reserves, 25, 49; locations, 57, 73, 142; Native (as colonial racial category), 34–35, 46, 50–53, 56, 63, 77, 79–80, 96, 99, 104, 108 (see also Africa and Africans: Black); "native race of Asia," 38
Native Affairs Commission/Department, 50–52, 56, 77
Native Marriages Act of 1950, 99–100
Navsari, 112

Ndebele: ethnicity, 9; identity, 142–43; language, 138, 150, 205n4; people, 34, 41, 141, 160; state, 41, 142, 187n67
Nehanda, 24, 176, 184n10
Ngcebetsha, Charlton Cezani, 145–47
Nkomo, Joshua, 1–3, 7, 137, 142, 149, 152, 157–58, 160, 164–65, 172, 182n10, 209n84
Nkosi Sikelel'i Afrika, 156
Nyasaland. *See* Malawi
Nyerere, Julius, 143

Operation Gatling, 166–67
oral history, 19, 22, 26, 29, 31–32, 141, 181n3; oral historians, 44; oral narratives and storytelling, 22, 18, 31; oral traditions, 2, 22, 31, 37
Orange River Colony, 34

Pakistan, 13, 118, 192n84, 194n51, 202n40. *See also* Partition; South Asia; subcontinent
Pan-Africanism, 142–43
Parliament, 41, 103, 125, 129–30, 144, 175
Partition, 13, 70, 81
Patel, Bharat, 114, 121, 122, 132, 178–79, 211n9
Patel, Hasu, 47, 60, 105, 112, 155
Patel, Kantibhai, 155, 209n94
patriarchy, 7, 13, 14–15, 22, 29, 34, 42–43, 45–46, 50, 53, 61, 65, 67, 69–70, 72, 76, 85–86, 88, 98, 101, 139, 141, 147, 150, 161, 173, 178, 189n35. *See also* males
peasants, 4, 74, 123, 143, 181n3, 204n75

pioneers: Indian, 4, 8, 15, 21–24, 31, 42–43, 45, 57, 82, 117, 135, 141, 146, 160, 173, 177; white, 4, 14, 22, 24, 29, 41–42, 116–17, 199n52
Pioneer Cemetery, 165, 199n52
Pioneer Column, 3–4, 23, 24, 116–17
Pioneer Street, 57, 77
polygamy, 91, 93–94, 97–101, 128. *See also* marriage
Portuguese, the, 4, 21–22, 28, 34, 36–37, 39, 77
postcolonial. *See* colonialism
precolonial. *See* colonialism
Property Owners (Residential Protection) Bill of 1971 (POP bill), 115, 126–30
prostitution, 50, 55, 189n31
purity: caste, 15, 69, 73, 77, 82, 89, 173; marriage, 69; racial, 15, 68, 76, 79–82, 84–85, 87–88, 173; schools, 15, 69–70, 76, 79–80, 82–86, 88, 93, 173; sexual, 85–86, 119, 153 (*see also* virginity)

Queen Victoria, 37
Que Que. *See* Kwekwe

race, 6–7, 10–12, 14, 18, 20, 35, 46, 61, 65–67, 77, 79–81, 85, 87, 92–93, 102, 104, 106–9, 124, 126, 153–54, 166, 169, 173–76, 182n18, 203n58; boundaries, division, and segregation of, 45–46, 49, 55, 57, 65, 70, 73, 75, 77, 126, 129–30, 135, 139, 144, 154, 157; categories, classification, and groups, 4, 6, 8, 10–11, 13, 20, 35, 43, 46, 55, 62–63, 65–66, 73, 75,

race (*continued*)
77, 103–4, 108, 115, 124, 126, 144, 157, 182n9; discrimination based on, 95–96, 102, 106–8; enclave of, 14; on grounds of, 39; hierarchy of, 8, 10, 13–14, 52, 62, 67, 75–76, 126, 147; identity of, 6, 8–10, 15, 19, 67, 69, 78–79, 115, 168, 173, 176, 182n14, 201n8; immigrants, 34; interracial relationships, 34, 51, 53, 56, 65, 79, 86, 104, 106, 111, 139, 146–47, 173; legislation and policies dealing with, 91, 93, 173; mixed, 45, 51, 63, 65, 75, 79–82, 87, 144, 193n29 (*see also* miscegenation); multiracialism, 81, 95, 111, 144, 177, 197n15, 208n64; "native race of Asia," 38; nonracialism, 103, 124, 155, 197n15, 208n64; purity of, 68, 76, 80–85, 88; racialized society, 9, 15, 18, 174; racism and prejudice, 18, 128, 134, 153–54, 165; rule based on, 93, 168; stereotype of, 104; superiority based on, 61, 205n8; violence on grounds of, 29

Raftopoulos, Gerald, 128

railways, 1, 4, 21–22, 25, 28, 36, 48, 49, 54, 57, 142. *See also* trains

Railway Street, 57

Ranger, Terence, 44, 105, 155

religion, 5, 6–7, 12, 16, 20, 35, 46, 64, 66–67, 69–73, 75–76, 77, 82, 89, 104, 121–22, 146; boundaries and restriction of, 81, 84; debate about, 82; education, 15, 78, 84; festivals, 73; grounds and justification based on, 83, 87–88; institutions, organization, and society of, 69, 71–72, 77, 82, 85, 125, 149, 176, 178, 198n34; purity of, 81; symbols of, 144; texts, 70; thinking and values based on, 88, 120, 122

reproduction, 16, 73, 86, 88, 189n32

reserves, 45, 49–53, 54, 80, 126, 132, 153, 173. *See also* Tribal Trust Lands

resistance: anticolonial, 10–12, 111, 119, 138, 141–43, 146, 149, 155, 160, 174; Black, 8, 135; Indian, 2, 39, 41, 88, 110, 130, 132, 141, 149, 178; legal, 102, 110, 115; network, 17, 138, 174

Rezende Street, 56, 177

Rhodes, Cecil John, 3, 24, 26

Rhodesia, Northern. *See* Zambia

Rhodesian Bush War, 115–16, 131, 134, 204n69

Rhodesian Front (RF), 19, 93, 111, 115, 129–31, 134–35, 138, 140, 147–48, 155, 166

Ridgeview, 106, 114–15, 123, 125, 155, 169, 177

Robert Tredgold School, 85

Roman Catholics, 77, 126. *See also* Christians

Rudd Concession, 24, 187n67

rural areas: Africans and peasantry in, 116, 134, 142–43, 150; belonging in, 9; existence in, 116; gardening, 47; in India, 25, 48, 112, 184n21; Indians based in, 45; land, and space, 5–6, 9, 44–45, 49–50, 53, 55, 60, 62, 101, 108, 142, 166, 173; land reform, 174; market and trade, 49–50; nationalism, 143, 155; segregation, 50, 115

Rusape, 1, 51

Salisbury. *See* Harare

sanctions, 119, 202n40

saris, 1–3, 72, 116, 120–22, 172

schools, 7, 74, 81, 107, 150; admissions, 70, 78–79, 81–82, 84–86; African, 76, 79, 208; age, 77, 86–88; colonial, 76, 84, 89; European, 54, 76, 79; Gujarati, 77, 78, 149, 177; Hindoo/Hindu, 77–78, 80–84, 87–88, 91; in India, 26, 28; Indian and Coloured, 68, 72, 76–78, 80–81, 85, 177, 195n58; Islamic, 77, 78, 177; mission, 76–77, 155; multiracial, 177; purity, 15, 69–70, 73, 76, 79–80, 82–86, 88, 93, 115, 173; Rhodesian, 118; secondary, 94, 122, 132; uniforms, 57. *See also* students; teachers

segregation, 7–8, 15–16, 45–46, 50, 56, 62, 66–67, 89, 91–93, 96, 101–2, 104–10, 115, 126–27, 132, 135, 138–39, 144, 154, 157, 173, 178, 199n62

Selbourne Street, 57

self-governing status, 3, 30, 41–42, 54, 72, 95

Selous Scouts, 166, 169

Senate, 130

servants, 54, 61, 71–72, 75, 109, 124, 126, 133; civil, 192n9

settlers: colonialism and imperialism, 9, 12–15, 18, 23, 29–30, 35, 40–41, 45, 50, 54, 62, 69, 124, 160, 173; colonies, 4, 23, 124; Indian settlement, 1–3, 5, 10, 14, 18, 20, 21–24, 28–30, 36, 38, 42–43, 47, 52, 55–56, 58, 60, 63, 69, 72, 82, 112–13, 135, 144, 172–73, 175, 182n14; nationalism, 93; "native settlement," 73; nostalgia, 24; rule, 5, 141, 204n75; urban settlement, 22, 33, 45–47, 50, 54, 116–17, 141–42, 157; white settlers, 3–5, 11–12, 15, 22–25, 29–30, 35–40, 42, 48–50, 53, 55, 64, 89, 91, 96, 102, 106–7, 116, 169, 174, 184n4, 196n4. *See also* migration

Shabani. *See* Zvishavane

Shamuyarira, Nathan, 154

sharia, 95

ships, steamer, 21, 25, 28, 33

shoemakers, 73, 75

Shona: -dominated government, 142–43; ethnicity and identity, 9, 142; language, 62, 204n69; people, 24, 41, 116; spirit medium, 116, 184n10

shops, 2–3, 5–12, 14–18, 22–23, 26, 31, 43, 44–49, 53, 57, 63, 65, 92–93, 101, 103–4, 106, 108, 113–15, 124–25, 131, 164, 168, 171–74, 176–79; as colonial institutions, 62, 75, 135; counters, 5, 7, 14–15, 46–47, 53, 58, 60–61, 67, 68–71, 86, 121–22, 140, 145, 149–50, 152–54, 159, 164, 173, 176, 179; hostility toward, 35–39, 45, 51, 63, 159; -keepers, 5, 150; laundry, 1; as racial enclave, 14; as site of political resistance, 135, 138–41, 145, 149–52; as social centers, 5, 15, 28–29, 33–34, 42, 46–47, 60–61, 68–72, 80, 87, 89, 91, 110, 114–15, 118, 120–22, 140, 156, 177. *See also* businesses; *dukkan*; stores

Shop Hours Act, 56

Singh, Nirmal, 145

Sinoia. *See* Chinhoyi

Smith, Ian, 117, 130, 165–66

Smuts, Jan, 41

socialism, 143. *See also* Marxism

South Africa, 3–4, 10, 14, 23, 25, 29, 31, 33, 38, 40, 41, 49, 61, 71, 74, 92, 94, 95, 106, 108, 112, 118, 119, 124, 135, 137, 145, 151, 155, 173, 181n3, 182n23, 183n32, 184n21, 185n31, 193n9, 193n29, 200n62, 205n9,

South Africa (continued)
208n64, 210n23, 211n2. *See also*
apartheid
South Asia, 75, 95; diaspora of, 9, 13,
74, 145; migrant from, 14; minority
of, 6; religion of, 7, 12, 15; tradition
of, 14, 69–70, 74, 89. *See also* India;
Pakistan; Partition; subcontinent
southern Africa, 6, 9, 10, 25, 65, 208n75
Southern Rhodesia African National
Congress (SRANC), 91, 153
Soviet Union, 143, 147, 151
stores, 2–3, 5, 28, 34, 36–38, 42, 44–45,
48, 51–53, 57, 58, 60, 64, 68, 70–71,
75, 103, 110, 112–13, 125, 137, 144–45,
149, 155–56, 171–72, 177, 189n40. *See
also* businesses; *dukkan*; shops
students, 20, 122, 142. *See also* schools
subcontinent, 2, 6, 8, 11, 13, 16, 30, 40,
47, 65–66, 69–70, 81, 95, 117, 140,
155, 175. *See also* India; Pakistan;
Partition; South Asia
subjects, 23, 29–30, 38–41, 64–65, 88,
94–95, 101, 110, 124, 172–73, 192n84.
See also citizens
Surat, 26, 83, 112
swimming baths and pools, 90–92,
104–9, 111, 206n22

Takawira, Leopold, 156–57
taxes, 49, 52, 58, 105–7, 129, 203n58
teachers, 26, 78, 83–85, 87, 121–22,
145, 153, 178, 195n58. *See also*
schools
temples, 72, 120, 125, 149, 169
terrorists, 134, 164–65; acts of terrorism, 164–65, 169
Thornicroft, Joseph, 129

townships, 15, 33, 45, 54–55, 59, 60,
62, 104–5, 112, 143, 156. *See also*
locations
trading, 15, 26, 48, 51, 55–56, 74, 125,
143, 190n58; businesses, 32, 35, 38,
42, 45, 72, 83, 137, 177; caste, 33,
74; class or communities, 52–53,
69, 151, 181n3; connections and
networks, 25, 49; districts or zones,
37, 85, 92, 101, 103, 116; economy,
149; families, 144; hubs, 5; licenses,
5, 36, 39, 50, 53, 56, 101–2; petty or
small-scale, 45, 48; sites or stands,
15, 21, 28, 36, 49, 55–57, 64–65, 113;
streets, 15, 45–47, 53, 56–57, 58,
60–63, 65, 67, 89, 104, 125, 144, 174;
traders, 2, 15, 21, 23, 35, 37, 42, 45,
49, 51–55, 60–62, 64, 92, 112, 129,
143–44, 1–5653, 172, 177, 186n59,
189n40. *See also* businesses; general dealers; hawkers
tradition, 2, 5–6, 8, 13–14, 16, 42, 54,
69–70, 72, 74, 76–77, 80–83, 87, 89,
93–95, 97, 110, 114, 116, 118–19, 121–
22, 124, 135, 140, 171–72, 196n82;
"traditional family," 68
trains, 28–31, 35, 84, 104; stations, 26,
30; tracks, 48. *See also* railways
Transvaal, 34, 38, 73, 187n79
Tribal Trust Lands, 49, 157. *See also*
reserves

Uganda, 25, 131, 168, 201n13, 203n47,
206n31
Umtali. *See* Mutare
Unilateral Declaration of Independence
(UDI), 111, 115, 117, 124, 138, 147
United Federal Party, 147

United Kingdom, 5, 94, 117, 166–67, 192n84, 202n40, 207n55. *See also* Britain and the British; England
United Nations, 119
untouchables. *See* Dalit
urban areas: history, 13, 143; housing, 55; life, 5, 45–46, 54, 62, 140; modernity, 115; municipalities, 20, 45, 129; politics and nationalism, 142–43, 151; segregation, 66–67, 92, 101, 124; space, 2, 5–6, 9, 13, 15–16, 33, 43, 45–47, 50, 54–55, 62, 70, 73, 86, 89, 92, 108, 114–15, 124, 126–27, 132, 136, 172–73, 176, 190n58, 207n45; trading, 23, 45, 49, 69; urbanization, 54; urbanized identity, 9, 47, 75, 94, 113, 123, 127
Urdu, 77–78

Vashee Hall, 72, 149, 207n44
Victoria Falls, 48, 146
virginity, 87, 88. *See also* purity: sexual
Viscount plane crash, 163–69, 211n24
voting, 123, 128, 130; Asian and Coloured, 128–31, 135, 168, 210n23; "one man, one vote," 142, 169; voter rolls, 63, 105, 126, 129, 203n58; white, 3, 103, 111, 125, 130. *See also* elections

Wankie. *See* Hwange
West, the, 74, 165; countries, 176; culture, 8, 118, 120, 122; customs and standards, 97–98; education, 145; fashion, 16, 113, 118, 122; identity, 114, 118, 123; legal standards, 97; modernity, 114, 119, 124; music, 119; scholarship, 17; values, 114
whites: authorities and administration, 12, 38, 41, 47, 50, 53, 62, 79, 88, 127; education and schools, 79, 122; farmers, 5, 33, 45, 166, 172, 174; history, 117; labor, 23; land, 5, 11, 43, 49, 124; liberalism, 145; members of Black nationalist parties, 208n65, 209n94; minority, 4, 6, 34, 203n58, 210n23; minority rule and settler state, 1–3, 6, 9–10, 23, 30, 40, 45, 110, 115, 117, 124, 130–31, 135, 138, 141, 143, 146–47, 149, 166–68, 173–74, 178, 182n10, 182n12, 184n10, 205n75; nationalism, 93; neighborhoods and space, 15, 45, 54–55, 59, 60, 62, 89, 91–92, 103–5, 109–10, 114, 116, 125, 131, 144, 154, 160; non-, 35, 76, 92, 103–5, 108–9, 115, 125, 134, 144, 146, 148, 173–74; people and settlers, 3–5, 9, 11–12, 14–18, 22–25, 28–30, 32, 34–36, 39, 41–42, 46, 48–50, 53–54, 62–63, 65, 69, 89, 90–91, 94–96, 100, 102–3, 105–7, 111, 115–16, 119, 124, 126–29, 134, 136, 164–67, 169–70, 172, 175, 185n37, 196n4, 204n69; pioneers, 4, 14–15, 22, 24, 29, 199n52; politics, 148; prisoners, 157; secret service, 151; settlement, 23–24, 40, 49, 55, 184n4; soldiers, 132–33, 199n52; supremacy, 37, 81, 135; trade, 5, 21, 33, 45, 53, 134. *See also* Europe and Europeans
Witwatersrand, 26
women, 7–8, 47, 121–22, 145, 152, 159, 161, 164–65, 171–73, 182n10, 184n8, 189n31, 200n2, 205n6; Black, 34,

women (continued)
    45, 50–51, 55–56, 80, 146, 186n53, 189n35, 207n55; Coloured, 69, 76, 80–81; Indian, 1, 7–8, 22, 25, 30, 42, 46, 50, 58, 60–61, 69–70, 72, 81, 110, 114, 119–20, 122, 128, 156, 178, 207n45; labor of, 61, 64, 71, 86, 100, 122, 152; marriage of, 16, 34, 60, 70–71, 86, 88, 91, 98, 100, 128, 150, 198n33; role of, 17, 34, 68, 120, 135, 140; sexual virtue of, 87–88, 120, 140, 146, 172; white, 50, 54, 128, 172. *See also* females
workers: Black, 5, 35, 48–49, 54–55, 61, 71, 142, 149, 211n4; female, 34; Indian, 33. *See also* labor and laborers
World War, First, 39, 112, 133, 199n52
World War, Second, 39, 113, 133, 142

Zambia, 73, 95–96, 117, 118, 132, 146, 155, 166–67, 200n70, 201n13, 207n51
Zhii riots, 156
Zimbabwe African National Liberation Army (ZANLA), 132, 134, 204n77
Zimbabwe African National Union (ZANU), 134, 140–43, 150, 154–55, 159, 166, 208n65, 209n94
Zimbabwe African National Union–Patriotic Front (ZANU-PF), 159–60, 165–66, 168, 206n31, 211n23
Zimbabwe African People's Union (ZAPU), 1–2, 17, 132, 139–43, 146–52, 154–57, 158, 159–60, 166–68, 182n10, 207n55, 208nn64–65
Zimbabwe People's Revolutionary Army (ZIPRA), 132, 151, 163, 165–66, 168–69, 207n51
Zvishavane, 112

RECENT BOOKS IN THE SERIES
RECONSIDERATIONS IN SOUTHERN AFRICAN HISTORY

An Age of Hubris: Colonialism, Christianity, and the Xhosa in the Nineteenth Century
TIMOTHY KEEGAN

Divided by the Word: Colonial Encounters and the Remaking of Zulu and Xhosa Identities
JOCHEN S. ARNDT

Violence and Solace: The Natal Civil War in Late-Apartheid South Africa
MXOLISI R. MCHUNU

Masked Raiders: Irish Banditry in Southern Africa, 1880–1889
CHARLES VAN ONSELEN

Sol Plaatje: A Life of Solomon Tshekisho Plaatje, 1876–1932
BRIAN WILLAN

Bound for Work: Labor, Mobility, and Colonial Rule in Central Mozambique, 1940–1965
ZACHARY KAGAN GUTHRIE

The Finger of God: Enoch Mgijima, the Israelites, and the Bulhoek Massacre in South Africa
ROBERT R. EDGAR

The Cowboy Capitalist: John Hays Hammond, the American West, and the Jameson Raid in South Africa
CHARLES VAN ONSELEN

Historian: An Autobiography
HERMANN GILIOMEE

Cradock: How Segregation and Apartheid Came to a South African Town
JEFFREY BUTLER, EDITED BY RICHARD ELPHICK
AND JEANNETTE HOPKINS

Imagining a Nation: History and Memory in Making Zimbabwe
RURAMISAI CHARUMBIRA

A World of Their Own: A History of South African Women's Education
MEGHAN HEALY-CLANCY

The Last Afrikaner Leaders: A Supreme Test of Power
HERMANN GILIOMEE

The Equality of Believers: Protestant Missionaries and the Racial Politics of South Africa
RICHARD ELPHICK

Slavery by Any Other Name: African Life under Company Rule in Colonial Mozambique
ERIC ALLINA

One Love, Ghoema Beat: Inside the Cape Town Carnival
JOHN EDWIN MASON

The Rise and Fall of Apartheid
DAVID WELSH

Art and Revolution: The Life and Death of Thami Mnyele, South African Artist
DIANA WYLIE

Murder at Morija: Faith, Mystery, and Tragedy on an African Mission
TIM COUZENS

The Afrikaners: Biography of a People
HERMANN GILIOMEE

Social Death and Resurrection: Slavery and Emancipation in South Africa
JOHN EDWIN MASON